LIVING
THE
COLD WAR

LIVING
THE
COLD WAR

MEMOIRS OF A BRITISH
DIPLOMAT

CHRISTOPHER MALLABY

AMBERLEY

This book is dedicated to Pascale, whose memory and help were invaluable, to my children, who gave me much good advice and to my grandchildren, who first suggested this book.

First published 2017

Amberley Publishing
The Hill, Stroud
Gloucestershire, GL5 4EP

www.amberley-books.com

Copyright © Christopher Mallaby, 2017

The right of Christopher Mallaby to be identified as the Author of this work has been asserted in accordance with the Copyright, Designs and Patents Act 1988.

ISBN 978 1 4456 6961 8 (hardback)
ISBN 978 1 4456 6962 5 (ebook)

British Library Cataloguing in Publication Data. A catalogue record for this book is available from the British Library.

Typesetting and Origination by Amberley Publishing.
Printed in the UK.

CONTENTS

ACKNOWLEDGEMENTS

The author and publisher would like to thank the following for permission to use copyrighted material.

Patrick Salmon, Keith Hamilton and Stephen Twigge, who edited 'German Unification 1989–90' Series III Volume VII of *Documents on British Policy Overseas*, published by Routledge in 2010. This was the source of some official documents quoted or paraphrased in this book.

The editors of Series III Volume VIII on 'The invasion of Afghanistan and UK-Soviet Relations 1979–82' published by Routledge in 2012; and Series III Volume X on 'The Polish Crisis and Relations with Eastern Europe 1979–82' published by Routledge in 2017. These two volumes were helpful to the author of this book.

Patrick Browne and The Times newspaper group for quotation from the obituary of Brigadier Mallaby, the author's father, in *The Times*, 14 November 1945.

The Miller Center at the University of Virginia, for use of the summary records of the Soviet leaders' meetings during the Cuba crisis in 1962: millercenter.org/search?q=malin

The Wilson Center in Washington, for quotation from the records of the Soviet leaders' discussions about Solidarity and Poland 1980–81 and their decision not to invade Poland: http://digitalarchive.wilsoncenter.org/11/1980–81-polish-crisis

Geoff and Kathy Murrell for quotation from their invaluable unpublished memoir.

The *Frankfurter Allgemeine Zeitung* for quotation of its comment on the Queen's State Visit to Germany, October 1992.

Every effort has been made to seek permission for copyright material used in this book. However if we have inadvertently used copyright material without permission or acknowledgement we apologise and we will make the necessary correction at the first opportunity.

I am most grateful to people who helped me with the writing, by criticising and suggesting improvements: Bruce Anderson, Sir Anthony Brenton, Sir Rodric Braithwaite, Sir Colin Budd, Sir Roger Carrick, Sir Brian Crowe, Sir Vincent Fean, Alfred Friendly, Lord Goodlad, Jeremy Hill, Olga Karetnikova, Princess Nina Lobanov-Rostovsky, Baroness Neville-Jones, Professor William Paterson, Hella Pick, Hermann Freiherr von Richthofen, James Stourton, Professor Horst Teltschick.

And to others who helped in equally valuable ways: Sir John Birch, Jim Daly, Edward Glover, Tony Longrigg, Norma Reid, Philip Short, Gina Thomas.

FOREWORD BY PETER HENNESSY

The Gods of Diplomacy smiled on Sir Christopher Mallaby from the moment as a Cambridge undergraduate he decided to sit the Foreign Office exam. For not only did they give him a profession he relished and a career he savoured from start to finish, they placed him in the right locations at the most significant times. A career official who was in Moscow as a young second secretary throughout the Cuban Missile Crisis and Ambassador to West Germany when the Berlin Wall toppled can only be described as an 'epicentrist' of the diplomatic trade.

Sir Christopher's professional life was shaped by the Cold War and this will rank among the most enduring memoirs of the great 40-year East-West confrontation. But there is also a very wide range of fascinations within these pages. For example, readers will be taken almost by the hand through the experience of how a front-rank embassy works – Bonn (later Berlin) and Paris. This is particularly important for an activity that is all too often parodied in the press as a kind of gilded out-relief for the clever and the polished at public expense.

Another treat in *Living the Cold War* are the cameos of the big figures; not least Margaret Thatcher. Sir Christopher ranks her as the greatest prime minister since Winston Churchill. But they were at opposite ends of the argument over German reunification. The pages dealing with it positively crackle. Christopher and his wife Pascale possess a great gift for friendship (a supreme asset for a diplomatic couple) and the accounts of these friendships, for example with the wonderful Simone Veil, are warm and fascinating.

At a time when our country's place in the world is, to put it neutrally, highly fluid and a top-flight Diplomatic Service a necessity not a luxury, it is both valuable and salutary to read a memoir of such quality and to realise the price we shall pay in the UK if we hollow out our Foreign and Commonwealth Office with still more cuts.

Amidst all the vicissitudes and uncertainties of current government and politics, sit back, relax and savour every word.

Peter Hennessy
Lord Hennessy of Nympsfield FBA
Attlee Professor of Contemporary British History
Queen Mary University of London.
July 2017

INTRODUCTION

In 1962 in Moscow, during my first diplomatic job, I witnessed the most dangerous moment of the Cold War, when the world came the closest it ever has to nuclear destruction. The Soviet leader, Nikita Khrushchev, began to install nuclear missiles in Cuba, a few miles from the United States. Some of President Kennedy's advisers thought that nuclear war was probably unavoidable. For thirteen surreal days, Pascale and I, recently married, went about our lives in Moscow knowing as the crisis deepened that we might be at risk from nuclear weapons – not the weapons of our Soviet antagonists, but those of our allies, the Americans. Even then, as a newly minted Soviet specialist in my mid-twenties, I knew diplomacy was the life for me.

For the next 34 years, my career in the Foreign and Commonwealth Office was everything I hoped it would be. I befriended Russian musicians, artists and political dissidents. I experienced life at Ground Zero of the Cold War: the fortified enclave of western freedom that was late 1960s Berlin. And I was involved in some of the geopolitical dramas of the late twentieth century, from the western response to the Soviet invasion of Afghanistan in 1979 to Margaret Thatcher's triumphant handling of Argentina's invasion of the Falkland Islands in 1982. Six years later I became Ambassador to West Germany; and before very long I flew into my old city of Berlin by helicopter to witness the collapse of the Wall. I still remember the sight of a small East German boy returning with his parents through Checkpoint Charlie from his first outing to a capitalist toy shop: he was pulling a trophy as tall as himself – a red plastic London double decker bus. That was the moment when I knew that the Iron Curtain had begun to melt. The tensions of life in Khrushchev's Moscow suddenly belonged to history. For someone who had spent most of three decades working in the Cold War, it was a giant relief and something of a vindication.

Is Diplomacy Still Necessary?

Looking back on his diplomatic life in 1936, Harold Nicolson thought diplomacy had always been necessary: 'Even in pre-history there must have come moments when one group of savages wished to negotiate with another... Even to our Neanderthal ancestors, it must have become apparent that such negotiations would be severely hampered if the emissary from one side were killed and eaten by the other side before he had time to deliver his message.'*

But what if we look forward? Does diplomacy remain necessary now, and will it still be needed in the middle of the twenty-first century? An insistent school of sceptics argues that the diplomatic arts have been made irrelevant by technology: why communicate with Washington through an expensive embassy when the Foreign Secretary in London can pick up the telephone? Another school of critics asks a different question: what is the 'national interest' that diplomats supposedly serve – has it not been superseded by supranational organisations such as the World Trade Organization or in my time the European Union, or hasn't it been blurred by globalisation? Both critiques, while understandable, are wrong.

One change of another kind has certainly diminished the importance of the work of British diplomats: the relative reduction in Britain's power in the world. The loss of Empire and the rise of the United States, and the weak performance of the UK economy from the Second World War to the early 1980s are factors which have demoted the UK from the top table of world affairs to a position which is still significant in many important ways but not at all what it was in the mid-twentieth century, when the UK in the age of Churchill was one of the Big Three with the US and the USSR.

---

* Sir Harold Nicolson, *Diplomacy*. 3rd edition 1969. Page 6.

As for the wider questions about the need for diplomacy, there have been two changes in the past half century. First, the meetings and the easy communication among Foreign Ministers of friendly states do mean that they can deal directly with really difficult and urgent decisions. But they are extremely busy and cannot take decisions at the top levels without facts and advice from diplomats. Each Foreign Minister needs the advice of Embassies on the decisions he is taking himself and on the attitude to them of the other Foreign Ministers. The value of Embassies is partly that they know the interests and the character, and indeed the hopes and fears and psychological hang-ups, of the country where they are working and can see which elements of that country's proposals or policies might be discarded or modified in negotiation. British policies, to win agreement, should be advocated with arguments designed to appeal to the other governments involved. You work to advance British views by first understanding the interests and views of the other country. That needs the expertise of our team on the spot. I call it letting the other side have our way.

The second change is that foreign affairs now include many subjects which used to be domestic ones. Embassies deal not only with international political problems and analysis of the politics, the economy and the policies of the country where they work, and the protection of British commercial interests and British travellers. They also deal with any subject with an international dimension, through NATO or the European Union or otherwise. In my Embassy in Bonn there were experts on international scientific matters, the European Common Agricultural Policy, environmental subjects and international labour and police matters, as well as Military Attachés and many others. The staff from other Ministries in London outnumbered the staff from the Diplomatic Service in the Embassy. The Ambassador supervises the work of all of them.

The result of these two changes in diplomacy is that part of the top icing on the cake of international relations is now handled by Heads of Government or Foreign Ministers, but the cake itself has become far larger than before. So the role of Ambassadors has diminished in independent responsibility but increased greatly in range and volume.

The second of the changes gives rise to another role of Embassies today. No Ministry in London knows about everything that all

Ministries are doing with the more important countries. The FCO and the Cabinet Office know a good deal, but not even the FCO knows everything. A British Embassy watches carefully to ensure that our policies in all fields are in line with our overall aims in the bilateral relationship. Also, a British Embassy is able, like no other part of government, to see where there are gaps in Britain's total relationship with another country and can take steps to fill the gaps in ways which will advance British interests. This sort of thinking gave me the ideas for my projects of founding a post-graduate institute of British studies in a German university and a programme of scholarship exchanges of able and ambitious graduates between the UK and France; and also my efforts to correct French ignorance of the many achievements of modern British art.

There is another important change which alters the work of many diplomats. They have always cooperated with like-minded countries in order to prevail in negotiations with other countries that have different aims. Some of this cooperative negotiation has long taken place within formal arrangements like international organisations or alliances. In the past half century, however, much more diplomacy has been conducted in multilateral organisations, whether global ones like the United Nations or regional ones like the European Union or NATO, which by the way is probably the most successful defensive military alliance ever.

So in many important fields the UK's influence is now exerted mainly in multilateral diplomacy. Many British diplomats work in this setting and have proved effective.

The very notion of 'public diplomacy' used to be an oxymoron. Diplomacy was conducted in private, not in public view. Today, negotiation and consultation among governments should still be conducted in private, but diplomats also have a public role. I often made speeches in public or was interviewed by the media, printed or electronic. This public diplomacy, the advocacy of British polices and achievements in the local language, often live on television, was a large part of my work.

Much of the huge increase in the international exchange of people, products, services, information and influence in the past half century has come about independently of governments – by trade, businesses, finance, the media and the Internet. In consequence the role of governments as coordinators and regulators has grown and will continue to grow if global contacts and cooperation continue to multiply. The further increase in international activity will increase the need for governments to negotiate the aims and rules of the game, in order to prevent major clashes of interest among nations or to reduce differences before they become acute and inflammatory. Governments will not be the only parties in these negotiations. International organisations, business interests and non-governmental organisations will need to be involved. So international negotiation will grow vastly in volume, variety, complexity and importance. Diplomacy and its special skills will play a large and necessary role, which will ensure their value as far ahead as we can see.

What about the National Interest?

A British diplomat's purpose is to advance and protect British national interests and to contribute to the success of British policies. Lord Palmerston in the 19th century declared that Britain had no permanent friends or enemies, and only its interests were eternal. Today our most fundamental interests are eternal – protecting the country's freedom, security and standard of living. But the meaning of each of these broad interests changes over time. Britain had many national interests which resulted from the Empire. One famous example was to protect the route to India from Russian or other encroachment. The security of India itself was a British national interest. It is obvious that the defeat of Nazi Germany and the successful containment and deterrence of the Soviet Union were existential national interests, but they too were not eternal because these purposes were achieved.

Indeed, national identity itself can evolve and change. Britain's national identity changed with the creation of the British Empire and again with its dismantling. And I think our national identity has changed through immigration; we have become more diverse ethnically and in religion and in the food we like. It can be argued that new immigrants are not themselves a part of Britain's national identity, but their descendants surely are.

Sometimes a government decides a major matter because it believes that the country's national identity or character requires a particular choice. When Argentina invaded the Falkland Islands in 1982, Margaret Thatcher's immediate instinct was that Britain must retake the Islands, by force if necessary, and also try by negotiation to persuade Argentina to withdraw without a war. This decision was justified by the British character and by the outcome.

In most matters, however, Governments try to balance the pros and cons of each course of action, and diplomats play a large part in this process when foreign affairs are the subject. But I have experienced few decisions which were based entirely on logic and cool calculation. Public opinion in the UK, as well as the views of the media, may well be influences. The views, even the prejudices, of supporters of the party in government are a likely factor too. This is necessary and right.

The UK's vote to leave the European Union in 2016 was based in popular dislike of immigration from EU countries and many less clear feelings about Europe. In my opinion, it ignored vastly important facts, not feelings, which made staying in the EU the right choice for Britain's prosperity and for our influence in the world. The national interest was greatly harmed by a majority of voters. They had the right to do this.

My view on this is rooted in tangible British interests. Idealism about building a united Europe has never been a part of my attitude to Europe.

Such is the nature of democracy: sometimes governments, like people, make questionable or regrettable decisions, but if you believe in the ultimate sovereignty of voters, it is right to respect these choices. Moreover, once a policy is decided, it is in the national interest that it be implemented as successfully as possible; and the duty of British diplomats is to work for that success. The bottom line is that furthering the national interest is a decent working definition of a diplomat's function, even when the policies reflect emotion or prejudice.

There may of course be exceptions to this verdict. If a diplomat hates a policy, for instance because he or she believes it is against the national interest, resignation may need to be considered. Richard Holbrooke, a gifted American diplomat with whom I worked in the 1990s, resigned from the State Department early in his career because he opposed the Vietnam policy. But that is rare. In my four decades as a diplomat, I always felt that I could serve my country best by advising and implementing on the inside, not by a public protest against a policy that had been decided by a democratically elected government. I never thought of resignation during my most significant disagreement on policy, when as ambassador in West Germany my views on German unification were diametrically different from those of the Prime Minister, Margaret Thatcher.

Britain's Future Relationship with Europe

I am an optimist, prone to seek silver linings in every cloud. Are there silver linings in the result of the British referendum of June 2016 when we voted by majority in favour of leaving the European Union?

There may be a chance of our staying in the EU and I still think that would be best for Britain. The chances of this outcome may be increasing, as the disadvantages of Brexit become more apparent. But it is more likely that we shall leave the EU and that the years of uncertainty before we have a new arrangement with it will do much harm to the UK's economy and influence. Our future trade arrangement seems certain to be less favourable than the one we have now. The only silver lining I can see is that our future cooperation with the EU as a non-member might suit our character better than our uncomfortable membership within it, which has repeatedly caused controversy with Europe and within British politics.

The Pluses and Minuses of a Diplomatic Career

In arguing that diplomats serve the national interest, and also that their role is undiminished by globalization, I am of course biased. I loved almost every moment of my career; I liked being surrounded by intelligent and cultivated colleagues; I enjoyed the culture of the FCO, in which ambitious people managed to work easily together, without an atmosphere of rivalry. Of course, there were disadvantages as well: the nomadic life made it hard for spouses to pursue careers, and more or less obliged children to attend boarding school; the workload was extremely heavy and the pay was low compared with jobs of similar responsibility in the private sector. But in my years in the FCO, there was barely a dull moment; and the satisfaction that I feel as I look back naturally disposes me to argue that my line of work should continue in the future. Readers will have to decide whether experience has distorted my judgment. But, especially at a time when Britain may be drawing in on itself, I hope this book will persuade some readers of the continued value of diplomacy. We live in an ever more interconnected world, and our relations with other countries are bound to affect us all profoundly. Those relations can be managed – or mismanaged – depending on the resources that the nation chooses to devote to advancing its values and its interests.

I

GETTING STARTED

My earliest memory is the start of the Second World War. I was evacuated from London in 1939, because German bombing was expected soon, to Camberley where my grandfather lived. I was three.

We left London to avoid the bombing, but still suffered bombing raids because Camberley was home to several important military targets. I remember fights between British and German aircraft in the night sky above our house. Occasionally I was brought out, wrapped in a blanket, to watch. Aircraft were shot down quite often and a house in our road was bombed. I collected fragments of the metal debris of crashed aircraft and exploded bombs. I still have a Players Navy Cut cigarette box of small bits of torn metal. I did not realise how strange and sad it was for a boy of six or seven to be a keen collector of the shrapnel from battles in a world war.

In our first four years in Camberley my father sometimes came for weekends but his heavy workload in the War Office, where he was Deputy Director of Military Operations, made it hard to get away. His visits were a highlight of our lives.

An unforgettable moment of happiness was a short visit in 1943 to Blue Anchor on the coast of Somerset. My mother and father and my brother Antony and I walked on twisting, rough paths across the cliffs. My father was a master of nonsense and kept us laughing all the time. He left a few days later for India, and joined

Field Marshal Wavell's staff as Director of Military Operations for the war against Japan. He was to visit London briefly once more, the last time Antony, Sue and I saw him. His last words to me, as he walked out of the front door, were 'Look after Mummy'. I hope that this unforgettable remark influenced my behaviour towards my mother.

The BBC announced on the six o'clock news on 30 October 1945 that my father had been assassinated in Indonesia. The War Office had not told my mother. The shock was terrible. The war was over, against Japan as well as Germany. He had survived it and had nevertheless been killed.

*****

My father was commanding a British Brigade of 6,000 Indian troops who had arrived a few days earlier in Surabaya in Indonesia to undertake three tasks. They were to disarm and round up the numerous Japanese troops who were still in the area and to liberate thousands of Dutch internees who had been used by the Japanese occupiers for hard labour. Finally – and crucially – my father's force was to prepare that part of Indonesia for the return of the Dutch colonial government.

This third task was the reason why his Brigade met bitter armed resistance. Indonesian nationalists had declared the country's independence when Japan surrendered. There were 22,000 nationalist soldiers on the streets of Surabaya including many irregulars who were not obeying their leadership. My father had only one option, to negotiate a ceasefire with the Indonesian Nationalist leaders and then to try to carry out his mission. He negotiated a ceasefire several times with Dr Moestopo, the nationalist leader in Surabaya. But there was still much hostility on the streets and my father, with an Indonesian leader, drove to the main square of Surabaya in the hope of explaining the ceasefire and getting it observed. He was shot at point-blank range by a fifteen-year-old nationalist with a Japanese rifle. He was 44. I was nine.

I was at prep school as a boarder when my father was killed. I was sent home. When I arrived at the house in Camberley my mother was in her bedroom. As I entered, she was bending over the washbasin, splashing cold water on her face. I said that I had been reading the many newspaper reports about my father's work in Indonesia and was very proud. Mummy wept a little and said 'they murdered him.' I was stunned. My grief took days to affect me fully. Antony was six and Sue was three. He was more upset than me in his immediate reaction. Sue was not told what had happened until later.

My memory of the next few days at home is full of the newspaper reporters who came constantly to the house and tried to ask questions. Mostly they were fended off by Miss Smith, the governess. But I sometimes did this job. I remember no difficult moments; being only nine may have made it easier for me to persuade them to leave.

For my mother and me another very moving moment came a few days later, when the postman brought a letter for her from my father. I took delivery of the post and realised that the letter was from him. My mother was resting in bed. I took her the letter and asked whether she could bear to read it. She managed a smile and read the letter there and then. My father had written it three days before he was killed.

Here is part of this letter, my father's last:

> I came ashore early yesterday morning and have been immersed in the most delicate and exhausting attempts to get the local Indonesians to cooperate ... I had a long interview yesterday morning with Dr Moestopo, the local head of the so-called Indonesian Republic. As these people are in complete control and have acquired all the arms which the Japanese had here, I have been obliged to try to play them along until such time as I feel myself in a position to become tough. This city has a population variously estimated at anything from 300,000 to half a million, and there are several thousand, I should say, who have arms of various kinds. They control all the public utilities and patrol the streets in large numbers. As a result of my interview yesterday I had Moestopo practically eating out of my hand, and although there were wearing and maddening delays in getting anything done, we were getting by degrees what we wanted and at least we succeeded in getting troops into the most important parts of the city without argument.

This morning, contrary to my wishes, a British plane came over and dropped a proclamation over the city. This sets up a military government under me, and makes death the penalty for carrying arms. It was for use when needed, but now it has utterly ruined all I had done!

I had three hours of most exhausting talk with Moestopo, who was very upset and doubtful if he could control the people. I gave him two days for the surrender of the arms, but without much hope that anything would come in. He finally promised to broadcast this evening and tell the people to accept and obey: I thought this might help; ... but he has not made his broadcast and has disappeared. Instead someone else broadcast a speech in very much the opposite sense. I think Moestopo has flitted, either because he dare not face his followers or because he has been put in the bag by someone more extreme than himself.

... I shall not be surprised if fighting of some kind starts at any moment, and once it starts there is no knowing how far it may spread! ... I think I have enough troops ... to prevent a massacre tonight – and pray that I am not being over-confident. I shall be glad when daylight comes and we can perhaps take stock of the situation, which is at the moment nothing if not obscure and explosive...

There were admiring obituaries of my father in the British press. Here is part of one in *The Times* by a colleague who had worked for him in the War Office before he left London:

The most vivid impression left by him is one of absolute single-mindedness and selflessness in all his work, and intense inner strength and courage which manifested itself in his unshakable calm and patience in every crisis. Besides these, his prodigious capacity for work, his accessibility and flawless courtesy at any hour of the day or night, his utter freedom from formality or pomposity, his willingness to listen to anyone (however junior) who had anything sensible to say, his quickness of apprehension and clarity of decision ... inspired those who worked for him with the deepest affection and admiration.

Sue and I visited Java in 2013. We saw my father's grave in Jakarta and the square in Surabaya, at the other end of Java, where he was killed. The Commonwealth military cemetery in Jakarta is enormous. Most of the graves are British, all in the same size and style, simple and modest. The endless lines of small, identical graves give a feeling of a multitude at rest. The place is peaceful, despite being in a noisy, dusty suburb of a big Asian city with a busy street of shabby shops along one outer edge and three nondescript skyscrapers on the other side.

The cemetery is alight with butterflies and tropical shrubs. Flowers in bright colours are disciplined into tidy clumps and rows along the walls and walkways. Five gardeners were at work when we arrived and the meticulous perfection of the garden, generously watered, was clearly a labour of love.

My feelings about losing my father when I was nine had begun with anger and grief, tempered by having seen many of my friends lose their fathers in the war. There were times in the next few years when I stayed with school friends and saw the role their fathers played and realised anew what I was missing. But before I grew up all that had become a familiar part of me – often in my passing thoughts but not often at the front of my mind. The visit to the cemetery in Jakarta all those years later gave me a feeling of reassurance. It was good to know that my father's grave is beautifully kept. I had always been touched by the lines from Wordsworth on his tombstone, and seeing the words on the spot was a deeply moving moment:

> More brave for this,
> That he hath much to love.

My father's death was followed by a tough battle between the British army and the Indonesian fighters. The British won but the Indonesians did well enough to strengthen their determination to achieve independence. They did achieve it only four years later. So in retrospect the British intervention looks unnecessary and ineffective. It seemed essential in autumn 1945 but a handful of years later circumstances were different. Other colonies in Asia, above all India, had meanwhile become independent with the cooperation of the colonial power. The long history of Europe's empires was entering its last phase.

* * * * *

The extraordinary and overwhelmingly important fact about my mother's life is that she was married for 10 years and a widow for 53. Moreover, for five of the ten years she hardly saw my father because of the war.

After my father was killed, she devoted her life to being a selfless and courageous mother. Love and determination were the keys. We children never suffered psychologically from the loss of our father, because of her care, love and example. She was indomitable, as my son, Sebastian, was to write after she died. She was good at conveying to us a vivid impression of my father and their extremely happy marriage. She often told us what she believed he would have done about a decision we were facing. She was also very amusing, intelligent and capable. She had received no formal education after the age of 17, but she read a great deal – biographies, history and novels. She was also self-disciplined and principled, and perfectionist about upholding standards, taking great trouble in returning hospitality, even when she could barely afford it; and she was always smartly dressed.

She received a commendation from the psychologist who was one of my interviewers in the Foreign Office entry exams in 1959. The psychologist asked me about my childhood and the effects of my father's death. I said that there had of course been a large gap in my life but I did not think I had suffered greatly, because my mother had been a marvellous influence and example, as well as a boon companion. The psychologist said that my remarks and his own deductions about me had persuaded him for the first time that a single mother could fulfil successfully the role of both parents. I of course reported this to my mother, whose eyes for a moment filled with tears.

My mother would not tell us children what kind of work she was doing in order to make ends meet when she was a widow. Antony and I discovered that she wrote humorous journalism for *The Times* and in *Punch*. There was a successful series in *Punch* called 'Mummy, Mummy'. Each article consisted of a breathless monologue by an excited and inquisitive child of four or five. I thought this series must be my mother's work; the style and wit were hers and the childish talk sounded like the chatter of my sister Sue. My mother denied authorship.

She also did industrial work, assembling large air filters for a vehicle company. Unlike the journalism, this work could not be kept secret from her children. The filter components were delivered to our home. My mother assembled them, and the filters were collected. I sometimes helped her in this work.

While we children were away at boarding school, my mother bravely reduced her expenses to the Spartan minimum by living in one room of the house. By saving money for more than half the year, she was able to give us one big treat every school holiday and a lovely summer holiday.

The most memorable holidays were spent at the Hotel Bonivard at Montreux on the Swiss shore of Lake Geneva. There were other British children and we made friends. We learned to fish in the lake for small inedible fish like dace and roach and we swam a great deal. One of my mother's gifts to her children was that she introduced us to travelling abroad and all three of us have had much enjoyment as a result.

My mother's sense of humour was frequently the main feature of a day. One part of it was her choice of words when telling light-hearted stories. Nobody died; they either perished or they upped and died. Once buried they were pushing up the daisies. Nobody left a room quickly; they always hurtled forth. Girls did not have boyfriends but besotted swains. Children did not play outside; they rampaged. The weather was not cold but bracing.

*****

My mother's father had had a distinguished career in the British Army in India. Then he lived in retirement in the Camberley house as a merry widower, travelling often to fish and shoot.

When out shopping one day in 1943 my mother was congratulated by a friend of my grandfather on his remarriage. My mother was astonished. But thinking over this strange revelation she guessed who her new stepmother must be, because of a puzzling conversation with her father some time before. He had asked her to dismiss the cook. She had agreed that the cook was a very bad cook and by no means clean, but said she would rather not sack this cook until another could be engaged. My grandfather had insisted that the cook must leave immediately.

Questioned by my mother about a second marriage, my grandfather admitted that he had secretly wed the cook and had insisted that she be dismissed so that his wife would not be a domestic servant with his family. Possibly as a result of his experiences when fighting in the First World War, he disliked responsibility and hated emotional moments, as this odd episode suggests. His new wife Violet had gone to Devon to find a home for them. He gave the Camberley house to my mother and left to join his bride. This was before my father was killed. It was hard then, and still is, to accept that my grandfather did not return to help my mother after that appalling bereavement. This episode left my mother hurt and angry.

About three years after he left Camberley my grandfather invited me to stay with him and Violet in Devon. As I stepped off the train, the first thing he said was 'She would like you to call her Granny. I hope you will.' I was happy to be with my grandfather again. He taught me to catch salmon on the River Taw, my first attempt at serious fishing. My stay went well and near the end I telephoned my mother. I said that my grandfather had suggested that she should drive to Devon to collect me at the end of my stay. I persuaded her that reconciliation was possible and she should come and spend two nights at the local pub. Her visit went quite well. I like to think of this as my first diplomatic assignment.

After that, Antony and I went to stay with our grandfather and 'Granny' a couple of times a year for many years. We fished for salmon and shot many rabbits. These visits were an important part of my teens. I enjoyed them and was glad to learn country pursuits. Today I continue to enjoy fishing and Antony shoots and fishes a great deal.

* * * * *

My mother had numerous admirers. In general she was not interested. One exception was the American statesman Adlai Stevenson. He and she got off a London bus outside the Ritz Hotel. They talked and got on well. He was clever, witty and debonair. He was Governor of Illinois from 1949 to 1953 and was twice the Democratic Party's candidate for President, losing both times to Eisenhower. My mother much enjoyed his company and might have been seriously interested but for one consideration. She told me that my father would have wanted his children to remain British rather than becoming American.

The most important point, I think, was a different one that my mother sometimes made to me. She said that her marriage to my father had been completely perfect in every way and she did not believe that a second marriage could be half as happy.

Our house in Camberley was frequently burgled when my mother was alone there. She saw outwitting thieves as a duty and a sport. In May 1960, she returned home to find a van driving away with our television and other booty. She blocked the way out with her car. The gang of burglars threateningly surrounded her. She let them go and immediately telephoned the police, who gave chase, at seventy miles an hour according to the press, and set up a road block on the bridge over the Thames at Staines. One of the burglars leaped into the Thames to avoid arrest and was drowned. The others were sentenced to seven years in prison, partly because they had threatened my mother with violence. The judge commended her for courage.

Eton

My mother and father wanted their sons to go to Eton. She could not possibly afford this as a widow. Antony and I were awarded bursaries which the school offered to the sons of fathers killed in the war.

Housemasters play an important role in the life of every boy at Eton. They are in charge of the well-being of the 45 boys in the house, as well as discipline and organisation. They play a major part in setting the atmosphere of the house, and they should get to know each boy, identify his talents and interests and motivate and encourage whenever necessary. Not all housemasters are effective and boys who have a good one can benefit greatly from the start. Francis Cruso was a good housemaster. He was also my work tutor until I took O-level at age 16 and was good in this role too.

Francis ran his house with tact and a light touch. He was humane, encouraging and humorous. He introduced us to us to amusing literature, reading *The Diary of a Nobody* by G. and W. Grossmith and *The Wrong Box* by R. L. Stevenson with verve and bursts of laughter. But I don't think that Francis really inspired his boys or awoke enthusiasm or exceptional effort, except in music or when producing a play.

There were a couple of aristocratic boys in my house but we were nearly all middle class, some from quite wealthy families. Among my seven or eight nearest contemporaries about four had more pocket money from their families than me, and I and the others had just enough to keep going. Being one of the less well-off was not a problem, though I was conscious of the difference.

I was hopeless at competitive sports and spent on them the minimum amount of time allowed. I enjoyed learning to row and to play squash but never became good at either. I was quite good at work by my second year. I then started to work hard. I advanced among my contemporaries from being a little above the middle in work results to near the top.

I was better at literary subjects than scientific ones. I liked Latin and Greek, especially some of the literature. I willingly learned passages of Cicero, Virgil and Homer by heart. I also enjoyed history. French was my favourite subject. When I was 14, a popular and effective master called Oliver van Oss took me aside and said, with a friendly smile, that French was my 'least bad subject' and I should do a second language. I began to learn German. I am glad I did, because I was to work for years in Germany as an adult, five of them as Ambassador. At first, however, learning German was a mixed experience. The teacher caught our attention by telling us that we would soon be able to join German words together to create perfectly legitimate new ones. He told us that there was a single word in German for 'an attempt on the life of a Hottentot Potentate', nine words in

English. His word was *Hottentottenpotentatenattentat*. Far less positive was the experience of learning German verbs; no sooner had we slogged through the regular verbs than we discovered that the irregular ones seemed at least as numerous.

Eton at that time did not do A-levels, relying on its own, rather harder, July Examinations for university entry. The few boys who were applying for County grants to help pay for university did A-level at Beaumont, a school in Windsor. I did French and German A-levels and performed sufficiently well to get the County grant I needed for Cambridge.

I enjoyed Eton in a quiet way. I liked the traditions and the beautiful buildings. I undertook fewer activities than many other boys, partly because I was bad at sports and music and was not religious. So I was not overstretched. My time was devoted mostly to friends, who were numerous, and to my work. I also fished often in the Thames and even published some articles in angling magazines. I enjoyed, in my final year, being a senior boy and in my last two terms being head of my house. I benefitted from this experience of exercising considerable responsibility, as I think did many others who had this privilege. This may be one reason why Old Etonians are often confident, willing to bear responsibility and ambitious.

I think of this confidence as one valuable legacy of Eton. It has helped me socially and also in being undaunted by difficult issues in my work. In my case, another benefit of Eton was to learn to organise my life and to work hard, concentrating on the purpose of the work rather than minding its cost in time and effort. Much of the work at Eton, after the first two years, was done in the boys' own time. So one needed to learn to organise the work for a week ahead at least. This was a valuable discipline for life.

The most important gain from Eton is also the most difficult to describe. You live closely with many different boys, and you learn to tolerate irritating characteristics and to value the good elements in those around you. You live in a world of effort and of humour, and you learn how to combine the two. You have a good chance of learning to distinguish what is displeasing behaviour in others from what is beyond the pale; and to recognise that the second category is by far the smaller.

National Service 1955–56

In my generation in Britain all men aged 18 were required to do military service lasting two years. I dreaded the basic training during the first months in the army, when learning to march and polish your boots were the main occupations; and discipline was fierce. But since National Service was obligatory, I said to myself that countless others had managed it and I should be able to manage it too.

I joined the army on 2 February 1955, six weeks after I left school. Hadrian's Camp at Carlisle was very cold. The basic training was indeed unpleasant. Square bashing, as marching drill was called, began before breakfast. The sergeant in charge of my batch of recruits was deliberately unkind, making young soldiers clean out the latrines before dawn as punishment for slight imperfections in their dress. He shouted obscenities at them with his face almost touching theirs. He particularly victimised the recruits with A-levels. This was not surprising because they were likely in six months to be officers and senior to him. Like others who were tall and slim, I was nicknamed Long Streak of Piss or Long Streak for short.

Mons Officer Cadet School at Aldershot, where I spent the next four months, was more agreeable. The drill sessions continued but other kinds of instruction, about armoured vehicles and their guns, tactics and the work of a junior officer, were more important. The staff who trained us were friendly and effective. Excursions to London for an evening were occasionally possible, and a modest taste of night life with a band of girls and army friends provided an exciting contrast to military training.

In summer 1955 I became a Second Lieutenant and joined the Ninth Lancers, a former cavalry regiment which now had Centurion tanks. We were stationed in Detmold, an attractive, sleepy town in north Germany. I was just nineteen when I took command of four tanks and about eighteen men. Leading my troop involved some responsibility, as we trained in the use in battle of our tanks and their radios, guns and engines. We practised all this, as well as map reading and tactics, in manoeuvres in the countryside and on shooting ranges where we learned to use the guns. These manoeuvres, often involving several days and nights in the open, were one of the army activities which taught me something valuable: it is possible to laugh with comrades in unpleasant situations, such as a series of mostly sleepless nights out of doors in cold, wet weather.

Many of my colleagues – officers and others – were good company. The atmosphere among the young officers, National Servicemen like me and our professional colleagues who were starting careers in the army, was defined by fellowship and frequent laughter and various sports, from riding horses to squash and billiards. We were part of BAOR, the British Army of the Rhine, which in turn was part of the forces of NATO, together with United States, French, German and other Allied forces. The role of this formidable deployment was to deter the Soviet Union from attacking westwards in Europe. The idea of the West's strategy of deterrence was that the Soviet Union would not launch aggression if it knew that it would be killing American and other Allied soldiers soon after an attack began, since this would run the risk of retaliation by the nuclear weapons of the United States and Britain and maybe France, and that would mean the destruction of much of the Soviet Union itself. My troop and I were a tiny element of that strategy. The training we did had two purposes – to learn the trade of a junior officer in case we should be enlisted again, after National Service, to fight a real war; and secondly to show the Soviet Union that the allied forces facing them in central Europe were serious and fully trained.

I wanted to take the opportunity to improve my German, in preparation for studying the language at Cambridge. I walked into the Grammar School in Detmold and asked if one of the teachers would talk German with me in the evenings to improve my knowledge of the language and literature. I went twice a week and I enjoyed it. The senior officers of the Ninth Lancers, however, did not approve of my absences in the town. The Colonel sent for me and began to say with a grin that he could of course understand that a young man like me would want a girlfriend in the town. I interrupted to say that I was not seeing a girl but a schoolmaster, and was taking lessons to improve my German. At this, the Colonel's mood of friendly chiding gave way to anger. He said the German language was not a reason for breaking the British Army's ban on fraternisation with Germans, in force for the ten years since the war. But the next day, he sent for me again and said with a smile that every important person had an interpreter and I should be his interpreter, as well as continuing to command my tanks and soldiers. This was a gesture of goodwill. I expected it to involve no work since the Colonel never spoke to any German.

There was however one occasion when I interpreted for the Colonel. I have told this story many times in the sixty years since then, and I may have embroidered it unconsciously. My regiment was on manoeuvres not far from Hamburg. The Colonel was curious to get a glimpse of Hamburg's famous red light district, explaining that he should see it briefly because he sometimes had to discipline soldiers who misbehaved there. He took a large army truck with me and a driver. We went to a bar on the Reeperbahn, the heart of the red light area but not in the parts which were out of bounds to British army personnel. The cabaret at the Lausen Bar consisted of young ladies without clothes, mounted on ponies, perambulating among the tables where guests were sitting.

As we sat at our table drinking beer and watching this tawdry show, the Colonel suddenly rose to his full height and bellowed a price in English. The manager, who had understood the amount offered, ran to our table, rubbing his hands in glee. He was happy to let the Colonel spend time with the girl for this ample price. The girl did not protest.

I interpreted for the Colonel who astonished me by explaining that he wanted not the girl but the pony. He thought it looked a promising mount for his beloved sport of polo.

At first the manager did not understand. The Colonel thought I was translating his simple proposition incompetently. Once I'd got the basic idea into the manager's head, the bargaining got going and I interpreted until agreement was reached on a rather higher price for the pony than the Colonel had first offered. We coaxed the pony noisily into our truck. I never heard that it was used for polo.

I visited various parts of Germany at weekends. I was excited by the metropolitan vivacity of West Berlin. This was 1955, six years before the Berlin Wall was built. It was an extraordinary experience to walk from the prosperity and the neon lights of

West Berlin to the war-scarred drabness of East Berlin, and experience within a few paces the division of Europe by the Iron Curtain. There were still piles of war rubble near Unter den Linden, East Berlin's main street, which I was to get to know well in 1966 and later.

My impressions of this first stay in West Germany were that stability and democracy had taken root and that prosperity, already impressive, was still growing. I could see no sign that Germany might become aggressive again. The worry of the young men from Britain who were doing National Service in Germany was that a third world war seemed rather likely, this time between the West and the Soviet Union. We thought that in the years following our National Service we might well be recalled to the army to fight. We did not doubt that West Germany would be on our side.

Cambridge University 1956–59

In my first year at King's College, Cambridge, I studied French and German, my main subjects in my last two years at school. In fact, the subject of study was not language but literature, although there were some lectures about the most excruciating parts of German grammar. Undergraduates were expected to improve their knowledge of the languages by visiting the countries concerned in the vacations. This was not unreasonable because the vacations lasted for more than half the year and there were some grants for travel and schemes for working in France and Germany. And the travel was enjoyable.

We studied seventeenth-century French literature. I worked hard, partly because I enjoyed it. The French writers we studied were interesting in themselves, as well as being the antecedents of many later writers whom I intended to read in due course. This part of my studies was the start of my devotion to French literature, which has given me much pleasure ever since.

In German, we studied some big names – Schiller, Gotthold Lessing, Goethe and the romantic poets. This too was interesting and I was keen, as with French literature, to learn about a significant part of Europe's cultural heritage. I was to enjoy modern West and East German literature at various times in my life, but, despite the many years I was to spend in Germany, the literature has not been as important to me as English, American, French or Russian literature.

I decided half-way through my first year at Cambridge to stop studying languages. It was possible to complete the first half of the degree in one year and I opted to do that and then move to another faculty. My reason was that I could continue to learn the languages by visiting France and Germany even if I changed my subject of study. Also, the study of literature was so intensive that there was a high risk of volume smothering enjoyment. To study in a week a play by Racine, reading not only the play itself but also critical studies and probably a biography, and then to write a long essay – this was not the way to digest and enjoy great writing. Especially if the next week required the same volume of effort on a work of Goethe. I knew I would continue in the future to read French literature, and probably German, at a more sensible and enjoyable pace.

Which faculty to choose for my last two years at Cambridge? One consideration was which course would prepare me best for the exams for the Foreign Office. I had wanted since about the age of 15 to become a diplomat. One reason was that there was a tradition of public service in my family; and the army, though I had enjoyed National Service, did not attract me as a lifetime career. Another reason was that I was good at languages. And the biggest reason was that I wanted to travel. I knew by my first year at Cambridge that the Foreign Office entrance exams were extremely difficult and I did not expect to succeed, but I still wanted to try.

I visited the personnel department of the Foreign Office to seek advice on my choice of faculty. The official I saw said understandably that the Office could not advise me which faculty to choose. But he told me which faculties at Oxford and Cambridge, the universities which then provided almost all entrants, had recently been most successful. The most successful faculty was PPE at Oxford. I would have loved to study politics, philosophy and economics, but there was no such faculty at Cambridge. History was the most successful Cambridge faculty, and history was also the subject which attracted me most. Cambridge agreed that I should switch to history. This change of faculty was the best decision I took before my marriage.

I chose as my main subject Modern European History, which began with the Renaissance. Within this I concentrated on Europe since the French revolution, including the later revolutions in France and Napoleon I and Napoleon III, the first unification of Germany, and the First World War and its causes. Another of my main interests was the Russian revolution. England in the 18th and 19th centuries, especially the Victorian period, gave me much enjoyment. Another subject which caught my interest was the expansion of Europe, about the creation of the empires of European powers and then their decline; this was rewarding for me because my mother's family had lived for generations in India. I was puzzled by parts of the course on Theories of the Modern State but Rousseau and Voltaire and John Stuart Mill made a strong impression. Marxism and its perversion into Leninism were explained in gripping lectures by Professor Sir Michael Postan, one of the outstanding academics whose arrival from Eastern Europe enriched British universities in the twentieth century. I became interested in the origins of the British Labour party. I saw the party then as a fine example of the combination of moderate socialism with democracy, a contrast to the Soviet Union where the leaders of the Communist Party ruled as autocrats.

I got a 2–1 in the examination at the end of my first year of history. As I had not studied the subject since I was sixteen I was encouraged. The more so since, in this first year of history, I had worked for only two days a week, because I wanted to broaden my knowledge of other subjects, especially literature and the arts. King's, with its highbrow atmosphere, had made me determined to make myself more cultivated. I prepared a wide programme of reading and followed it with much enjoyment. Thanks to Kings, I came to see myself as a bit of an intellectual.

My reading covered modern English and American literature, from George Eliot to Hemingway, Russian novels in translation and many French novels and short stories, especially from the 19th century. I also read some literature from earlier times, including Boswell's Life of Johnson, Machiavelli and Benvenuto Cellini. Often I devoured more than one novel a day in the terms or the holidays. This was the greatest pleasure and has continued at a less hectic rate ever since.

In my final year at Cambridge I worked flat out on my history, usually eight hours a day in libraries. My special subject, European diplomacy in the 1870s, was fascinating. Among other things it covered the Russo-Turkish war in the late 1870s and the subsequent Congress of Berlin. For the first time I researched primary sources, mainly diplomatic correspondence from the British Embassy at Constantinople and in the archives of the foreign ministries of Russia and Germany.

Having worked hard, I had mild hopes of getting a first, but another two-one was clearly the most likely result. And a high two-one was what I got. This was a respectable outcome. It was enough to confirm my place at the Foreign Office, so it was certain (since I had passed the FO entry competition), as I left Cambridge, that I would become a diplomat within a few weeks. My knowledge of French and German, developed by periods spent during Cambridge vacations in Paris and Cologne, was of course a useful asset for diplomacy. And some of the history I had studied, such as the Russian Revolution and Marxist-Leninist ideology, was to prove directly relevant to my first diplomatic assignment in Moscow.

I enjoyed Cambridge immensely. It was a greater influence than Eton on the person I was becoming. My time, as at school, was devoted mainly to friends and to work. A big difference was that girlfriends were a major part of my enjoyment of life. Religion, sports, music and acting played no part.

My rooms for my first two years were in the house near Magdalene Bridge of Mrs Agnes Smith, a generous and humorous landlady who was in her fifties. Agnes and I got on extremely well and joked that we were engaged and I was marrying her for her money – amassed, according to her student lodgers' teasing, from the excessive sums she charged us. Far from overcharging, Agnes provided, for no extra payment, enormous breakfasts, with mixed grills and mushroom omelettes among our favourite dishes. She also spoiled us with teas of toast and large chocolate cakes. This delicious and filling fare enabled us to skip lunch often, and thus reduce our cost of living.

For my final year I lived in King's, in the courtyard beside the River Cam. I loved the beautiful surroundings, with two masterpieces of architecture – King's Chapel and Gibbs Building – very near my rooms.

My friends at Cambridge I got to know in various ways. Some were friends from school or National Service. Many of these were members of the Pitt Club, a rather posh place frequented by men from independent schools. I met friends there for lunch a couple of times a week. The second source of friends was King's College itself, where I dined most evenings. Many friends came from the modern languages faculty and then the history faculty. And I met many others by chance.

Endless conversation was important in my friendships, both light-hearted and serious. Like so many students, we meandered from love to religion to the meaning of existence. We argued about books and films and plays. Our attitudes to current affairs, notably the uprising against Soviet communism in Hungary in 1956, which was squashed by the Red Army, and the British-French-Israeli intervention at Suez in the same year, were influenced by our recent experience of military service and the fact that the fathers of many of us, like mine, had been killed in the war. Most of us were in favour of the UK's intervention in Suez but everyone realised after its failure that it had been a humiliating mistake.

My political views began to take shape. I was right of centre, a moderate conservative who favoured reform, and was willing to like some policies of the other parties. The political position of my Pitt Club friends was to the right of mine – most were committed Tories and opposed to other views. My other friends held various views but none were far from the centre of politics. None were attracted by communism, which did appeal to some Cambridge students at that time. Fascism, the enemy in the war, was reviled. My pragmatic, right-of-centre politics have stayed with me all my life. I look carefully at the policies of the parties before each election and have usually voted conservative, but not always.

My Cambridge friends were rather sensible and sober. At parties there was wine and beer and sometimes spirits. I can remember only occasional moments of drunkenness among us. We had never heard of drugs.

At Cambridge I developed my interest in art. I was inspired by the lectures of Professor Sir Niklaus Pevsner on the history of art and architecture. His lectures were a phenomenon at Cambridge, with a devoted following among undergraduates from many faculties. I started visiting galleries much more frequently and taking time to think about the pictures that I saw. By the end of Cambridge, visits to exhibitions and museums had become a major occupation.

I also began, with the help of friends who were interested, notably Paul Cornwall-Jones and Mark Glazebrook, to learn about contemporary British artists who were virtually my age – David Hockney, Patrick Caulfield and others. This interest in art was to lead me to collect dissident art in Moscow in 1961–63 and, twenty years later, English watercolours of the late eighteenth and early nineteenth centuries; and nowadays British painting of the early twentieth century. Museums and exhibitions continue to be a major interest and from 1997 to 2003 I had the privilege to spend six years on the board of Tate when we created Tate Modern. That was the most substantial of my various roles in the art world.

The three stages of the entry competition for the Foreign Office took place in the first half of 1959, my last year at Cambridge. The final interview was daunting but my confidence had been strengthened by job offers I had by then received from Shell, BP and Unilever. I sat at a large round table with a hole in the centre, through which the feet of my seven interviewers were incongruously visible. Sir David Scott, a distinguished former diplomat, was in the chair. He asked me a tricky question. After noting that I had been at Eton and then in a smart regiment in National Service, he asked whether I had found it difficult at Cambridge to get to know undergraduates of other backgrounds. I said truthfully that I had made friends among many kinds of people, in my college and my faculty and socially. He looked at me sharply and asked 'So you dug down?' I replied that I was glad I had broadened out.

I enjoyed the interview and was for the first time quite hopeful about passing into the Foreign Office. I heard 10 days later that I had been successful. I was utterly delighted. This was a difficult thing to achieve. There were thousands of applicants and fifteen of us got in. It was the first notable achievement of my life. I had never expected to succeed, so I had not been worried about failing.

My elation at success was far stronger than my disappointment would have been if I had failed.

Early in 1958 at Cambridge my friend David Williams invited me for a drink after dinner to meet a French girl from Paris whose cousin was his girlfriend in London. He lived on the top floor of a large house. The light on the stairs went off when I was near the top. There was a sound of rushing water, a door opened, light filled the stairway, and a girl fell headlong out of the lavatory door, just in front of me. I helped her up.

Pascale and I fell in love within days. We met constantly till the summer when we stopped for no reason except that our relationship did not seem to be going well. The following spring I was In Paris on a travel grant from King's. I contacted Pascale. Immediately we met the attraction was there again; we got on fantastically well and I enjoyed every minute of it. By the time we had dined and talked and arrived in a nightclub it was obvious that we were falling in love again. After that we went to the Pied de Cochon restaurant in the market of Les Halles and stayed till dawn. Pascale and I met every day for the rest of my stay in Paris. We spent a happy afternoon at the Jeu de Paume gallery and an evening at the Comédie Francaise, where we saw an appallingly stodgy production of *La Reine Morte* by Montherlant. We talked endlessly and were happy.

I spent several weeks in the summer of 1959 staying with Pascale and her family near Le Havre in northern France. A few months later Pascale and I dined at a London restaurant. We discussed the future and agreed that we wanted in due course to marry. At Waterloo station, where she was catching a train to France, we talked for 20 minutes. Suddenly I found myself proposing to her. It simply could not remain unsaid; it came out unselfconsciously and unexpectedly. And Pascale said yes. Waterloo, platform 10, was hardly a romantic place to propose marriage so, as her train began to move, I promised to re-enact the scene on bended knee in more suitable surroundings.

2

MOSCOW 1961–63

For centuries, western travellers have described Moscow as European yet not European, Asian yet not Asian. In my time the city was more European than Asian, but very unlike Western Europe. A city of six million people who seemed shabby, cowed and expressionless; passive, fatalistic and sad. Many people were lazy, unreliable and late for everything, and the men were often drunk. There was a pervasive smell, a mixture of low grade petrol, cheap tobacco and cabbage.

Shop windows were often empty and always colourless. There were far fewer cars than in western cities. Everywhere were communist party slogans on enormous red banners. One common slogan was 'Long Live the Great Soviet People, Builder of Socialism'. Apart from lists of film and theatre performances, the only advertising I saw was the occasional small sign on the back of a van urging baldly, 'use restaurants'. Neither the slogan nor the two-word advertisement seemed at all persuasive.

The bad sides of Moscow begin with the depressing climate. In our time the temperature in winter fell frequently below minus 20° C. Daylight lasted from about 10.30 am to 3.00 pm. Snow lay everywhere for months, piled up by snow ploughs along the sides of the streets. In the spring the city was awash with muddy melting snow.

Moscow is a city of despotism, from the Tsars to the Communist Party, from Ivan the Terrible to Stalin. It has also been a holy city. The Kremlin, the historic seat of despotism, has beautiful palaces and churches, but also threatening fortified walls; for a westerner mysterious, even eerie. Under these outward features there was endurance. For there was much to endure. Overcrowded, verminous homes, shortages of many goods, dictatorship and its instruments – lying authorities and media, ubiquitous informers for the KGB, punishment for anyone who did not obey the party line in speech or behaviour. No wonder people lied like the authorities and corruption was rampant in everyday life: bribes to get a flat or medicines, or a spare part for your factory's machine, or someone to repair a lorry.

In this city of hardship, corruption and lies, there were good things too. Many highly educated people whose conversation, deliberately avoiding politics, sparkled with passion and wit in discussing books, films or plays. Splendid cultural joys: ballet and opera at the Bolshoi, many excellent concerts, good theatre.

For western diplomats and journalists there was above all the fascination of learning to understand and predict the policies and actions of the Soviet Union, of the main antagonist of western freedom, the main threat to peace. This professional thrill more than outweighed the disadvantages of life in Moscow.

Before arriving in Moscow in January 1961, I spent a year on two absorbing things. I learned Russian and then I participated from September to December 1960 in the General Assembly of the United Nations in New York. These two experiences provided an ideal start to my career; the first was essential for me and the second was exciting and both were valuable for my future work.

Learning Russian

I joined the Foreign Office on 21 August 1959. We ten recruits were each to learn one of the harder foreign languages. My fate was Russian, with eight months' study in London and then a couple of months in Paris with a Russian émigré family, and finally a posting to Moscow. My reaction was that a career biased towards the Iron Curtain countries would be fascinating and useful.

My Russian teacher was Frank Esterkin. He had left Russia in his teens after the revolution, found his way to London, and served in the British army as an interpreter in the war and at the

Nuremberg trials of the Nazi leaders. After the war he worked for the Foreign Office as an interpreter and instructor in the Russian language.

Frank made his two students learn and laugh. He made even the driest grammar lesson agreeable. We started from scratch, with the Russian alphabet and some of the grammar covered within days. Frank sped us on to read Russian literature. I enjoyed Pushkin's *The Captain's Daughter* and Lermontov's *Queen of Spades*, and later Turgenev's *Sportsman's Sketches*. To be devouring the simpler works of great Russian writers within weeks was satisfying and enjoyable. By the end of Frank's course of eight months I could write and read Russian with a dictionary and talk fairly fluently.

The second part of my Russian course lasted ten weeks. I stayed in Paris with Princess Eka Dadiani. She was about 55, unmarried, gregarious and good company. A Georgian aristocrat, she was making her living in exile by taking in British diplomats and army officers who were learning Russian. She taught Russian effectively by sharing her daily life with her students. I spent much time with her, in the dusty, cluttered flat decorated with Tsarist uniforms on tailor's dummies, living and talking in Russian with her numerous guests. They were mostly the children of Russian nobles who had left Russia after the revolution in 1917. The oddity was that in Russia Eka and the other aristocratic exiles had spoken French among themselves and Russian only with their servants. Now they spoke Russian among themselves and French with everyone else.

One incident illustrates the quaint lives of the émigré milieu. All the men at one dinner party had left Russia between 1917 and 1920 as young lieutenants or cadets in the Tsar's army. In exile in Paris, when the Tsar's army no longer existed, each had promoted himself rapidly through the military ranks. No-one knew who had made himself a general first, so they bickered about the order of precedence at the dinner table.

I read a great deal in Russian, and my interest in the literature and history kept growing. When I left Paris I could speak Russian fluently and read even the complex Russian of Dostoyevsky's novels without a dictionary.

The United Nations

For my first diplomatic work, I was a junior member of the large British delegation at the annual General Assembly of the United Nations. My role was to write summaries for the Foreign Office of the innumerable speeches made in the Assembly. One notable example was the speech of Fidel Castro, the new revolutionary leader of Cuba. Castro's speech was a marathon lasting six hours. My summary was only a few hundred words. I thought there must be more to report from Castro's torrent of flamboyant rhetoric, so I read the speech again. Nothing else in it save bluster and repetition. I did not amend my report.

The UN General Assembly has many limitations, but its sessions are important, being the nearest thing to a world parliament that has existed. The session in 1960 was much more important than usual because the leaders of many countries participated and made speeches designed, not always successfully, to impress each other and the media. Khrushchev, the Soviet leader, was the first to announce that he would attend, and the leaders of the other communist countries in Europe immediately said that they would come too. A galaxy of others then decided to attend. China was represented by Prime Minister Chou en Lai, and Yugoslavia by Tito. Nehru from India and Nasser from Egypt were among the many leaders from the developing world. The United States was represented at the start of the Assembly by President Eisenhower and later by the new president, John Kennedy, who spoke with brilliance and charm. The United Nations Secretary General, Dag Hammarskjöld, played an important role. Kennedy and Hammarskjöld were the two statesmen at that extraordinary gathering whom I found truly inspiring. Both were to die violently within three years.

The numerous national leaders were clearly glad to be participating in such a newsworthy world gathering. Those from newly independent countries were particularly proud. Into this self-important throng erupted an angry display of rank vulgarity.

The British Prime Minister, Harold Macmillan, responded to Khrushchev's attacks on western imperialism by saying that the Soviet leader was ignoring the empire he knew best, the one consisting of the eastern European countries under the domination of Moscow. I was sitting a few rows behind the Soviet leader.

I saw him leap to his feet, shout, remove his shoe and bang the desk. Macmillan turned to the President of the General Assembly and asked languidly 'Mr President, perhaps we could have a translation; I could not quite follow.' Far from being critical of Macmillan's superior style, the General Assembly was cross with Khrushchev's violation of its dignity and applauded the British Prime Minister.

Arrival in Moscow

When I arrived in Moscow in January 1961, I was 24 and had left Cambridge 18 months before. I had a very Soviet experience immediately on arrival. Using my Russian in Russia for the first time, I asked a waitress in the airport café 'Gde tualet?' 'Where is the loo?' She examined me intently from head to foot, and asked 'Men's or women's?' She had evidently understood my question, so this was not a language problem. I learned later from the Embassy driver who met me at the airport that the terminal had had both sorts of loo for only a few weeks, and wanted to make sure that travellers were aware of the new sophistication.

Starting work the next day, I found an Embassy dedicated to its work and conscious that the work mattered. The Soviet Union was the great threat to the security of the West, and Khrushchev, the fiery leader of the Communist Party and the country, fulminated frequently about the iniquities of capitalism and boasted that communism would overtake it; he threatened that the Soviet Union would 'bury' capitalism.

The impression in the Soviet Union and among many people elsewhere at this time was that the USSR was on the up in the world and was gaining influence. Its important part in the defeat of Nazi Germany fifteen years earlier had begun to establish its position as one of the two superpowers. Following that, it had gained control of Eastern Europe. It had become a nuclear power. It had led the world in sending the first satellite into space in 1957, and in April 1961 was to send the first man into space. Living standards were far behind those in the West but had begun to improve.

The people in our Embassy who were doing substantive work – political, commercial, consular and so on – were immersed in significant subjects. Especially for the many Russian speakers, the interest of the work outweighed the daily difficulties and the nastiness of Moscow life. The work of the junior staff was essential to the whole Embassy, but it was less interesting and the bad sides of Moscow loomed larger. I think most still managed to enjoy the experience of a different world and the daily confirmation that Soviet communism was dictatorial and unsuccessful. Curiosity is an important quality for diplomatic life and its enjoyment.

Beginner's Work

My vague idea of diplomacy until this time had featured fascinating travel, interesting people and some luxuries. Although I had read several books of diplomatic memoirs and a good deal of diplomatic history, I had not really registered that the office workload would be heavy and require many hours of concentration on files every day. The lucky thing was that I found that I loved this dominant part of a diplomatic career.

My first job in Moscow was as Private Secretary to the Ambassador, Sir Frank Roberts. He was energetic and experienced, with an agile and fertile mind, rapid in his style and incisive in his talk. I was impressed, even daunted, by the time he devoted to the work, managing to combine a demanding office job with an active social life. I organised his diary, making engagements to visit Soviet ministers or lunch with other foreign Ambassadors; and even trivial things like booking haircuts. Frank had had dealings with Stalin in the past and was now having conversations with Khrushchev about Berlin. He knew and understood the Soviet Union; his only missing attribute was that his Russian was not strong.

Frank expected me to be available, in Moscow or when we were travelling, at absolutely any time. I lived in a flat in the Embassy courtyard, so I could normally meet this requirement. But one weekday afternoon I took two hours off to see *Clear Skies*, a new Soviet film about public reactions to the death of Stalin eight years before. When I returned to the Embassy, Frank was understandably seething. Later, I told him about *Clear Skies*, which was one of a number of good Soviet films that appeared in the early 1960s. It showed Stalin's death as a relief to many people. This contrasted with the usual portrayal of Soviet leaders in films and books, but chimed with Khrushchev's own claim that Stalinism had been a cruel aberration, and that he was now trying to humanise the system. Frank was interested by my account of the film; he said no more about my truancy that afternoon.

I have said sometimes since that time that 90% of what I know about diplomacy I learned from Frank and the remaining 10% from Cella. They were indeed very professional and effective. They remained friends of ours for the rest of their lives. She was Lebanese, small like Frank, and clever and cultured; and she could be good company. She seemed to the Embassy staff to have a sharply commercial side, demonstrated when she sent the Ambassador's Rolls-Royce round to the flats of Embassy families, trying to sell fur coats and other clothes and objects which Cella did not wish to take to West Germany, where Frank was to be Ambassador next. Cella's note to Embassy wives made it difficult for them to refuse to buy her surplus gear. There was mild resentment at this use of rank to sell jumble to subordinates.

Among the Embassy colleagues I worked with closely were several who were notable authorities on Russia and the Russians. Having learned Russian before coming to Moscow and read much Russian literature and history, I was eager to learn more and benefitted from the erudition of Michael Duncan, Geoff Murrell and others. Michael and Geoff were members of the research cadre of the Diplomatic Service, devoting their careers entirely to the Soviet Union and related subjects.

I shared a flat in the stables behind the Embassy with Michael for my first eight months in Moscow. His knowledge of Russian literature, including the best from the Soviet period, was exceptional, and I lapped up his guidance on what to read. He once took me to dine at the club of Soviet writers; this was not allowed because we were not members of this prestigious place, but we sat down brazenly at an empty table and soon got into conversation with people at nearby tables. They seemed as much interested by us as surprised by our presence. This kind of minor infringement of Soviet rules was not seriously risky for foreign diplomats who spoke Russian. If we had been asked what we were doing in the writers' club we would have apologised and said we thought it was a public restaurant.

Sir Frank Roberts was succeeded as Ambassador by Sir Humphrey Trevelyan, one of my two or three favourite bosses in 37 years of diplomacy. Humphrey was very energetic, engaging and amusing as well as eminently qualified. He was an extremely effective Ambassador, deeply interested in Russian history, literature and language. One endearing characteristic was that Humphrey, who was frequently animated in conversation, would wiggle his ears to emphasise a point.

After Pascale and I were married in September 1961 in Paris, we went together to Moscow and were very happy. I was no longer Private Secretary to the Ambassador but was one of the analysts of Soviet foreign policy in the Embassy's Political Section. My field was Soviet policy in the developing world. It turned out to be an active subject.

Soviet foreign policy was driven mainly by the state interests of the USSR, but ideology also played a role. The Soviet leaders not only trumpeted constantly in propaganda that Marxism-Leninism was destined to be the future of mankind, but probably also believed it at this time, and saw it as their ideological duty as well as their interest to advance this cause. It is true that the doctrine had appeal in some countries, and Castro's revolution in Cuba was seen in Moscow as evidence of this and as an example which other developing countries would follow.

Khrushchev had been a cruel subordinate of Stalin, in charge of mass murder in the purges in Ukraine. When Stalin died, he behaved differently, and denounced Stalin's repression as an aberration which he would correct. This was part of his bid to gain public approval and outplay his colleagues to become the new Soviet leader. The terror Stalin had imposed for years was ended, though the labour camps remained and the system was still dictatorial.

Khrushchev was boastful, erratic and impatient. He was also vulgar and had an earthy sense of humour. In my few direct contacts with him I found that he had a human side. In May 1961, he gave a reception in the Kremlin for a large group of British business leaders who had come to Moscow to show their wares in a British industrial exhibition. Khrushchev made a clever, flamboyant speech, teasing the businessmen with allegations about excessively high prices. Then the businessmen formed a queue to shake Khrushchev's hand, and most of them gave him some gift concerned with their products. There were catalogues and miniature models of machinery. Khrushchev accepted each gift with a cursory nod. He beamed when the head of the British company Wilkinson Sword gave him a huge pair of scissors. He stuffed them carelessly into his jacket pocket. I was standing ready to interpret while his interpreter was out of the room. He turned to me and said, 'At last, something for the grandchildren!'

It was daunting to be interpreting, even briefly, for a cruel and powerful autocrat. This remark provided not only relief for me in a challenging moment but also a glimpse of the little known family man who coexisted with the merciless man of power in this complex personality.

The one and only great international achievement of the Soviet Union was its immense role in the victory over Nazi Germany in 1945. Having acquired then an empire in Eastern Europe, Moscow wanted now to push further across Europe. But the creation of NATO, the western military alliance formed to ensure the security of Western Europe and North America, and Stalin's climb-down over the blockade of West Berlin in 1948, were major setbacks. Khrushchev then tried threats; he issued ultimatums to the western powers in 1958 and 1961 to withdraw their forces from West Berlin. The West did not yield and the Soviet and East German tactics became defensive, with the building of the Berlin Wall to halt the mass emigration from communist East Germany to the West via Berlin.

These experiences made clear to the Soviet leaders that their aim of spreading Soviet power and Marxism–Leninism westwards across Europe and beyond would not be achieved by full frontal aggression, or the threat of it, with troops and tanks attacking into West Germany and towards the Atlantic. The risk of American nuclear retaliation, not to speak of British and French, made that strategy impossible.

So Khrushchev tried a different approach in the Cold War. He attempted to out-flank the West from the south, by gaining influence in major developing countries. At the United Nations General Assembly in late 1960, described above, Khrushchev had made an energetic bid for cooperation and influence with India, Egypt, Nigeria and other countries which wanted to find new friends and to distance themselves from the colonial powers from which they had recently gained independence.

Khrushchev's drive for influence in the developing world made my job in the Embassy of analysing Soviet policies in this field both topical and active. The disadvantage of the work was that our main tool for analysis was the Soviet press. I had to read the coverage of foreign affairs in *Pravda* and *Izvestiya* and other Soviet newspapers every day. It was stodgy, blatant propaganda, with no attempt to inform Party members and the public about the facts, but only telling them what they should think about international developments. Rather than explaining the reasons for a Soviet policy, Pravda would often resort to the meaningless assertion that 'life itself' showed that the Soviet view was right. The value of reading the press was, however, that the policies or intentions of the Soviet Union could often be deduced from the propaganda line combined with other information. So I found this work laborious but rewarding.

The Cuba Crisis

For thirteen days in October 1962 Khrushchev's policy of exploiting developing countries against the West brought the world to the most dangerous crisis of the Cold War. Khrushchev attempted to install nuclear missiles with ranges up to 2000 kilometres in Cuba, a few kilometres from the United States.

It is clear that Khrushchev believed that the nuclear missiles could be installed in Cuba and made ready to be used before the United States discovered what was happening, and that he would be in a strong diplomatic position if they were ready to use by the time Washington reacted. In fact, a US observation flight over Cuba discovered the presence of the missiles on 14 October 1962, before they could be made ready. On 22 October President Kennedy called publicly on the Soviet Union to remove the missiles and declared a quarantine at sea to prevent Soviet ships from bringing more military equipment to Cuba. Soviet representatives continued to declare, privately to the US and publicly to the world, that there were no nuclear missiles in Cuba. This was a lie. Work to make the missiles operational continued until the very end of the crisis and made President Kennedy and his colleagues sceptical about Khrushchev's first indications that he was willing to withdraw the missiles.

I think Khrushchev's main motive in taking this enormous risk must have been to achieve the strategic goal of shifting the balance of forces in the world in Soviet favour and against the US, giving the Soviet Union greater leverage for dealing with Berlin and many other matters. I have recently found that Anatoly Dobrynin, then Soviet Ambassador in Washington, gave the same interpretation in his memoirs.[*] It is also confirmed by the fascinating summary records of the Soviet leaders' meetings at the time, which are available on the website of the University of Virginia (millercenter.org/search?q=Malin).

My colleague Geoff Murrell saw additional motives: Khrushchev 'may have concluded from the Vienna summit with Kennedy a few months earlier that the new American President was weak and indecisive and that an aggressive move would wrong-foot him. He may have hoped that such a bold stroke would make a strong impression on the international communist movement and thoroughly disarm Chinese criticism of Moscow's alleged weakness and defeatism.'

Khrushchev was impulsive and excitable but not mad. He had taken a huge risk to win a potentially important power advantage. He had miscalculated. I thought he would not risk a nuclear war in which he and his beloved family would be destroyed along with millions of other victims. He would not order Soviet warships to confront the US ones which were blockading the sea approach to Cuba. He would not be responsible for the greatest disaster ever caused by human beings.

Pascale and I, newlyweds in Moscow, were fully aware that there was a risk of nuclear war, in which we might fall victim to American nuclear weapons. We saw the risk but we did not believe there would be a nuclear war. We were riveted, not afraid. We spent the evening and much of the night of 27 October, the last hours of the crisis, in the US Embassy in Moscow, eating with friends there, playing a little absent-minded bridge and following word by word the inconsistent messages from Khrushchev to Kennedy, which were delivered in Russian to the Embassy at intervals through the night.

---

[*] Anatoly Dobrynin, *In Confidence*, Times Books New York 1995.

The diplomacy was dramatic. It is worth noting the main moves, with the help of the Soviet archive on the website of the University of Virginia. On 25 October Khrushchev and his top colleagues decided to offer to remove the missiles from Cuba if President Kennedy undertook that the US would not invade the island. On 26 October Khrushchev conveyed this proposal to Kennedy. On 27 October he added another condition: the removal of US missiles from Turkey. On 27 October Kennedy, ignoring Khrushchev's latest message, agreed to a deal where the Soviet missiles would be removed from Cuba and the US would undertake not to invade Cuba. The Soviet leaders, judging from the notes of their discussions, were inclined to accept this arrangement. But the Soviet Ambassador in Washington asked Bobby Kennedy, the President's brother who was his main adviser in the crisis, about the US nuclear missiles in Turkey and Bobby Kennedy indicated that they could be removed.

So Khrushchev agreed to withdraw the missiles from Cuba in return for two actions by the US. But these two actions cost the US nothing. The President had already decided not to invade Cuba again, after the disastrous attempt in the Bay of Pigs incident in April 1961. And he had wanted for some time to remove the US missiles from Turkey because they were obsolete. Turkey had resisted this. This element of the momentous deal, which probably saved the world from nuclear disaster, was kept secret for a time so that the US could inform Turkey.

I learned more about the Washington side of the crisis several years later from *Thirteen Days*, a book by Bobby Kennedy. He states that the President's expectation on 27 October was that there would be a military confrontation within the following three days and that there was a one-in-three chance of nuclear war. This remark was made *after* the Soviet leaders had decided, as the Soviet papers show, to settle the crisis in return for US concessions. The President put the risk of war much higher than I myself had thought. I'm glad I learned of his view only later![*]

* * * * *

---

[*] *Thirteen Days* by Robert F Kennedy. WW Norton and Company, New York 1969. See especially pages 87 and 110 of the paperback.

President Kennedy's success in facing down Khrushchev in an extremely dangerous crisis restored the initiative in the Cold War to the West. Khrushchev was perceived among developing countries as having let Cuba down by yielding to Kennedy over nuclear weapons, and some drew the conclusion that the Soviet Union was an unreliable patron. President Castro of Cuba did not hide his fury about Khrushchev's 'betrayal'.

After the Cuba crisis Khrushchev abandoned his high risk policy of brinkmanship in dealing with the US. He became more conciliatory, notably in his public withdrawal in 1963 of his threat of further ultimatums about West Berlin.

Khrushchev's failed attempt to install nuclear weapons in Cuba also had major repercussions within the Soviet Union. His colleagues accused him of 'hare-brained schemes' when he was sacked two years later. They meant the Cuba crisis among other actions.

It never occurred to Pascale or me that we should ask to leave Moscow after this dangerous crisis. One reason was that the crisis was over and another of similar danger did not look likely. Also, I was enjoying my work and we were happy together in Moscow and anyway due to move to London nine months later.

Cultural Work

My work on Soviet foreign policy took up more time and concentration than the more enjoyable second part of my job in Moscow from September 1961 to July 1963. I was the Deputy Cultural Attaché in the Embassy. A British-Soviet Cultural Exchange Agreement had been signed in 1959. The Embassy had a major hand in selecting and arranging the British activities under the Agreement. The Agreement was an example of the British policy of trying to enable more information about life in the West to reach people in the Soviet Union. It was in the interest of Britain and the West as a whole to do what we could to increase knowledge of our higher standard of living and our freedom.

One element in this Agreement was that each year twenty British postgraduate students would spend an academic year in Soviet universities, and the same number of Soviet postgraduates would study in Britain. The British students had a harder life than we did at the Embassy. We saw them socially and invited them for Christmas and helped them in other ways. My feeling about this exchange was that the students going both ways learned some useful truths. The British saw the absence of freedom and the low standard of living in the Soviet Union and shed quickly any illusions about communism. The Soviet students saw that the propaganda they were fed at home about poverty and the rule of big corporations in Britain was untrue.

One article of the Cultural Agreement was especially intriguing. The Soviet side 'took note' that the British Council would invite up to fifteen Soviet cultural figures to Britain. It was understood that the Soviet authorities would have no say in our choice. This was significant because totalitarian states insist on having total control over everything. Even this one small exception from total control was highly unusual. The Embassy suggested to the British Government the candidates for these special invitations. We proposed innovative writers, composers, film-makers and others who were becoming known in the Soviet Union during Khrushchev's 'thaw' under which new and more experimental artistic activity was being tentatively permitted. Our thought was that such people were likely to suffer from official reprisals when, as seemed inevitable, the thaw ended and conformity with the Communist Party's line was again enforced without exceptions. If people like this went to Britain and had some publicity there, they would be somewhat less likely to be victimised when the thaw ended. This was because action against them would become known in the West, and the Soviet authorities would prefer not to stimulate criticism abroad when they resumed repression of young talent in the arts.

One of the most interesting people we invited to Britain was Zhenya Yevtushenko. He was a poet and one of the leaders in the new writing being published during Khrushchev's thaw. His best-known poem, 'Babiy Yar', was to show that not only the Nazi invaders but also the Soviet authorities had been guilty of anti-semitism in Ukraine during the war.

I am each old man here, shot dead.
I am every child here, shot dead.
Nothing in me shall ever forget!

I saw quite a lot of Yevtushenko. His company was exciting. In our social conversations he spoke rather freely about cultural matters and was opinionated, witty and entertaining. He was sometimes rude and he drank every kind of alcohol on offer when he came to our flat. But the main point for me was that I was hearing a well-known Soviet writer criticise aspects of Soviet power, especially in the Stalin period. I was experiencing something that till fairly recently had been punished by banishment to a labour camp in the Gulag. Yevtushenko has been criticised for being too favourable towards Soviet power on some subjects in later years. But in the early 1960s he was a daring and highly refreshing talent in Russian literature.

Khrushchev himself decided that *One Day in the Life of Ivan Denisovich* by Solzhenitsyn should be published in 1962. This short, vivid novel about hard labour and terrible conditions in the Gulag was a sensation in the Soviet Union and abroad. Pascale and I read it with astonishment at the revelations and with admiration for the prisoners and the author, who was clearly an important new voice in Russian literature. Khrushchev's motive was not freedom of expression but to permit revelations about the mass cruelty of Stalin's camps. *One Day* was a landmark and I think the most important fruit of Khrushchev's thaw.

A major setback hit the thaw in December 1962, thanks to a ruse by the official Union of Artists. Khrushchev visited the Union's large official exhibition of socialist-realist art in the Manège Hall next to the Kremlin. The official artists had also arranged a small exhibition of new, experimental art. They shepherded Khrushchev into a side room to see it. They got what they wanted: Khrushchev exploded with earthy expletives. Witnesses said that he spat on one of the pictures and declared several times that the non-realist artists were pederasts (though he apparently mispronounced the Russian word). That deliberate gambit by the orthodox artists turned Khrushchev against innovation in the arts and ended the heyday of the thaw.

A Special Friend

Six weeks later, the closest friendship Pascale and I had found among Russians was interrupted. Some months before, the Second European Department of the Soviet Foreign Ministry, which dealt with relations with the UK and some other countries, had invited a few of our Embassy staff to see a new film by the gifted and experimental directors, Alov and Naumov. Various people involved in making *Peace to Him who Enters* were there, and among them was the composer of the music for the film, Nikolai ('Kolya') Karetnikov. He and I talked and got on well. Soon afterwards he came for a meal in our flat.

Kolya's real vocation was to compose complex, high-brow, innovative, often dodecaphonic music, including major pieces for the Russian Orthodox Church. That music could not be performed, even in the thaw, but he kept on composing it all his life. In 1958 he had begun his second profession, as he called it, of composing scores for Soviet films. This was how he earned his living, but there were times when he was denied work and faced hardship including hunger. We became friends. Kolya, born in 1930, was of medium height, shy, a little awkward in his movements and a heavy smoker. The main impression he made was of high intelligence and passion about everything that interested him. That meant music and freedom of expression and friendship. He was a strong Christian and deeply concerned by religion and ideas.

Kolya invited Pascale and me to the premiere of his first ballet at the Bolshoi. It was a one-act ballet called *Vanina Vanini*, based on a story by Stendhal. It was in twelve tone and therefore controversial. On the morning of the premiere, Kolya telephoned me and said that his mother-in-law had an in-growing toenail and therefore he could not host us at the premiere that evening. This excuse was deliberately absurd and we thought that Kolya had decided he should not see us because the setback to the thaw had made contacts with Western diplomats too dangerous for him. Alternatively, he might have been ordered by the KGB to cancel the invitation. Pascale and I were sad to lose touch with a friend whose company we greatly enjoyed. Kolya was demonstrative and agreeable as well as highly talented.

In our remaining 10 months in Moscow, I saw Kolya only once. By chance we came face to face in the interval during a concert. He spoke only for a moment and asked me softly 'Ty ponyal?' 'You did understand?' I said I had understood the message about the toenail.

Twelve years later, when we returned for our second period in Moscow, Kolya told us that he disliked the Soviet system and its arbitrary treatment of anything experimental in the arts. He had friends among dissidents but was not himself a dissident. He thought he could again see westerners in Moscow without suffering reprisals. We often saw him and his beautiful wife, Olga, and their infant son, and our friendship deepened.

There was a sequel after the end of the Soviet Union. I was in my office in the Embassy in Paris in 1993 when I received a totally unexpected telephone call from Kolya. He said that the world premiere of one of his most important classical works, the opera *Till Eulenspiegel*, would take place a few days later in Germany, and I simply must come. I said, miserably, that I could not leave Paris on the day in question but I hoped to see him as soon as possible. He followed up with an affectionate letter suggesting a meeting in Paris. Months later he died of a heart attack. We have kept in touch with Olga and love to see her. Today, their two sons, my godson Kolya Jr and Anton, come frequently to London and we enjoy their company.

In 2015, I received from Olga some writings by Kolya which show that his reason for interrupting our friendship in 1962 was not exactly what I had thought. He had been approached for the second time by the KGB about his friendship with me. The KGB offered him, in exchange for information about me, publication and performances of all his works, travel abroad and money. Kolya was determined never to become an informer for the secret police. That was why he stopped seeing Pascale and me.

Flowers, Tears and Blood

In my work as Deputy Cultural Attaché in Moscow in 1961–63, I sometimes helped to manage visits of British cultural groups. There was a tragicomic moment when I accompanied Margot Fonteyn, who was appearing in Moscow with the Royal Ballet, to call on Galina Ulanova, the greatest Soviet ballerina of the period. My role was to interpret the conversation between these two world-famous dancers. When we arrived at Ulanova's flat, Fonteyn presented an enormous bunch of flowers. I interpreted a few words of greeting on each side. The two ladies sat down.

Ulanova began to sob through her smiles. Fonteyn joined in the sobs and smiles. Neither could complete a remark during our twenty minutes in the flat. It was a touching scene and I had nothing to interpret.

Pascale and I went to Kiev with the Royal Philharmonic Orchestra and its handsome, exacting conductor, Sir Malcolm Sargent. My role was to deal with any problems between the British group and the Kiev authorities and to interpret as needed. 'Flash Harry', as Sargent was known in the press, was an energetic womaniser and he made a brisk pass at Pascale, who was then 22. She brushed this aside with a laugh. What she remembers more vividly is an encounter with a senior administrator of the Kiev orchestra. This man came up to her at a reception and stroked his suit. He explained that Harold Macmillan, when he visited the Soviet Union as Prime Minister in 1959, had brought with him a tailor from a well-known London firm. When Macmillan wanted to give a thank-you present to a man who had been helpful during the visit, he summoned the tailor and directed him grandly to 'measure that man'. The Kiev administrator had received a made-to-measure suit a few weeks later and remained proud and grateful for Macmillan's unusual gesture.

On another occasion I accompanied Benjamin Britten and Peter Pears on a visit to Leningrad. Mstislav Rostropovich, the great Russian cellist, came with us. When we boarded the Red Arrow overnight train in Moscow, Rostropovich produced a bottle of Soviet champagne. This was a notoriously unpleasant beverage, and he explained urgently that he had not brought it for us to drink. The water on the train was not safe, and the champagne was for cleaning our teeth!

*****

A tragic incident occurred one afternoon at the Embassy, when a dishevelled man somehow got past the Soviet militia guards who manned our gates and prevented Soviet citizens without special authorisation from visiting the Embassy. This man told me that he had written a book which he would not be allowed to publish in the Soviet Union. He wanted to go to Britain, a free country where he could try to publish. I looked at the crumpled manuscript which he drew from his pocket. It seemed incoherent.

In any case, whatever the merits or otherwise of his manuscript, the Embassy could not help Soviet citizens to leave the Soviet Union. I explained gently that he would have to leave the Embassy. After a long conversation he accepted unhappily that he must go. I walked beside him to our front door and suddenly he drew a small knife from his pocket and cut his throat.

Geoff Murrell participated in the scene outside the Embassy door. Geoff writes:

> The Embassy doctor ... and I were among the first at the scene and for some time I helped to hold the wounded Russian down while the doctor cheerfully inserted tubes into a gaping hole in his throat. Not the least unpleasant aspect of this incident was the laughter of the Soviet militiamen as they looked on from the gates. The doctor had saved the man's life but he was not allowed to visit him in hospital, nor did we ever learn what happened to him.

I see that incident as an example of the innumerable human tragedies that are caused by the rigidity of a repressive system that tolerates no opinions or activities which are not authorised by the communist party.

Daily Life

Foreign diplomats and journalists in Moscow lived in blocks of flats segregated like ghettos from the Soviet population of the city, as a key part of the authorities' efforts to prevent contact between Russians and foreigners. These flats had no charm and many were very noisy. The rooms were small and there were mice and cockroaches.

This accommodation was infinitely better than the conditions the Muscovites themselves had to endure. One family we knew was a typical case. A woman, her husband, his son and the father of her previous husband all lived in a single room. They shared a lavatory, a bath and a gas ring for cooking with several other families in other rooms. They told us that one of the difficulties of this overcrowding was that each person had to queue for at least an hour each morning to make tea and use the lavatory.

In the rather hostile atmosphere of Moscow, westerners formed lasting friendships among themselves. This happened within the British Embassy and also between us and other embassies and the foreign correspondents. Many of the parties of the westerners were enjoyable. One I remember was the birthday party of my Embassy colleague and friend, Anthony Loehnis, who was popular in the western community. Anthony invited a large number of non-Russian friends to meet one Saturday morning in Red Square. About 30 foreign cars convened there. Anthony served very strong Martinis from an enormous thermos jug. He gave us instructions in riddle form on how to find our picnic place, which was in the country outside the city. The picnic took place in sunny weather and we swam in the river and much enjoyed the day. My feeling looking back on this excursion is that we made ourselves too conspicuous on Red Square that morning and that the quaffing of Martinis would not be likely nowadays. But it was the greatest fun.

The shortages or the total absence of many products in the Soviet Union were caused above all by the hopeless inefficiency of the state-run economy. For many Russians this was made bearable by their belief that Marxism-Leninism would in time produce a better life. The shops were dull, the products few, the sales staff surly and the queues long. One infuriating rule was that you had to queue three times: first to choose your purchase and get a ticket showing the price, then to pay the cashier and finally to collect your goods.

In the early sixties the main source of provisions for foreigners in Moscow was a state store portentously named Gastronom Number One. Every week we were supposed to order what we wanted from a long list of products which never varied. Nearly all these items were never available. The only things which were usually available were cabbage, scrawny chickens, mineral water and matches. We occasionally got steaks, which were rather blue inside and tasted slightly sweet. Horse meat.

One day, Pascale and I could not resist venting our frustration by ordering several dozen partridges; they were always on the shopping list but never available. We got a very large delivery and thought we had our partridges. But they were seagulls, complete with plumage.

The so-called peasants' markets in Moscow were fun to visit and you could buy some fresh goodies – yoghurt, cream and smetana, a delicious sour cream; and above all honey and many varieties of mushrooms, most of them new to us. Part of the attraction was that this was the only chance in Moscow to taste some of the products and then choose.

These goods were sold by plump women in rural garb with head scarves. The goods were mostly produced on the personal allotments permitted by the authorities as an exception to state agriculture. Farm workers worked hard on their allotments because they could make a little money by selling some of the produce in the peasants' markets, so that this exception to state farming gave a useful boost to production.

A feature of Moscow in these years was the queues one saw everywhere – in shops, on the streets, in rail stations and many other places. Muscovites often joined queues without knowing what was on sale. They would buy more than they needed of whatever it turned out to be and would sell on most of this booty to others who had missed the chance to buy. Pascale once joined a mid-winter queue and asked her neighbours in the line what product was on sale. No one knew but all stayed in the queue. On this occasion the prize turned out to be watering cans, a useless possession in a Moscow winter.

Pascale had a similar experience in GUM, the famous department store. Word had spread in Moscow of a delivery of women's shoes from Czechoslovakia. A queue formed in the store. Each customer could buy several pairs of shoes but was not allowed to try them on. Pascale watched as a woman bought six pairs, sat down on the floor nearby and openly started to sell all pairs but one. A short queue quickly formed in front of her. Her price was higher than GUM's but her customers were delighted because she allowed them to try the shoes for size.

As this account shows, shopping for daily needs, like many aspects of life in Moscow in those days, was wearing and depressing. But we managed to keep going without feeling really low. Partly this was because we had only two to three years there, with home leave in the middle, so that there was always light somewhere ahead in the Moscow tunnel. Another reason was that life had satisfactions in addition to the absorbing work.

Good Things to Do

We could always get tickets for the Bolshoi Opera and Ballet. We came to know the museums well, notably the Tretyakov Museum of Russian Art, where Humphrey Trevelyan and I agreed that Russia's great landscape painters of the 19th century were really good and must one day command high prices. That has now happened on the world art market, since the end of the Soviet Union.

The Commission Shops were another source of mild enjoyment. They sold antiques and bric-a-brac for private sellers and took a commission for the State. I had heard that the Commission Shop on the Old Arbat Street in central Moscow had attractive things. I walked there in the dark on my third evening in Moscow. The shop was closed but I had a good look at the objects on view in the windows. A short man wrapped in a heavy scarf came close to me and spoke softly. He asked if I wanted 'Eeky'. I was puzzled at first but then guessed that this word must be slang for icons. He asked me to meet him in the same place next evening. I said yes and walked quickly away. Needless to say I did not turn up for the rendezvous. This furtive approach at the start of my time in Moscow was unnerving. I could not guess whether the man was just a tout or maybe a tout working for the KGB with the aim of ensnaring foreigners in illegal purchase of icons on the black market.

The embassy's Dacha, a large log cabin by the river on the edge of Moscow, provided a haven for occasional week-ends. We also gave parties there in summer. Every spring the Embassy staff spent a Saturday cleaning up the house and garden. We painted, repaired and threw out rubbish. This was a moment of comradeship among us. I remember Rory Chisholm acting as a powerful foreman, organising us firmly and efficiently for the work. Even Lady Roberts would put in an appearance.

Pascale and I often drove out of Moscow and explored the surrounding area within a radius of 40 km, most of which diplomats were allowed to visit. There were some attractive monasteries and pretty village churches with onion domes. We tried cross-country skiing in the winter and swam in the Moscow River in the summer.

The most important monastery we could visit without a permit was the Trinity Monastery of St Sergius at Zagorsk. The large orthodox monastery has many lovely churches and was almost always crowded with worshippers. It was touching to see this expression of belief at a time when Khrushchev was engaged in repression of Christianity and was closing many churches. Most of the worshippers were elderly women. Five years and ten years later the same was true. So people were evidently starting to go to church in later life. Yet we knew from Russian friends that many younger people were believers too. Some did not go to church when younger because of the risk of reprisals, probably at work. When they grew older they had less to lose.

One Sunday in winter Pascale and I drove out of Moscow to visit a monastery. When we arrived we got out of the car and, without exchanging a word, crossed in front of it and each got back in on the other side. There was a high wind. This, combined with a very low temperature, produced an icy chill which was totally incompatible with sight-seeing. We drank a dram of brandy from the flask we kept as a restorative in the car and drove straight back to Moscow.

Once or twice, Pascale and I spent a weekend at the 'Diplomatic Sporting Base' at Zavidovo on the Volga, to walk in the forest and row on the river. We remember particularly a weekend there in February 1963 with Kathy and Geoff Murrell, my colleague Anthony Loehnis and Rob Armstrong of the US Embassy. We were all absorbed in Nabokov's latest novel, *Pale Fire*, and we read aloud from it in turns one evening, with enjoyment and emotion.

Getting away from the pressures of Moscow to Zavidovo was a relief, even if our break was in a very Soviet institution. It was infuriating when we found mushrooms or wild strawberries in the forest and, requesting them at dinner, were told that none were available from the state supplier several hours' drive away in Moscow, where the sporting base was obliged under Soviet rules to get all supplies. We went out and picked strawberries or mushrooms and the kitchen reluctantly agreed to provide them for our dinner in the restaurant, but the manager was rightly fearful that other diplomats around the room would ask for the same treats, which the staff could not supply. Experiences like this were frequent, and we were appalled by the distortion and incompetence caused by the Soviet economic system.

Travelling in other parts of the Soviet Union was more interesting and often a real pleasure. The atmosphere in the provinces was somewhat less oppressive than in Moscow and Soviet people were more ready to chat with foreigners; they were insatiably curious about life in other countries.

About half of that enormous country was closed to foreigners. It was nominally possible to visit the rest. The Embassy had to register each intended trip with the Foreign Ministry. If the Ministry did not reply the trip was 'registered' and could go ahead. But often the Foreign Ministry informed the Embassy at the last minute that the trip was not registered, so we could not travel. In order to preserve the official position that the area in question was not closed to foreigners, the Ministry would give the totally uninformative explanation that the refusal was 'for reasons of a temporary character'.

Pascale and I visited Leningrad, now St Petersburg, many times. It is in part a beautiful city with much Italianate architecture built in the 18th century by the Italian-French architect, Rastrelli. We visited the palaces in and near the city. We also went to the Kirov opera and ballet and often to the museums.

We made one epic trip, with my colleague Michael Duncan, in the south-west of the Soviet Union. We went first to Odessa on the Black Sea, where we explored among other things the former Jewish quarter, which is the scene of Isaak Babel's wonderful short stories. Then we went to Izmail on the Danube Delta and to Kishinev, the capital of Soviet Moldavia.

On an overnight train we knew vermin were to be expected in the bunks. Pascale wrapped herself up carefully but was terribly bitten by bedbugs. The fourth person in our compartment was a youngish Soviet woman, blonde and attractive, who said she was a schoolteacher. She swore that we could not be foreigners because we were not black.

In Izmail we were shown a new estate of public housing. The flats were cramped and unappealing. They did not have the charm of the 'izby', the wooden cottages which were the traditional housing of Izmail. The old and the new housing was much like what we saw in parts of Moscow and almost everywhere we travelled in the Soviet Union. In Izmail, however, we came upon one oddity which we did not find elsewhere. Local farmworkers who had been moved into the new flats did not like them but were not allowed to return to their izby, which were to be destroyed. They especially disliked the bathrooms and lavatories. But they found a use for these facilities; they installed pigs there but were forced to stop.

Two days later we were due to move to Kishinev by bus. We were informed by Intourist, the notoriously obstructive official travel agency for foreigners which worked closely with the KGB, that there would be no buses 'for reasons of a temporary character', so we could not visit Kishinev. Michael went to the bus station and discovered that there would be a bus very early next morning. We asked Intourist to book us on this bus. They denied its existence. We went to the bus station at dawn and found the bus. Travelling across country we saw crops in a bad state. The authorities tried to prevent foreigners from seeing agricultural and other failures, and the sodden crops may have been the reason why Intourist lied about the existence of the bus. Our hotel in Kishinev was shocked when we arrived after all. Such independence of action by Russians or foreigners in the Soviet Union was rare. We had taken a small risk and had outwitted Intourist.

Cars

In the freezing winters of Moscow it was essential to have a reliable car, with snow tyres to reduce the risk of skidding. I took with me to Moscow a bright yellow Ford Anglia, a small car suitable to my means and my status as a beginner diplomat.

Early one morning, when driving to work at the Embassy, I had a nasty collision with a Soviet lorry. I banged my head against my windscreen but was not seriously hurt. My little car was a write-off. This was in August 1962. The winter was looming and there was no time to import another car before the freeze set in. It was not permitted in those days for foreign diplomats to buy Soviet cars, so I had to find a car to buy from another foreign diplomat in Moscow. Only two cars were available. One was a vast pre-war Mercedes, discarded by the West German Ambassador. The other was an old, but less old, Cadillac discarded by the US Ambassador. I bought the Cadillac for £100. It is the only superior car I have ever owned. It was black and elongated, with a glass partition between the small area at the front for the chauffeur and a vast compartment behind, large enough to fit a bridge table and four chairs between the glass barrier and the passenger seats. Pascale and I sat in the front, leaving the large space unoccupied behind us. All went well until we were nearly due to leave Moscow in summer 1963.

As I drove across the Kameny Bridge and began to descend the slope towards the Embassy one morning, the Cadillac's brakes failed completely. The traffic lights ahead changed to red, and hordes of pedestrians on their way to work sped off from both sides of the wide road to cross it. All I could do was to sound my horn and steer down the middle of the road between the crowds advancing from each side. I got through before they converged and no one was hurt. At the bottom of the slope, I crossed the junction ahead and jabbed my front right wheel repeatedly against the kerb, stopping the car after a dozen thumps.

We tried to sell the car before we left Moscow, but my story of the unstoppable Cadillac quickly did the rounds of the diplomatic community and nobody wanted such a dangerous and conspicuous vehicle. After Pascale and I had returned to London, the Embassy managed to sell the car to Mosfilm, the state film production organisation where, presumably, it was used as a prop in propaganda films about American capitalists or gangsters, both incidentally the same in the Soviet portrayal of America.

KGB

The Soviet Ministry of State Security, the notorious KGB, played a frequent role in our Moscow lives. One strange aspect of our life concerned a few Soviet people who clearly were licensed by the authorities to meet foreigners socially. One purpose of the authorities, I think, was to avert complaints from the diplomats that they could never meet Russians. The more important purpose was to gather information about western diplomats and journalists which might be useful to the KGB for blackmail purposes. Some of these Russians were intelligent and had interesting jobs in culture or education.

We had to assume that any Russian we met inside or outside official activity might be cooperating with the KGB and we would always be careful in our conversation with them. We would be especially careful with the Russians who were obviously licensed to meet foreigners regularly, and these Russians knew this. The paradox was that we could sometimes enjoy their company and even learn interesting things about Soviet life. I think the Russians enjoyed these conversations too.

This highly artificial situation was not difficult for Pascale and me to manage. There were many subjects to chat about which had nothing to do with my work. I learned interesting things from Victor Louis, a clever Soviet citizen with a British wife, who had spent ten years in Stalin's labour camps and may have begun to cooperate with the KGB on his return to Moscow. He took me round the churches of Moscow to experience the all-night services at Easter. Pascale and I did not make friends in this social penumbra, but we were glad to chat to Russians. We made the best of a depressing situation.

The KGB hid microphones in the flats occupied by Westerners in Moscow. We were always careful to say nothing in front of the microphones which would interest the KGB. That rule was easy to apply to my work in the Embassy. I was never in the habit of returning home of an evening and declaring 'Darling, the Foreign Secretary has sent us a new instruction about fisheries policy'. But what was more difficult was gossip. It would have been harmful if I had said to Pascale 'Did you notice at dinner that the Belgian Third Secretary was complaining that he was broke?' or 'Did you notice that the US Counsellor's wife was flirting with the Italian First Secretary?' The microphones would have recorded our conversation and the KGB might well have tried to exploit the information by offering the Belgian money or offering the flirtatious diplomats attractive Soviet partners, in encounters contrived to seem accidental. Anyone who fell for such a ploy would be in danger of blackmail by the KGB.

There were frequent incidents when Western diplomats, travelling in the provinces, were given a drugged drink in a hotel restaurant and consequently passed out. In the morning, the diplomat would awake with obvious signs of sex in the night. Love bites in embarrassing places were a particularly crude device. The KGB's method was to approach that person a week or two later and mention pointedly that the photographs were good; and then ask for some unimportant information, such as the job of a particular person in the Embassy, a fact which anyway was published. That harmless enquiry would be followed later by the real thing, questioning about confidential matters.

The rule in the Embassy was that anyone who had an incident like this should inform a senior colleague, and there would be no disapproval. Knowing what KGB follow-up was usual, the Embassy simply sent the unlucky member of our team back to Britain to avoid a very unpleasant experience.

* * * * *

The most prominent Western diplomat to fall into a honey trap during our time in Moscow, so far as I know, was Maurice Dejean, the French Ambassador to the USSR. Pascale and I knew Dejean and his wife. He was ordinary in appearance and arrogant in style with lesser diplomats, but definitely clever. She was a raving beauty.

The KGB must have had indications that Dejean might be susceptible to a pretty girl. They arranged for him to meet, as if by chance, a young dancer in the Bolshoi Ballet. Dejean duly took the bait and had an affair with this Swallow, as ladies in this specialised branch of international relations were known in Moscow.

After a time, the supposed husband of the Swallow burst into her flat where Dejean was with her in the bedroom. The husband beat up the Ambassador. Dejean apparently panicked. He contacted a senior Soviet Air Force officer, with whom he had become friendly, and asked for help. The Air Force General, who had probably made friends with Dejean under instructions from the KGB, said he would try to arrange that nothing more should happen. Nothing did. The Soviet authorities probably expected that Dejean would go back to Paris after Moscow and would have an important confidential position in the entourage of President de Gaulle. This would have been a reasonable assumption, since Dejean had worked with de Gaulle in London during the war. The Soviet plan would have been to blackmail Dejean on the basis of his ballerina fling in order to obtain secrets of real importance concerning de Gaulle's government and its policies.

When the French government found out about the exploits of Dejean he was summoned back to Paris and President de Gaulle sacked him. There are several versions of the words used by the President when he dismissed the errant envoy. One version is: 'Eh bien Dejean, on baise.' In English this would be roughly 'Well, well Dejean, we screw, do we.'

* * * * *

Many Western diplomats in Moscow experienced nasty incidents set up by the KGB. A lesser operation was mounted against Pascale and me. When we arrived in Moscow in September 1961, after being married in Paris, Pascale wanted to learn Russian. Teachers, like all Soviet employees of Embassies, could only be hired through a special department of the Soviet Foreign Ministry. We applied for a teacher, and a young lady called Tatiana came to teach Pascale. She was tall, with a shapely figure, dark hair and lovely green eyes. She was a good teacher and also clever and good company and well-read in Russian literature. Pascale and I liked her. We took her out to dinner once or twice, and I remember an evening of laughter in a restaurant on a barge on the Moscow River, when we enjoyed a very Russian meal of vegetable soup and salted herring.

After a few months Tatiana stopped me on the stairs of our apartment block and said she must talk to me outside. This meant that she wanted me to think that she did not wish to be heard by the microphones in our flat. Outside, she told me that, as I must have realised, she had been tasked by the KGB with reporting useful information about Pascale and me. She told me that she had found nothing to report and, if she could not do more to please the KGB, she would be punished. Tatiana then begged me to help her get away 'from this horrible country' by smuggling her in my car to Finland. I knew that such an escapade would be discovered by the Soviet police at the Finnish border and I was sure that Tatiana was carrying out a provocation on behalf of the KGB, with the purpose of discrediting Pascale and me and subsequent blackmail. I sacked Tatiana then and there. I did not enjoy doing it and Pascale was understandably sad to lose a good teacher who was becoming a friend.

Some weeks later, a young Austrian diplomat, a bachelor, approached me at a reception and said with a grin, 'I am being taught Russian by your mistress.' He meant Tatiana. The allegation of adultery was totally untrue. I suppose Tatiana had told the Austrian this lie in order to arouse his interest. She had clearly been assigned to another KGB operation.

* * * * *

When travelling outside Moscow, westerners were followed by KGB agents, whom we called 'goons'. Once, when visiting Kiev, Pascale and I were followed by three obvious goons. As we walked around the city centre, they would dart frequently into doorways and change their berets for a different colour, in the naïve hope that this would prevent our realising that they were tailing us. Goons always ran to catch us up if we visited a second-hand bookshop. I suppose they thought we might find a book which had been banned by the authorities but not removed from the shop. When we reached a well-known bookshop in Kiev, I went in first and started looking at one of the books on display. The goon in his beret, a maroon one at this moment, must have sprinted 30 metres, for he entered the shop only a moment after me. He came up beside me and pretended to look at a book, but in fact he looked across to see what I was reading. Pascale then came into the shop and stood on the other side of the goon and pretended to look at a book but actually looked at the book the goon was pretending to look at. This was too much for Comrade Goon's self-respect and he darted shiftily away. Such were the pleasing pranks we resorted to in the strange conditions of the Soviet Union half a century ago.

* * * * *

One of the most important Soviet spies for the West in the Cold War was Colonel Oleg Penkovsky. He was an officer of the Soviet Military Intelligence Service, the GRU. He spied for MI6 and the CIA from April 1961 to October 1962. He said his motive was that Khrushchev was increasing the risk of world war. His behaviour may also have been caused by resentment at his failure to be promoted beyond the rank of Colonel. He had the non-military job of managing scientific exchanges between the Soviet Union and Western countries, and this gave him the right to meet people from western Embassies. Penkovsky took serious risks in obtaining highly secret information about the Soviet Armed Forces and nuclear weapons programme, which he passed to the Americans and the British.

The person in the British Embassy who maintained clandestine contact with Penkovsky was Rory Chisholm, greatly helped by his wife, Janet. They were our immediate neighbours in our block of flats but we had no inkling that they were engaged in a really important espionage operation. The Chisholm family were happy and numerous. I remember Rory and Janet giving a birthday party for their young son, Alistair, known as Aliboy. To reduce the risk of riot among a large group of excited children in a cramped flat, Rory began the party with a competition to see which child could continue jumping on the spot the longest. Rory claimed that the winner, obviously the most energetic of these small children, had then been given half a glass of beer to make him sleepy.

Pascale's and my wedding in Paris in September 1961 played a small role in the Penkovsky affair. Before leaving Moscow for Paris, I had invited everyone in our Embassy to come to the wedding. I expected that few if any would be in Paris, and indeed the only acceptance was from Rory Chisholm. He said he would love to come and he let it be known that he was going to Paris to attend our wedding. Actually, Penkovsky was visiting Paris that day in a Soviet scientific delegation and Rory went there to meet him secretly with American and British officials. There was an extremely successful discussion with Penkovsky, who handed over Soviet secrets of major value to the West.

After this Rory arrived at our wedding very late, at the end of the reception. He looked tired and bedraggled. I fetched him a glass of champagne, and Pascale and I left immediately for our honeymoon. The Soviet indictment of Penkovsky revealed later that our wedding was Rory's cover story for having to be in Paris on that day.

The CIA has revealed much about the Penkovsky story. I think his key contribution was that the detailed information he provided about the Soviet Armed Forces showed President Kennedy that the Soviet Union had far fewer and less advanced nuclear weapons than the USA. This was confirmed by US aerial photography. It was important because there was a scare in Washington at the time about a so-called Missile Gap, a false theory that the Soviet Union had overtaken the US in nuclear missiles. The CIA has stated that Penkovsky also supplied information about Khrushchev's plan to deploy nuclear missiles in Cuba and how much time the Soviets would need to make them operational. All this helped Kennedy greatly in handling the Cuba crisis in October 1962.

Penkovsky thus contributed to the avoidance of a nuclear war. He was arrested by the KGB in October 1962 and executed in May 1963. The day of his arrest happened to be when President Kennedy first announced that the Soviet Union was installing nuclear missiles in Cuba.

* * * * *

On our last night in Moscow, our close friends in the Embassy gave a farewell party for Pascale and me. This lively rout lasted all night till we left for the airport and flew to London early on the morning of 1 August 1963. Geoff and Kathy Murrell have recently reminded us that we stopped on the way to Moscow airport with some of our friends from the party, to swim in a country stream. Pascale swam in her underwear, which she took off afterwards in the airport because it was uncomfortably wet. She popped the sodden garments in my briefcase and flew to London without underclothes.

Our feelings about the experience of Moscow as we departed were positive on balance. We had coped without difficulty with the adverse aspects of the experience, from the climate to the antics of the KGB. We were curious about how the USSR would develop and we agreed that we would like to be posted there again in a few years.

Professionally I had learned much from this first diplomatic posting and I was conscious that the experience had matured me. I was more sure than ever that I would enjoy a diplomatic career and that I could do the work. I saw a career focussed mainly on the Soviet Union as an opportunity to be useful to Britain.

Pascale and I were looking forward eagerly to living in London. We wanted to see our families often, to choose our first home and arrange it, and to enjoy London. Above all, we were longing to have a baby.

Sebastian was born on 9 May 1964. Since that thrilling day parenthood has been the most important and most joyful part of our lives.

3

FOREIGN OFFICE 1963–66

My first job in the Foreign Office in London was in the Central Department. Its name was misleading: it dealt with Europe, but not the central part. In fact it covered the countries around the edges of western Europe which were not in the Common Market. I worked at different times on Britain's relations with Iceland, Portugal and its colonies, Turkey, Greece, Austria and Switzerland.

My first head of department was Derek Dodson and the second was Alan Davidson. They could not have been more different. Derek was tall, elegant and conventional, the picture of a smart army officer, which he had once been. In his sleek appearance he reminded me of a greyhound. Alan was shorter and squarer; he had a passion for cooking and was to leave the Diplomatic Service early in order to write successfully about fish and how to cook them. He compiled the *Oxford Companion to Food*. His eccentric interests and informal style made working for him enjoyable.

The staff were expected to be at their desks by 10 o'clock every morning, much later than became usual soon afterwards. We normally stopped work at about 6:30 pm, but some of us stayed later because of volume of work. The working conditions were not good. There were four of us in my office, each with two telephones. Often, one or more of us was dictating to a secretary. This created constant cacophony. One just had to learn to concentrate despite the din.

In that crowded, noisy room we worked hard but we also laughed together. Lunch in the canteen was a combination of a sparse meal and lively conversation. A typical lunch was a cheddar cheese salad and a cup of instant coffee.

I found myself dealing first with trouble between Britain and Iceland about fishing in the sea around Iceland. There had been serious disputes between Britain and Iceland because of Iceland's wish to extend the restricted fishery zone around its shores. In 1963–64, when I was handling this subject, the difficulties between the two countries were not as bad as they had been in the first so-called Cod War in 1958, nor as bad as they would become a few years later. But there were incidents between British trawlers and Icelandic fishery protection ships. On one occasion an appropriately named Icelandic sea captain, Captain Bang, fired at a British trawler.

This is an example of defending British interests in a bilateral dispute with another country. The subject was important to the fisheries industry in Britain and to the Ministry of Agriculture, Fisheries and Food. I participated in the discussion of policy among ministries in London, putting forward the views of the Foreign Office and our Embassy in Reykjavik. I briefed senior officials and Foreign Office Ministers about what was happening and as needed I proposed changes in our policy in the form of draft memoranda, called submissions, for signature by my head of department. These functions were typical of the work of a political department in the Foreign Office and I was glad to learn to do them.

After Iceland I worked on a wider canvas, dealing with British relations with Portugal, Austria and Switzerland as well as economic relations with Greece and Turkey. My main role was to make proposals, for the approval of senior officials and Ministers, on policies to advance British interests in our relationships with these countries on various subjects. The work was less enjoyable but much more responsible than my role in Moscow. It is a complicated exercise to obtain the views of various British government departments on a particular problem and to try to persuade any department which disagrees with the Foreign Office that they should accept our view. Then I would put together all these views and those of our Embassy in the country concerned, and propose what British policy should be on the matter in hand. If I could not get agreement at my level, there would be discussion or correspondence among government departments at a higher official level, and if agreement was still not reached, there would be Ministerial discussion to reach a decision. I was responsible, once a policy had been decided, for ensuring that it was properly applied at each subsequent stage and that the government's other actions towards the country were compatible with the policy.

This work was very varied. I participated for three years in deciding the level of British economic aid and defence aid to Turkey. I drafted replies to many Questions in Parliament about British policy towards Portugal and its colonies in Africa. In a single day I might prepare a speech for the Foreign Secretary to make at an event in honour of a visiting Austrian minister; a brief for our delegation at the United Nations to guide their speeches in a debate about the Portuguese colonies; and an account for Ministers of the attitude of Portugal to the Rhodesian problem, with suggestions on how we might try to influence Portugal to act more positively towards our policy.

There were moments of amusement. For instance, the first occasion when I spoke for Britain in an international forum was a conference in Paris about aid to Turkey, comprising the western countries with an interest in the growth of the Turkish economy. I had a very short statement to make, informing the conference how much aid Britain would give Turkey in the coming year and on what terms. I was used to dictating to a secretary when of course you say what punctuation you want. I was worried that I might inadvertently read out the punctuation in my short statement to the conference. I therefore had it typed with no punctuation. This nervous precaution worked.

A different oddity in my performance came when I was writing a paper on the likely developments in Portugal and its colonies in the next few years for the Foreign Secretary, Sir Alec Douglas-Home. I dictated a careful analysis of the various factors, political, economic and so on. My conclusion was going to be that nothing much would change until Portugal's then leader, the autocratic Dr Salazar, died. In my relief at finishing this careful piece of dictation, I ended by saying nothing would happen until Dr Salazar kicked the bucket. On re-reading this text, before sending it up the line to the Foreign Secretary, I thought that the expression I had used provided an agreeably light touch and I sent off my memorandum. No-one objected.

While working in the Central Department I was involved in the organisation of State Visits to Britain by two foreign leaders, the Presidents of Iceland and of Austria. State Visits are formal and elaborate occasions. It fell to me to draft the speeches at events in honour of the visiting presidents for the Queen, the Prime Minister, the Foreign Secretary, the Lord Mayor of London and others. I did much research, to find historical, literary and other nuggets which would enliven the speeches.

In the case of Austria one thing went wrong (and proved that repetition can be important for comic effect). The speech I wrote for the Lord Mayor included compliments about Austria and its culture, its scenery and its economy. The Lord Mayor, after one mention of Austria, referred to Australia instead. The hundreds of guests, dressed ultra-formally in white tie and tailcoats with medals, looked startled but probably reflected sympathetically that anyone could make the slip of saying Australia instead of Austria. The trouble was that the Lord Mayor then ploughed on solemnly saying Australia time after time. The guests became more and more irritated and embarrassed. When the Lord Mayor praised the great Australian composer Haydon, meaning Haydn, there were guffaws from all directions. After the meal, I scuttled round the table to check that the speech, typed in my office, did refer all through to Austria and nowhere to Australia. I was relieved to find that only Austria was mentioned.

These three years in London were very happy for Pascale and me. Sebastian's birth was an absolute joy. We lived at first in a pretty mews house just north of Hyde Park. Then we moved to Gloucester Avenue near Primrose Hill. We were very tight for money, but supplemented our income by letting the large garage of the mews house to a car hire firm which kept hearses there. Sebastian demonstrated good taste, when taken to Hyde Park in his pram, by laughing aloud each time we passed the Albert Memorial. (I have come to like that exuberant confection, so I would not be so pleased today if one of my grandchildren laughed at it.)

We had an au pair girl, the first of many, who was obviously a kleptomaniac. She would come home with a brand-new handbag containing expensive cosmetics and numerous toothbrushes. Pascale solved this problem by explaining to Helen that there was a new method in the National Health Service for curing her medical problem. The treatment, Pascale explained, required a week in hospital. Helen declined the treatment with a look of horror, and she never stole again while she was with us.

Our next au pair girl was Lisbet, another Scandinavian. She was fair and pretty and she rapidly found a boyfriend. He was Pip, a handsome London policeman. When Lisbet took Sebastian for walks in his pram on Primrose Hill, Pip would walk proudly beside her; we felt that our son was secure with his uniformed bodyguard.

My mother was now living in her 'grace and favour' apartment at Hampton Court Palace. It was good to see her established there. She loved the buildings and the park, and she had no money worries for the first time in twenty years. We visited her often and borrowed her apartment occasionally when she was away. Later we were to live near the Palace, and that lovely and very English place has played a lasting role in our lives.

* * * * *

Some months before I was due to go abroad again I sent a note to the Foreign Office Personnel Department listing the fifty foreign postings which Pascale and I would prefer. My thought was that this tactic should have a better chance of getting a place we wanted and avoiding the others than if I suggested only two or three top preferences. The secretary who typed my list omitted one of my choices – Berlin. We were duly sent to Berlin and we were delighted.

This first period in the Foreign Office was instructive and useful for me. We loved living in London and saw many friends. I was still sure that diplomacy was the right life for us, although the discipline of living on a modest salary limited our scope for enjoying London's theatres and other cultural treats.

4

BERLIN 1966–69

We had a very happy period of 2½ years in West Berlin. I enjoyed my only diplomatic assignment when the pressure of work was not severe.

Emily

A big moment for our family came early in our stay, when Emily was born. She was due to arrive on 1 April 1967. I booked to fly on 3 April to London for my sister Sue's wedding the next day. Since Emily had not arrived by late morning on 3 April I cancelled my air tickets and telephoned to tell Sue with sadness that I could not come to the wedding. Emily then arrived in the early hours of 4 April. She was born in the British Military Hospital in West Berlin, formerly barracks of Hitler's SS. The British Army doctor on duty was not around and the one nurse was dealing with two young mothers who were in labour. The other birth was complicated and Pascale's delivery promised to be straightforward. Luckily, it was indeed straightforward, because I was the only person helping. Emily was born easily and Pascale and I were thrilled to have our first daughter.

A few hours later that night I went to Berlin's Tempelhof Airport without a ticket. I managed to get a flight via Frankfurt to London. I arrived at Hampton Court with an hour to shave and change before escorting Sue down the aisle of the Chapel Royal for her marriage to John Peake. I enjoyed the lovely service and the reception, slept one night in my mother's apartment in the Palace and flew back to Pascale, Sebastian and Emily in Berlin.

Work

After the defeat of Germany in 1945 Berlin was divided into four sectors, each to be occupied by one of the four victorious powers: the Soviet Union, the United States, the United Kingdom and France. The rest of Germany was divided likewise into occupation zones, each held by one of the four powers. Berlin was surrounded by the Soviet occupation zone but was not part of it.

The three western sectors of Berlin became democratic and prosperous. The surrounding Soviet occupation zone, which became communist East Germany, and the Soviet sector of Berlin, which became East Berlin and capital of East Germany, were under Soviet autocratic control and achieved only a poor standard of living. So West Berlin stood out as a beacon of freedom, prosperity and modernity in the centre of unhappy, undemocratic and backward communist East Germany.

It was fortunate that the area which had formed the capital of Germany since the 1930s was not only the city itself but also a large belt of forests, lakes and farms around the city. This Greater Berlin was the area divided among the four powers in 1945. The West Berliners therefore had access to countryside as well as the city itself.

The Soviet Union detested the presence of democratic West Berlin within East Germany. Stalin tried to force the western allies to abandon the city by blockading it for 11 months in 1948. Access to West Berlin by road, rail and water was cut off. In the famous air lift, the American and British air forces flew 200,000 flights to Berlin from the West, bringing everything the western sectors needed during the blockade. This included the astonishing example of all the machinery and components needed to construct a large new power station in West Berlin, replacing electricity from East Germany which had been cut off. This power station was still producing electricity in 1988 when I became Ambassador in West Germany.

After the failure of the blockade, Khrushchev tried by ultimatums to threaten the Western allies and force them to leave Berlin. This too failed. In 1961, the Soviet Union and East Germany resorted to a different tactic, a defensive one: they built the Berlin Wall to close off East Berlin from the Western sectors and this ended the haemorrhage of working people from East Germany and East Berlin to West Berlin. The Berlin Wall became the great symbol of the failure of communism in Europe: the only way the East German Communist regime could keep its people was by shutting them in.

One major reason why West Berlin continued to succeed was the toughness and the courage of the Berliners themselves. They were positive and determined throughout the whole long story. There is a lovely Berlin expression, dating from long before the war: '*Uns kann keiner!*' which in English means roughly 'nobody can outsmart us!' That was exactly the feeling I had about the courage of the Berliners when we lived there in the 1960s.

The next reason for West Berlin's success was the Allied commitment to the freedom of the city and the presence of our forces. The Soviet Union could not try to seize the city without fighting American and allied forces, which would probably have started a world war between the Soviet Union and the West, with the risk of destruction of the Soviet Union by Western nuclear weapons. This was the doctrine of deterrence: we made it too dangerous for the Soviet Union to use force against us or to threaten the use of force.

The third reason for West Berlin's success was large financial subsidies from the Federal Government in Bonn, forming a high proportion of the money in use in the city. The West German taxpayers were generous, and the support was never in question.

The governance arrangements of West Berlin were the fourth reason for the city's success as a beacon of freedom within East Germany. The three Western allies were careful to base the continued presence of their forces in West Berlin on agreements reached with the Soviet Union at the end of the war. The allies retained ultimate authority in their sectors, in line with the post-war agreements, and those sectors did not become part of the Federal Republic in West Germany. The allies remained responsible for many important activities, notably the defence and the external relations of West Berlin, including relations with the Soviet Union and the East German authorities. But the allies delegated the running of West

Berlin to the democratic city government and elected parliament. Laws enacted by the Bonn Parliament for the Federal Republic in West Germany could be extended to West Berlin, but each law had to be approved by the Allies when it was taken over by the city Parliament, and sometimes we modified or blocked a law.

In Berlin, my work, as always, was about protecting British interests – in this case as one of the officials whose role was to help to keep West Berlin viable and free, and thus to prevent further Soviet encroachment westwards and maintain the security of western Europe including Britain. My particular role was to represent the United Kingdom in the day-to-day discussion with the city government about Berlin matters affected by Allied Rights. I worked with officials representing the US and France. There was close coordination between our three governments on Berlin matters, through our diplomatic offices in West Berlin and through our Embassies in Bonn, which also ensured cooperation with the Federal German Government.

The Allies consulted daily with the Berlin city government, with two main purposes. We wanted to ensure that decisions by the city did not undermine the continued validity of the post-war agreements on which our military presence in Berlin was based, since the Soviet Union might have claimed that the agreements had been rendered invalid by our actions and our presence in Berlin was therefore illegal. And we wanted at the same time to enable the city government to exercise as much of the normal responsibility of a democratic government as those agreements could be held to allow. This was an intricate process involving highly expert discussions and legal arrangements, which created over time a complicated contrivance which many observers might have thought artificial.

In diplomacy, artificial contrivances are better avoided and often do not last. This contrivance worked, and it lasted all the way to German unification in 1990. I have often said in lectures and speeches that West Berlin in the Cold War was a wonder of the modern world. It was a wonder of freedom and prosperity and courage in adversity. The intricate complexity of its governance was a wonder of ingenuity.

The work I did, coordinating constantly with the city government, was varied and necessary. Everyone involved wanted to reach agreement on arrangements that would keep West Berlin safe in its exposed situation beyond the Iron Curtain, while making life for Berliners as normal as possible. We worked together in friendship.

One matter which concerned me actively was that the division between East and West Berlin meant that families whose members lived on both sides of the Wall could not meet, even on special family occasions like births or funerals. Before Easter and Christmas each year, the city government, acting under authority from the Allies, held negotiations with the East Berlin authorities to obtain special passes for West Berliners to make brief visits to see relatives in East Berlin. There was strong public interest in West Berlin over whether passes would be available for next Christmas or Easter. The allies wanted to see agreement on passes but also insisted that this should be done under the umbrella of allied rights in Berlin. That is an example of the complexities which arose in operating the governance arrangements necessary for West Berlin.

The tension between the Soviet Union and the West over Berlin diminished in the mid-1960s because the Russians realised that threats would not make the western allies leave the city. In this easier climate, Berlin's worldwide fame as a hero city resisting Soviet dictatorship became less obvious and the Berliners, very naturally, began to worry about their own problems. The departure of the popular Mayor, Willy Brandt, contributed to this mood. He left in 1966 to become Vice Chancellor, then Chancellor, of the Federal Republic in Bonn, and a great figure in the history of post-war Germany. The new fretting of the West Berliners was expressed in many ways, such as concern about the city's economy and its falling population. It was my job to analyse the new mood and consider how the Allies should react.

One example of the new mood presented particular concerns for the Allies. In 1968 there were major demonstrations by students and others in Berlin, as in many cities in the western world. In Berlin, as in some other places, one of the purposes of the demonstrations was to protest against US participation in the war in Vietnam. The Berlin demonstrations had many other motives; a major one was to protest against the way Berlin's universities were run; with little contact, the students said, between the teachers and themselves. The movement was joined by many left wing intellectuals and other sympathisers. There were sit-ins in the universities and violence between demonstrators and police.

On 1 June 1967 a student participating in a demonstration against a visit by the Shah of Iran was shot dead by a plain clothes West Berlin policeman. This happened outside the opera house where Pascale and I were enjoying a performance of *The Magic Flute* in honour of the Shah.

It was shocking and inexplicable for a policeman to kill an unarmed demonstrator, and there was sharp criticism in the West German media. Decades later, in 2009, it became known that the policeman was an undercover agent working for the Stasi, the East German Secret police. Some observers have made the obvious suggestion that the Stasi must have ordered the killing, with the purpose of inflaming the clashes between demonstrators and the police in West Germany and West Berlin. There is no indication of this in the Stasi files now available after the end of East Germany. It is, however, clear that the killing of Benno Ohnesorg was one of the influences which prompted the rise of left-wing terrorism in West Germany in the 1970s.

The clashes on the streets of West Berlin were a concern to me for wider reasons. The West Berlin police had difficulty in coping with the large demonstrations. The police had no reserves to call on in a crisis. The only possible resource were the Allied forces in Berlin. There was moreover a question whether there might be demonstrations near the Berlin Wall and demonstrators might try to move into East Berlin. That would have brought into play the relationship between West and East Berlin, a matter of Allied responsibility. The Allied forces were in Berlin to deter Soviet aggression against the city. They were not there to keep public order within Berlin. The idea of using them against West Berliners was appalling.

One evening a large demonstration marched in the direction of the Wall. I was on duty and the West Berlin Police Chief asked me to join him at his command post near the demonstration. I told the British army what was happening and they told the other allies.

Thank goodness the demonstration turned back before it reached the Wall. Public order in West Berlin never deteriorated to the point where we would have had to take the agonising decision whether our forces should help the police.

For my work with the city government I needed to know everything important that was happening in West Berlin politics. I made friendships among the ministers and the officials. The politicians I knew well came from the main party then in government in Berlin, the Social Democratic Party, or SPD. After a time I was also made press spokesman for the British authorities in Berlin, and I made friends among the foreign and German press in the city.

I began with a distorted view, derived perhaps from German literature, that German officials might show inflexible conformity, obsessive devotion to hierarchy and pedantic legalism. I found nothing of the kind. The politicians and senior officials were energetic and adaptable. I enjoyed their company. I also benefited from the experience of this first job where I was a kind of public figure. The Allied Liaison Officers were VIPs on the political and public scene of West Berlin, and in my other role as British press spokesman I spoke in German at press conferences and was interviewed on television about allied policies. After some experience I became confident in this work.

Daily Life

West Berlin at this time was an exciting city. We had an agreeable, airy nineteen-thirties house in Charlottenburg, the heart of West Berlin, which was ideal for our young family and for entertaining my work contacts and our friends.

Berlin's famously invigorating air stimulated energy and a feeling of well-being. The theatres were good, the museums were excellent and walks and picnics in the country areas of West Berlin provided a contrast to our life in the city centre. We also visited East Berlin from time to time. We found this communist capital less oppressive in feeling than Moscow but at the same time a sad contrast of grey backwardness in comparison to swinging West Berlin.

Our Berlin period was a high point for friendships. As well as my friends through work, in Berlin politics and the media, we had good friends in the British army, some of whom I had known before. Our main group of friends were West Berliners, mostly with an interest in the arts.

Foremost among them were Bernd and Gisela von Keyserlingk, he an architect and she a teacher. They were clever and amusing and they had children a little younger than ours. Bernd and Gisela were to settle in East Germany when communism collapsed in 1989. Bernd's architectural business played an active role in the modernisation of the city of Leipzig. Tragically, he was drowned in a canoeing accident there. I shall always remember his handsome smile and enthusiastic attitude to life. Gisela still lives in Leipzig, as does my godson Felix, who now has a family.

Through the Keyserlingks we met many others in Berlin, notably Volodya Lindenberg, a fascinating Russian emigré, much older than us, who was a gentle sage with an aura of saintliness and serenity. He was deeply religious and erudite, a good artist and a moving and prolific writer of autobiography and books on philosophy and medicine; and on yoga, which he taught.

Volodya's Russian father was a Prince Tschelishchev. When the Russian revolution took place in 1917, Volodya was 15, living in Moscow with his mother and stepfather, a German industrialist. He was arrested by the Bolsheviks and put before a firing squad, but was freed by one of the executioners who was a house servant of his family. He emigrated to Germany, studied medicine and became a neurologist and psychiatrist. After visiting Africa and South America as a ship's doctor, Volodya practised in Berlin. He was arrested by the Gestapo in 1937, held in a concentration camp and then released in 1941.

We went often to Volodya's small wooden house in the woods in the north of West Berlin. He had built the house himself after the war. It was like a Russian dacha, full of icons and other Russian objects. There was usually an overcrowded lunch with lively conversation in German, Russian and English and always Russian food – borsch, beef stroganov and vodka. The guests, all squashed round the small table, were intelligent people of all ages and activities. Many had aristocratic backgrounds and many were academics, artists, or students. Several were related to participants in the failed attempt to assassinate Hitler in July 1944.

Volodya continued to see psychiatric patients until shortly before his death aged 95 in 1997, when I was among the pall bearers.

I helped to arrange for a gallery in Berlin to hold David Hockney's first exhibition in Germany, a complete showing of his prints. David stayed with us for the opening. We gave a riotous buffet dinner. One of our guests was George Rickey, an American sculptor spending a year working in Berlin. His constructivist sculpture had struck us as particularly beautiful when we first saw it at the Documenta exhibition in West Germany not long before. George and Edie became boon companions of ours and we saw them in London, New York and East Chatham, Massachusetts many times afterwards. He was modest and diligent and erudite. She was tall and flamboyant and had a loud laugh and a wonderful way with small children.

We had a dear elderly body called Gretchen Volkhaus as our cleaning lady. She had been trained for domestic service in a German bourgeois family before the war. She was proud that she knew the skills of her role and she always addressed Pascale in the third person. Her daughter had married a soldier in the British Army and she had learned English from this son-in-law. The problem was that she did not realise that some of the words she used frequently were unprintable. The best example of this involuntary comedy was when Frau Volkhaus, as she liked to be addressed, was helping with a lunch party of some thirty official guests in our home. She walked with dignity and deference among our guests with trays of Pimms. When the meal was ready, she took up a prominent position on one side of the room and declared 'Madam's bloody lunch is bloody well served!'

After 2½ years in Berlin I was called back to the Foreign Office. I was reluctant to leave Berlin, where we were happy and my job was enjoyable. But the head of the Eastern European and Soviet Department, our dear friend from our Moscow days, Howard Smith, wanted me to be the new desk officer covering Soviet foreign policy. That would mean much more responsibility than before, and I was pleased.

Pascale flew to London to sort out our flat in Primrose Hill. We had let it to several young ladies who described themselves as physiotherapists. After Pascale moved back in, the telephone never stopped ringing day and night, with men requesting appointments. We learned a lesson: if you move into a home where prostitutes may have worked, the very first thing to do is to change the telephone number!

5

SOVIET DESK, FOREIGN OFFICE 1969–71

My new job, for my second period working in the Foreign Office in London, was to be the in-house expert on Soviet foreign policy. I had to watch Soviet statements and actions concerning all major subjects and analyse them and predict what the USSR would do, and to suggest British or western responses and initiatives. I was also the FCO's coordinator for the wide subject of relations between the Soviet Union and the NATO countries. I wrote papers on many aspects of this vast subject and how British interests might better be advanced.

My subject was central to British international interests and my output was read by senior officials and ministers in various government departments, as well as many senior people in the FCO itself.

During my first year in this job the Foreign Office was amalgamated with the Commonwealth Relations Office. From now on I shall call it by its new name, the Foreign and Commonwealth Office, or FCO.

My work on Soviet affairs required cooperation with many parts of the FCO, for instance the Middle East Department when there was a new move in Soviet policy in that region; or the Western European Department if Soviet rhetoric on Berlin seemed to be changing; or the Arms Control Department if an analysis of the Soviet position on some issue in that field was needed.

I was helped immensely by the Embassy in Moscow and the Soviet Section of the FCO Research Department, the latter staffed by lifelong experts on the Soviet Union. They knew the factual background and the Soviet interests behind any new Soviet policy or initiative and they played an invaluable role in the FCO throughout the Cold War.

* * * * *

Soon after I began this job, an astonishing development occurred. In March 1969 there were armed clashes between the Soviet Union and China on their frontier on the Ussuri River, with hundreds of casualties on each side. There was intense interest in the British Government and there were major questions to consider about the clashes and their likely effects. John Boyd, the desk officer for China, and I played the central role in forming the FCO contribution to the Government's assessments of this new development and its likely repercussions.

The public dispute about ideological questions between China and the Soviet Union had now become also a military clash about a state matter, the frontier between them. The Soviet Union, our antagonist in the Cold War, now faced a crisis on its south eastern frontier. Would this lead to a major war between the Soviet Union and China?

John Boyd and I deduced that China had instigated the first armed clash. The motives included anger about Soviet positions in the dispute about ideology and a wish to stimulate patriotic cohesion within China. It became clear later that these two judgments were correct. We also thought that neither China nor the Soviet Union would want a major war. Yet we did not quite exclude that the Soviet Union might be tempted to use the military clashes and the furious Chinese propaganda as an opportunity to destroy China's nuclear weapons facilities, thus putting an end for years to this potential threat to itself. This did not happen.

Would the Soviet Union, facing a crisis versus China, become more interested in improving relations with the West? And might China, in a crisis with the Soviet superpower, be interested now in a new relationship with the United States? The Vietnam war, which might have made them reluctant to make such moves, had ended four years earlier. John Boyd and I thought that both communist powers would now seek better relations with the United States and the West. Indeed, we therefore saw the Sino-Soviet clashes as a potentially promising development for the West and a weakening of the Soviet Union in the world, especially in its leadership of the world communist movement.

It soon became clear that the Soviet Union did want to improve relations with the West. And by the summer of 1969, secret talks began between the United States and China about a new relationship.

Another example of my work was to participate in the consideration in London the question of whether the UK with the USA and France should try to engage the Soviet Union in a negotiation about Berlin. There were several reasons for thinking that the Soviet Union had become more interested in reducing tension between East and West. Moscow might therefore see advantage in an agreement which would relieve the tension concerning Berlin, the focus of several serious East-West crises. I also thought that the Soviet Union might be persuaded that improved access to West Berlin from the west would be a necessary part of an agreement designed to reduce tension about Berlin. So would greater contact between families divided between West Berlin and East Germany and also local cooperation between West Berlin and the surrounding area on practical matters. These views were among many – British, American, French and of course West German – which contributed to the decision to attempt a negotiation.

One of the complexities of this negotiation was that the Soviet Union on the one hand and the United States, Britain and France on the other could not agree on the words for describing the area to be covered by an agreement. The Soviet Union wanted to confine the agreement to West Berlin, but the western powers could accept nothing which implied that the post-war status of Berlin as a whole had ended. Evasive expressions such as 'the relevant territory' had to be used in the agreement. This diplomatic difficulty was thus circumvented and a really useful agreement was reached in June 1972.

By stabilising the situation of West Berlin and making life better for the West Berliners and access from the western world to West

Berlin much easier, the Quadripartite Agreement contributed to the continued success of West Berlin through to the end of the Cold War and thus to a major western and British interest. Moreover the Agreement signified Soviet abandonment of the policy of threats to West Berlin, and a major source of East-West tension was eased. I think it is fair to say that the Quadripartite Agreement was not only a valuable achievement in the work to relax East-West tension at that time, but also, by helping to ensure West Berlin's continued success, was one of the roots which contributed to the terminal crisis which overtook communist East Germany 17 years later, bringing German unification, which in turn was an essential part of the ending of the Cold War.

Another important subject in which I was much involved was the Soviet call for a European Security Conference. This idea had been floated several times by Moscow, and the West had ignored it because the Soviet Union wanted recognition of the existing frontiers in central and Eastern Europe, meaning Soviet power in the area, and not much else. We now tried the idea of a new policy based on adaptation of the Soviet proposal in ways which would suit western and British interests. I was asked to write a paper on European security that would review the whole vast subject and suggest the aims the West and Britain should adopt in a negotiation, in order to increase stability and reduce tension in ways that would advance our own interests. After lengthy consultation among the NATO countries the decision was taken to attempt a negotiation. This was to lead eventually to the Helsinki agreement of 1975, described in Chapter 7 about our time in Moscow from 1975 to 1977.

One of the suggestions which I put forward in the study of European Security and Cooperation (as we re-named the Soviet proposal) was for a permanent forum where international disputes in Europe could be discussed. The purpose would be to reduce misunderstandings and lessen the risk of impetuous action without consultation. This was a germ of the later creation of the Organisation for Security and Cooperation in Europe.

The most important addition by the west to the Soviet idea of a conference was to include human and political rights and greater cultural, commercial, scientific and other exchanges across Europe.

One of our major purposes in this was to increase the information about freedom and prosperity in the West which would reach the peoples of the Soviet Union and the other communist countries in Europe. This subject became a major part of the subsequent conference and the Helsinki agreement. It contributed to the pressures for freedom in the communist states and then to liberation from Soviet domination, as later chapters will describe.

In many other subjects too, I was trying to suggest better policies for the UK and the West in dealing with Soviet moves. All this involved contacts with Sir Alec Douglas-Home, the Foreign Secretary, and other British ministers. Once I was participating in a meeting between the Soviet Foreign Minister, Andrei Gromyko, and Sir Alec in the latter's splendid office. My role was to take a note of everything that was said and to prepare a summary afterwards for the information of other ministers and ministries in the British government. To my horror, my ballpoint pen ran dry after about ten minutes. The only thing I could do was to leave the conference table in extreme embarrassment and borrow one of the pencils standing in a silver cup on the Foreign Secretary's desk. When the meeting was over and Gromyko had left, Sir Alec, true to his reputation for charm and consideration for staff, said to me 'I am glad you borrowed a pencil. I'm not sure I would have dared but you were right.'

My work during this period in London was far more varied, difficult and significant than any I had done before. It was also the first time I had held a job which was prominent in the daily affairs of the FCO. I was told by the Personnel Department that I had done it well and that I was now seen as a good performer with prospects of one day doing top jobs in the Diplomatic Service.

Pascale and I loved our life in London. We moved from Primrose Hill to a pretty house by Bushy Park at Hampton Court. Julia, our third child, was born just before we left London for New York, to join Sebastian and Emily as the focus of our life and love.

6

BRITISH TRADE OFFICE,
NEW YORK 1971–74

I wanted to work in the promotion of British exports, which would give me a complete change of subject. At that time our Personnel Department wanted people who had a future in the Diplomatic Service to do this kind of work at roughly my age.

The most substantial export promotion job at my level seemed to be the one dealing with industrial exports to the United States, based in New York. But I didn't know anything about business or exporting and I needed some quick way of reducing this vast gap. I had to make myself credible in dealing, without relevant experience, with business people who had worked for years in their fields. They knew everything about their work and I knew nothing. How can you get round that disadvantage? The FCO had a policy then of sending one person to the Harvard Business School every summer for a highly intensive course in marketing. I was chosen for the New York job and the Harvard course.

I did the course with some thirty keen business people from many countries. We didn't do the whole MBA course, which lasted two years; for instance, we were spared accountancy. But we did the marketing element of the MBA course and parts of the management element, and we did this in three months under extreme pressure. It was absorbing and very difficult.

The course was brilliantly taught. For me its particular value was that it was a way of learning something about American industry, because the business cases which Harvard used in teaching marketing were set in American companies, many of them in industry. So I was able to gain some knowledge of US industry and its ways and mentality before starting to work on helping British firms to sell to customers in that field. I also benefited in a wider way from that great institution, the Harvard Business School. Its basic principle was that firms should not produce what they think they are good at and then try to sell it. They should think in the opposite way, finding out first what the market wants in their general field and then producing and marketing that. This is a principle which I have found valuable in many fields, not only business, ever since.

I was at Harvard throughout the summer of 1971 and in September I moved to the British Trade Development Office in New York to do the export promotion job. I did it for three and a half years. I was delighted to be living in New York, having fallen in love with that thrilling city when I spent three months at the United Nations in 1960.

The case work we did at the British Trade Development Office was a kind of business consultancy provided to British firms by the Government in order to increase exports. Our advantage was that between us we knew a good deal about the US market and had many contacts there. I had seven commercial officers in our New York Office, two of whom were career diplomats and the others were engineers and other technically qualified people employed on contract. About fifteen more commercial officers in the British Consulates in other US cities reported to my office.

I delegated the bulk of the case work to the Commercial Officers. Much of this consisted of requests from British firms for advice on selling in the US. A company would seek our view on whether its products would sell and what sales arrangements – such as agents – would be best. One of my commercial officers would research the market, finding out whether American manufacturers of the types of product in question were so successful that a newcomer would have little chance; or whether the British product had attractions of performance or quality or price which might enable the UK firm to succeed in the US despite the competition. When the UK firm had considered our advice they might ask us to find agents to market the product. Often, different agents would be needed for different regions of the US and our Commercial Officers in other American cities made suggestions.

Another frequent type of case work was when a UK firm wanted to sell a licence to a US firm to manufacture and market a product which had done well in the UK or other markets. We did the research and made enquiries in the US market and introduced the UK firm to possible US partners.

I supervised this casework carefully. There were also cases where I played the lead role myself, for instance when the British company seeking our help was an important one, or where there was a political interest from the firm's MP.

It was not hard to persuade US companies to consider importing British products. If profits looked possible from marketing the products, a serious negotiation about the terms of a partnership could be mounted. I had more difficulty in persuading British companies to look seriously at the US market. Some British firms were too complacent about selling in the US, believing that with the common language and shared traditions, business in America would be similar to business in Britain. Other British firms were nervous of launching into the largest and most efficient and competitive market in the world. The first of these attitudes was naive. The second could be mistaken, if the UK firm had good products with competitive prices. The job of my team in New York was to explain these things to UK firms and to introduce them to potential partners in the US whose business style would show how things were done in America.

I did not believe that this work, where we were responding to UK firms' ideas, was all we should be doing. I wanted to be proactive as well. There was already a scheme where British export promotion staff abroad looked for specific sales opportunities for British exporters. In the US we scanned the press, especially industry magazines. We quizzed business and government contacts galore. We wrote short notices about the opportunities we found, which were conveyed by the Department of Trade and Industry in London to firms across Britain. The sales opportunities in the US market are limitless and we tried to select the most promising ones for Britain. The responses from British firms were rather disappointing.

So I thought we should try another method, which was not part of our instructions from the ministries in London. We should look not only for individual short-term opportunities but also for wider sectoral ones which might last for some time. In the vast US market we could surely find many possibilities. We researched the US market for industrial products. This was a major task, and we did it with our existing staff. When we found a clear possibility for Britain we wrote a paper describing the opportunity and our reasons for seeing scope for UK firms. We suggested how firms should tackle the opportunity and how we, as the UK's export promotion service in the US, could help with detailed advice and by making introductions to customers and intermediaries like sales agents. I hoped by this method to arouse the interest of more British firms in exporting to the US.

The sectors of US industry where we found opportunities were quite numerous and very varied. There were several possibilities in the field of energy: for example, modern technology and equipment for longwall coal mining and gas turbines and their components. In transport we saw openings for certain types of aircraft and air engines, and for automated signalling and control systems for city rail systems. There was scope for British machine tools, components for cars and trucks, textile machinery and numerous types of scientific instruments.

One of the promising fields for British exports was medical equipment. I saw this as an opportunity to persuade British companies to look seriously at the US market. American hospitals until then had generally wanted the most advanced equipment and had given less attention to the price. They now began to take more care about prices and to look for good products which were less expensive.

British medical equipment, sold principally to the National Health Service, clearly had new opportunities. Senior British doctors working in various parts of the US were glad to tell me about the opportunities they saw for British products. Then my team and I wrote a detailed report about the American market for British health equipment, from hospital beds to diagnostic instruments, describing the American needs and explaining how a British exporter would best sell its products. I attended a trade fair in London of the British medical equipment industry. There I visited the stands of many British manufacturers, gave them our report and explained what we in New York could do to help them sell in the US. British exports to the US in this field grew considerably. It was a good feeling to see tangible results from our initiative.

A British product which I thought would have a market in the United States was Dunlop's moving pedestrian beltway. Transport interchange stations were being planned on the outskirts of many American cities. Commuters would park their cars there and take a rapid transit link, probably an overground railway, for the last part of the journey to work. It seemed to me that passengers leaving their cars and walking through the transit building to the trains would benefit from a moving walkway. I put this idea to Dunlop's US company, which said it was not interested because its role was selling tyres. I wrote to Dunlop in the UK but received no reply. Then I had a piece of luck. I met at a party in New York a young woman whose father was head of Dunlop. I told her about the opportunity I saw for the company. Her father got Dunlop to look carefully at the planned interchange stations. The results of this effort were disappointing, partly because fewer interchange stations were built than had been intended.

I did some public speaking and interviews on US radio and television about the UK and British products which I wanted to promote. I hoped that some business listeners might be attracted by the products. At a time when rising energy prices had prompted public debate about how families could reduce their heating bills, I was asked in a breakfast interview on television in Upstate New York whether the central heating was kept on at night in British homes. I replied that the central heating was usually turned off, to save heating costs. I added unwisely 'There are other ways of keeping warm in bed.' I was thinking of blankets, hot water bottles and so on. But the interviewer seized the opportunity to tease. He guffawed that a British diplomat had made a naughty suggestion live on American TV.

There has long been a debate about which organisation in Britain is best placed to undertake the promotion of exports and of foreign investment in Britain. Both types of promotion need to be undertaken by some sort of dedicated service. The Diplomatic Service, with its adaptability and worldwide presence, was and is well suited to this work in terms of its deployment and the keenness of its people. But it has a key weakness: most of its people do not have readymade knowledge of business. So the Diplomatic Service, as well as training its own staff for this work, tried in my time to bridge the gap by hiring, in foreign markets, people like my commercial officers who did have the right expertise to do the case work. In addition, the involvement of senior people from British business in non-executive and other roles in London has been a real help in recent years. The idea of passing the role of export promotion to some other organisation has been considered in depth several times and has always been set aside. My conclusion about this was that the Diplomatic Service was the only viable candidate for the work; we simply had to work flat out to find opportunities and to try to get British firms interested in them.

* * * * *

Life in Manhattan was good for our family. Charlotte was born on 14 October 1972, the youngest of our four beloved children. We lived in an apartment on Fifth Avenue, just south of Harlem and beside Central Park. Sebastian went to a school only a few steps away and could walk there unescorted – a rare advantage in Manhattan in those days. St Bernard's was and is a fantastic school. Sebastian really took to his studies. At the age of eight, he had the best or nearly the best teacher he ever encountered.

Manhattan was as exciting as I remembered. We made many friends, some of them parents of our children's schoolmates. Our closest friends in our apartment block were David and Pat Read. David was the popular and erudite Minister at Madison Avenue Presbyterian Church. We often went to services there, and Sebastian and Emily went to the very lively Sunday School. This was the only period in our lives when we went regularly to church. David's charisma and his excellent sermons were the attraction.

Pascale and I went for walks in many parts of Manhattan and got to know it rather well. We visited many of the impressive modern buildings. The few blocks on Fifth Avenue just north of

Grand Central Station, dominated by the Pan Am (now MetLife) building, formed the most splendid modern urban view I knew then. We visited the main museums and we got to know the galleries where the leading younger artists of the day, including Alex Katz and Philip Pearlstein, were being shown. We went often to the movies and sometimes to the theatre. We had favourite restaurants in various parts of town.

We had a crummy little weekend cottage for our first summer. It was beside a lake near the town of Poughkeepsie in New York State. The children and I enjoyed the outdoor contrast to our weekday life in New York City, but our log cabin was dilapidated and cramped. Later we had a much nicer weekend place: we rented at bargain price a large, shabby house by the Atlantic in a village called Center Moriches on Long Island. It took 70 minutes to drive the 70 miles from the city. We enjoyed the garden and the sea fishing, and were happy.

I had a very New York incident with Julia, then aged three. One weekend she fell off the washing machine in our apartment, hitting her head on the hard floor. I wrapped her in a blanket and carried her to the emergency center at Mount Sinai Hospital, just along 98th Street. Nothing was seriously wrong and I was soon on my way back with Julia in my arms. In 98th Street a car was driving much too fast towards us and behind it was a police car with policemen shooting at the first car. I dived with Julia into a doorway and the speeding cars went quickly past us. The incident was over before Julia and I had time to be afraid. When we returned to our block a couple of minutes later the Irish doorman quipped that we should not have worried, because the hospital would surely have given us a discount if Julia had visited the emergency center twice in one evening.

I enjoyed my work in New York. It was gratifying to achieve some tangible results. The experience broadened my interests and I learned a lot. I enjoyed the company of business people and have done so ever since. I also had great pleasure travelling in the US for my work. To get to know Washington, Chicago, Los Angeles, San Francisco, Atlanta and other cities was a privilege. My experience in New York also stood me in good stead when much later the promotion of British exports was a large part of my work as Ambassador in Germany and France, although then I was providing strategic advice to major British firms rather than detailed advice to smaller ones.

This stay in New York deepened my love of the United States. My devotion has to do with the excitement and the efficiency of the country and above all my gratitude for America's vastly important role in defeating Hitler and then ensuring the security of Western Europe including Britain during the Cold War. I have continued ever since to admire the United States in many ways and to enjoy frequent visits.

When we were about to leave New York after 3½ years, I was approached by two British companies with offers of jobs. One was a major UK group which wanted me to head its medical equipment company and the other was an investment bank which wanted me to work with them in New York. Both offers had attractions, but I had decided that diplomacy was my career and Pascale did not want to stay in New York. I turned down the offers.

The FCO at that moment told me that I would be sent next to Moscow. I was to be Head of Chancery, or number three, in the Embassy. Pascale and I were curious and glad to experience the Soviet Union again after twelve years.

7

MOSCOW 1975–77

We arrived in Moscow for our second stay in January 1975. We lived in a flat on the ground floor of a charming house near the Old Arbat, one of the central streets of the city. It was one of the many pretty houses built around 1820 to replace buildings destroyed when the Muscovites burnt the city in 1812 before Napoleon captured it. Our side street was called Skatertny Pereulok, meaning table cloth lane. Tradition says that table cloths were made there for the Tsars.

Twelve Years On
The big change we found in Moscow was that since our first stay people had lost their belief in Marxist-Leninist ideology. They no longer believed that the system would in time deliver a better life. That optimism had vanished and had been replaced by cynicism. The economy worked poorly and where it worked barter and bribes, even more than before, were what made the wheels turn. If you wanted something mended you gave the shop or garage a bribe, whether money or vodka or a foreign product. A black market flourished.

Here is a small example of the death of ideology. In 1962, during our first stay, I went to GUM in Red Square, the city's best known department store, and innocently asked for razor blades. As I expected, they had none, but the sales person said something optimistic. She said one Russian word, *'budet'*, meaning 'it will be' or 'we shall have razor blades in due course'. I tried the same experiment again in 1975. Asked for razor blades, the sales lady at GUM simply answered '*netu*', meaning 'got none'.

Work

My new job in Moscow was called traditionally Head of Chancery and today is known as Political Counsellor. I had two roles. One was managing the embassy and coordinating its work. The other was to head the team doing the political job of analysing and trying to predict Soviet foreign policy for the Ambassador and the FCO. The political team also made numerous suggestions about British policy towards the Soviet Union.

As always in my diplomatic career I found that the new job was stretching, because I needed to learn new functions, and I was never bored. This effect was increased because the position immediately above me, the Minister or deputy to the Ambassador, was vacant for eleven months during our time, when I did that job as well as my own. I much enjoyed working for two very different Ambassadors. Sir Terence Garvey was friendly, clever, flexible and deeply interested in Russia. Pascale and I admired and loved Rosemary Garvey for her down-to-earth views and tastes. Sir Howard and Mary Smith were dear friends since our first period in Moscow. He was a superb official – very acute and accurate intellectually.

The Soviet Union was now more cautious than Khrushchev had been. There was no big East-West crisis, like the Cuba crisis we had experienced in 1962. The Cold War continued but it was a few degrees less cold than it had been during our first stay in Moscow.

The Embassy did a great deal of reporting, sending several telegrams about developments in Soviet policy every day. When I was doing this work in Moscow twelve years earlier we relied almost entirely on the Soviet press and the deductions we could draw from it. The task of analysing Soviet policies and actions now became more rewarding.

Harold Wilson as Prime Minister and James Callaghan as Foreign Secretary visited Moscow in February 1975, shortly after our arrival at the Embassy. The visit was successful, and both sides declared that it was the start of a New Phase in British-Soviet relations. One of the documents the leaders signed was a Protocol on Consultations, which announced that the United Kingdom and the Soviet Union would increase their discussions about international matters, including contacts between our Embassy in Moscow and the Soviet authorities. This gave me a lever for opening doors to Soviet organisations and for meeting people in the Russian foreign policy machine with whom the Embassy had not had contact.

I wrote to many organisations, and some did not reply. But many did agree to hold discussions with the Embassy. So we visited for the first time other parts of the Foreign Ministry than the one which dealt directly with Britain, for discussions about many subjects including European security, the Middle East and arms control. I held meetings with other ministries with interests in international affairs, with the Soviet think-tanks which dealt with foreign policy, with senior academics and journalists specialising in foreign affairs; and once or twice with members of the International Department of the Communist Party's Central Committee. Some conversations were dull and stilted, but others yielded more detail about Soviet policy than was given in public statements. We asked questions about new Soviet policies or the meaning of particular points in speeches by the Soviet leaders. We were able sometimes to quote to London the insiders who were recommending what the Soviet Union should do. These conversations made our reports to London more informative and useful: and much more interesting for us in the Embassy to write.

That is not to say that the Soviet press was no longer essential reading. A young diplomat in the embassy noticed that an article on the Cyprus problem in *Pravda* was different in one word from earlier articles on this subject. Instead of saying that foreign forces must withdraw from the *Republic* of Cyprus, which meant the Turkish forces in the north, Pravda suddenly said that foreign forces should withdraw from the *island* of Cyprus; and that meant also the British military bases, which were on the island but not part of the Republic of Cyprus. So we predicted to London that there would be a change of Soviet policy and Foreign Minister Gromyko would criticise our military presence in Cyprus at the next United Nations General Assembly, which was a couple of months away. That is indeed what happened. It was bound to happen because *Pravda* did not publish anything by chance, but only on instructions from the authorities.

In addition to our new contacts with Soviet organisations we in the political team tried to learn more about Soviet policy from individual officials whom we met socially in Moscow. One friend of mine was Roland Timerbayev, a senior Soviet diplomat dealing with arms control negotiations between the Soviet Union and the West. Roland and I went to the theatre a few times together and talked in a friendly way about many things. I did not learn anything confidential about Soviet policy, but I was able to ask him to explain and justify points about arms control which had appeared in statements by the Soviet authorities. Roland gave helpful and reliable explanations.

I also had many talks with my opposite number in the Chinese Embassy in Moscow. He was well informed and very active, and I enjoyed learning from him. The Chinese Embassy of course understood the Soviet system particularly well, despite the sharp differences between the ideological positions of these two communist powers. The Chinese diplomat often told me about new points in Soviet policy which had not yet been made public. Perhaps he saw an interest in encouraging a western diplomat to work against certain Soviet policies which China too disliked. Sometimes I sent reports to the FCO which gave three points of view on a key current question. One was the official Soviet view stated by the Soviet press. The second was the account we heard from Soviet organisations, which was often more detailed or easier to understand than the public statements. The third view of Soviet policy was the one I heard from the Chinese Embassy. These reports helped to show the differences of view between the Soviet Union and China on specific subjects and contributed to the British Government's effort to understand the important but sometimes obscure Sino-Soviet dispute.

The West and the Soviet Union wanted to reduce the tension between them. The effort to relax tension, known as détente, was developing quite well. During our stay in Moscow the first two Soviet-American treaties on nuclear arms control were concluded: one limiting the number of long-range nuclear missiles on each side and the other banning missiles for destroying the other side's offensive missiles in flight. The view of the US and the Soviet Union at that time was that these anti-ballistic missiles, if developed and deployed, would have led to even greater expenditure on developing new offensive missiles and might have dangerously destabilised the nuclear balance between the two superpowers.

There was also a joint interest between the Soviet Union and the NATO countries in preventing the spread of nuclear weapons to more countries, and we cooperated with the Russians in the United Nations and elsewhere on the diplomacy of this subject.

The West had a major purpose in pursuing détente. We wanted to get more information through to the Soviet people about our freedom and our much higher standard of living. This would reduce somewhat the monopoly of information enjoyed by the Communist party and its mendacious propaganda about western life.

Moscow, like the West, wanted to reduce East-West tension so that the risks inherent in the adversarial relationship could be reduced and the world become a safer place. The Soviet Union also wanted to strengthen East-West relations as a counterweight to the major difficulties in its relations with China. And the Soviet leaders wanted to increase trade, partly in order to obtain access to new western technologies which they hoped to copy.

It would, however, be very wrong to think that détente was the only important part of Soviet policy towards the West. The Soviet Union maintained its efforts to prevail in the Cold War, especially by trying to outflank the West from the South by gaining influence in developing countries. Some of this involved military aid to revolutions in Africa and Latin America. Moscow aided Ethiopia in a war against Sudan, and the Sandinistas in their revolution in Nicaragua, who in turn fostered revolutionaries in Guatemala and El Salvador. There were sizeable Cuban interventions in Angola and Mozambique, Portuguese colonies in Southern Africa which had gained independence. The Soviet Union saw these two activities – détente and energetic efforts to gain influence in the third world – as compatible elements of their doctrine called Peaceful Coexistence, defined as a struggle against the capitalist world by all means short of war.

The biggest event in East-West relations during our second period in Moscow was the signature in August 1975 of the

Helsinki Final Act. I'll describe this in a moment, but first I want to relate an incident in the British-Soviet discussions about it. When Harold Wilson and James Callaghan visited Moscow in February 1975, I was present at talks between Callaghan and Foreign Minister Gromyko, where one purpose was to agree the text of a British-Soviet declaration on the international situation. In this the two sides set out the points on which they agreed concerning the main issues in the international arena at the time. One paragraph concerned the negotiations on security and cooperation in Europe which were to lead later to the Helsinki agreement. The British draft text said that good progress was being made in the Helsinki negotiations. Gromyko adamantly refused to accept these words. We knew that the Soviet Union agreed that good progress was being made, so why was Gromyko refusing to say so? Thinking about how the English words would come out in Russian, I realised that a translation of 'good' would produce a Russian word which means good in quality and says nothing about quantity. So we suggested that the text should say that 'much progress' was being made. Gromyko immediately agreed. The moral of this incident is that, even with excellent interpreters, one needs a Russian speaker in one's own delegation to make sure that the words we propose in English will readily give the same meaning in Russian, rather than the meaning being lost or distorted in translation.

The Helsinki Final Act was not a binding treaty with legal force but was politically and morally binding. The participants were all the European countries (except Albania) and the United States and Canada. The Final Act began with a Declaration on Principles which should govern relations among the participating states. These principles included:

- respect for sovereignty
- refraining from use or threat of force
- inviolability of frontiers
- peaceful settlement of disputes
- non-intervention in the internal affairs of other countries
- respect for human rights and freedoms including freedom of thought, religion and belief.

Several of these principles obviously went against the Soviet claim that any move away from socialism in a socialist, meaning communist, country was a matter of concern to all the socialist countries; in other words the Soviet Union had the right to intervene by force in a socialist country where it did not like the way things were developing. That principle was known as the Brezhnev Doctrine. Yet the Soviet Union signed the Final Act, which proclaims principles which are not compatible with the Brezhnev Doctrine and therefore undermine it. This was a gain, in theory at least, for the West and especially the countries under Soviet domination in central and eastern Europe to which the Brezhnev Doctrine most clearly applied.

The third principle was the one the Russians wanted; they interpreted it as meaning that the frontiers of the communist countries were inviolable and that the West was undertaking not to try to change them. This was not a problem for the West, which had no intention of trying to change the frontiers. The principle of international law which says that frontiers may be changed with the agreement of the countries involved remained in force.

The last Helsinki principle about respect for human rights and freedoms was the key aim of the West. We had insisted before the conference that its agenda should be extended by adding this principle and others which in our view were not observed by the Soviet Union.

The essence of the Final Act was therefore that the West confirmed its de facto recognition of the frontiers in central Europe and the Soviet Union for its part undertook to apply principles which contradicted a major element of its power system in central Europe and also the very nature of its own political system.

The Final Act also set out many proposals for building East-West confidence in military matters and for contacts and cooperation in many important fields: economic, scientific, environmental, youth exchanges, sport, culture, education and others.

It is easy to dismiss the Helsinki Final Act as naïve – a collection of pious principles and ideas for cooperation which the Soviet Union would ignore in practice. But the Final Act gave much encouragement to the critics of the regimes, known usually as dissidents, in the Soviet Union and the other communist countries in Europe. When criticised or attacked by the authoritarian governments they could and did point out that their activities were fully in line with an international agreement signed by those governments. This helped them to continue their work in opposition to the authorities and emboldened them to do more. Committees supporting the Final Act were founded in several communist countries. As a result of the Final Act, more information about prosperity and freedom in the West reached the people in communist countries. Mainly because of this last effect, I have no doubt that the Final Act was among the factors which contributed to the decline and later the collapse of the communist regimes in Europe. Our work to reinvent the Soviet proposal of a European Security Conference as a western proposal which advanced our interests was a success, and I was glad to have played a role in this.

My job at this time also included work on the British-Soviet bilateral relationship. The Helsinki Final Act was helpful here. It included many points which the Embassy could use in making new suggestions in the field of cultural exchanges or trade and we could propose new exchanges of information through publications and so on, always saying that we were trying to fulfil the requirements of the Final Act. This produced some results.

Daily Life

In general Pascale and I found the city and the lives of Muscovites similar to conditions in 1963. But some things were a bit better. The atmosphere of the city was a little less oppressive and bleak. There was more colour in people's clothes. Oranges sometimes appeared in the shops and other new goods had become patchily available. There was more new housing round the city but it did not look better than the housing built under Khrushchev in the early sixties. There were far more cars. Some pet dogs were to be seen.

Many more foreigners, especially business people, were now living in Moscow. For us there was one distinct improvement: there were now special food shops for foreigners that sold attractive luxuries such as smoked fish. We found life easier than during our first stay.

Pascale and I had the same kinds of enjoyment as we had a dozen years before, with some improvement. We made lifelong friends among the western diplomats and journalists, and made more Soviet friends than before. We found more to interest us in the cultural life of Moscow, especially films and art exhibitions and the innovative productions at the Taganka Theatre directed by Yuri Liubimov.

Family

Sebastian, now nearly 11, started prep school as a boarder at Woodcote House School in Windlesham, an hour's drive from London. I was there as a boy and the school was still run by the Paterson family and was a happy place. Sebastian flew to us in Moscow for school holidays.

Emily was eight, Julia three and Charlotte two when we arrived in Moscow. Charlotte's very first memory is of being woken up with Julia one night by Pascale and me, bundled in blankets and taken to an upstairs window to watch fireworks. The fireworks were part of the celebration of the communist festival on 1 May.

Our house had a helpful doorman who cleared the snow and washed the cars and did other jobs about the place. He was called Volodya, the usual diminutive for the common Russian name Vladimir. Julia and Charlotte called him not Volodya but Bloodier.

Sebastian says today that he quite enjoyed the school holidays. He remembers skiing in the forest near Moscow and country picnics in summer by the Moscow River. He liked the Moscow circus which starred an amazingly skilful North Korean conjuror.

He remembers a prank which he and Emily perpetrated a couple of times on Moscow buses. The buses were full of standing passengers. People entering the bus would pass the fare of a few kopeks (pence) from passenger to passenger, and the passenger nearest to the pay box would drop the kopeks into the box and pass the ticket back. Sebastian realised that you could take a ticket without putting money into the box. He and Emily took position beside the box. When they received a passenger's kopecks they would pocket the money and pass the ticket back. Had I known then of this petty illegality by my children I would have been concerned: a British diplomatic family should not break local laws and the Soviet authorities would have been delighted to embarrass me by lodging an official complaint and having the story published in the Soviet press.

We waged war against mice and cockroaches in our flat. Julia liked the mice and would feed them scraps of cheese. That was bound to make them multiply and become even more of a nuisance. The mice, however, were highly strung and I found that one sharp stamp on the floor of the kitchen would make all mice in the room jump a centimetre into the air and die of heart attacks.

We were always spraying the flat to kill cockroaches. Once I used Pascale's hair spray by mistake. This fixative fixed the insects where they were on the walls. They were then difficult to scrape off and Zina, our Russian maid, had one of her bad moods. Zina, incidentally, told us that she had had over a dozen abortions, which was usual in the Soviet Union then, because contraceptives were not available.

Julia and Charlotte often went to playgrounds. These were not nearly as large or modern as their playground in New York. But there was enough to amuse them and they played with Russian children. These local children were looked after by grandmothers, as usual in the Soviet Union, while both the parents worked. I found a way of getting into conversation with the grandmothers. If Julia or Charlotte was showing even a small amount of skin between socks and trousers or glove and sleeve in winter, the grandmothers would say sharply that we should not allow this harmful exposure to the cold. We immediately corrected the children's dress. The advantage of such incidents was that they helped Julia and Charlotte to join the play of the Russian children and gave me the opportunity to chat with Russian grandmas about daily life. They chatted normally, complaining about this and that and asking avidly what life was like in other countries.

The things which Julia and Charlotte enjoyed in Moscow included the circus and the conjuror mentioned above; and in the winter sledging, which was a frequent weekend occupation. We usually did it on a steep slope outside the Novodevichy Monastery, where we could also visit the churches with their crowds of worshippers.

KGB

My job as manager of the Embassy's work included the security against the KGB of the Embassy building and staff. The security of the building was difficult to maintain. Quite a few Soviet people were working there, from drivers to telephonists and junior administrative staff. The building was flanked on three sides by buildings controlled by the Soviet authorities. It was obvious that microphones could be inserted from under our premises into the walls of the rooms where we worked. All our British staff knew this and we were careful about what we said. We also had several so-called safe rooms, where we could hold our meetings or dictate to a secretary without risk of eavesdropping. These rooms consisted typically of a transparent soundproof box large enough to accommodate a meeting of eight people. Between this box and the actual walls, floor and ceiling of the room was a space filled with noise. This 'cocktail party noise' came from tapes of conversations among many raucous people, recorded and then rerecorded several times on the same tape to produce appalling cacophony. This ensured that any microphones in the outer walls of the room would record nothing but ear-splitting babble.

We discovered that a thick cable had been introduced into a closed tunnel under the Embassy, no doubt for eavesdropping. We wanted to sabotage it, so as to make the work of the KGB more difficult. It was desirable to make this operation a surprise to the KGB so that they could not remove or booby-trap the cable before we started work. They were less likely to guess our intentions if there were other activities in the Embassy compound. We organised a picnic lunch there on a Sunday. The compound was crowded with cars and families, with children zooming about. Under cover of this commotion a small team of our technical staff went down to the tunnel, broke into it quickly, removed a section of the cable for analysis and disabled more of it. An unusually exciting family picnic!

I was also responsible for efforts to keep up the morale of staff in the Embassy. Morale was understandably vulnerable, given the difficulties of working in Moscow, especially the harassment by the KGB and the depressing climate. The meagre opportunities for shopping were another reason for people feeling low. The senior staff of the Embassy took a great deal of trouble to help with this. The main purpose was to keep the staff contented. We were also conscious that the KGB might well notice if one of our people was lonely and might think him or her susceptible to making friends with Russians, who could then try to compromise the person and demand confidential information.

All our British staff had a right to annual leave in the UK. We held many social events and excursions to the country round Moscow and we provided plenty of opportunities for sport. The heads of sections in the Embassy made sure that they got to know not only their staff but also the families of the staff. The Military Attachés, with their experience of caring for morale in military units, were particularly good at organising events and keeping staff content. I remember Captain Richard Turner, the Naval Attaché, and his wife Mimma as stars in this field. They were our neighbours in the house on Skatertny Pereulok and the four of us became fond friends for life.

The frequent attempts by the KGB to entrap members of the British and other Western embassies in compromising situations, in the hope of blackmailing them for confidential information, were described in Chapter 2 about our first posting in Moscow in the early 1960s. This hazard was still part of Moscow life in our second period there. The Embassy warned new staff about the danger and said that anyone who was subjected to an experience of this kind should report it to me and the incident would not be held against them.

Until this time, the Embassy had sent home to Britain anyone who suffered an incident like this, to spare them the nasty experience of a blackmail attempt. This practice had two disadvantages. The Embassy lost the services of one of its members and there was bound to be a gap before that person could be replaced. And it was disappointing for many people, especially Russian speakers, to have their time in Moscow cut short prematurely.

I am glad to say that we found a better way of dealing with this hazard of daily life in Moscow. The first case we handled differently concerned a young man in the Embassy who gave a lift home after a staff party to a young Soviet woman, a telephonist in the Embassy. This pretty girl, incidentally, had a characteristic frequent among Soviet staff who worked with the KGB: she had a good degree but was doing a junior job.

My young colleague went to her flat and something happened between them, not much but something which might have been photographed and then used in an attempt to compromise him. He told me about the incident. I thought he had been unwise. But this experience would have taught him to be careful and I did not want to lose him. Rather than returning him to the UK, what we did was to make clear to the KGB that he had reported the incident both to the Embassy management, meaning myself, and to his wife. I had a long telephone conversation with her, which would certainly have been recorded by the KGB, who would have learned that she knew about the incident and had forgiven her husband and that I knew this. I also walked round the Embassy grounds in the snow with the husband, obviously talking about something serious. The KGB were bound to deduce from this conspicuous activity that the young man had told his wife and me and that therefore there was no scope for blackmail. The couple stayed for their full term in Moscow, and the KGB did nothing.

The next incident concerned another young man from our Embassy. Travelling in another Soviet city with a colleague, he passed out as a result, obviously, of a fixed drink he'd been served at dinner in the hotel restaurant. The usual ritual continued: he awoke next morning to find conspicuous evidence of sex in the night. He and his travelling companion returned to Moscow and he told me about the incident. In this case the young man had done nothing wrong. He was a victim of a typical KGB entrapment operation and had immediately reported what had happened. We reacted in much the same way as in the first incident. I had a telephone conversation with this young man's wife and drove the next day to their flat where I spent an hour chatting with them both. My visit would certainly have been noted by the KGB who would have deduced, or learned from microphones in his flat, that his wife and his boss knew about the incident so there was no scope for blackmail. The colleague concerned, an expert on Soviet affairs and a Russian speaker, stayed for his full posting in Moscow and was not bothered by the KGB.

* * * * *

Another theme of my work was the repeated attempts by the Soviet authorities to persuade us to give up our handsome Embassy building opposite the Kremlin across the Moscow River. They allowed us shorter and shorter leases, and finally leases of only six months. I was summoned to the Foreign Ministry to be told that electricity and other utilities and also central heating, which is a public utility in Moscow, were important necessities for which the Embassy was dependent on cooperation from Soviet organisations. I was told that the Embassy should bear this important point in mind when deciding whether to agree to give up our Embassy building in return for another building in the centre of the city. Returning to my office in the Embassy, I checked that the Soviet Embassy in Kensington Palace Gardens was dependent on London utilities for essential services. When I next met a member of the relevant department of the Soviet Foreign Ministry on a social occasion I took the opportunity to mention in a semi-humorous way that the Soviet Ambassador's residence in London got its electricity and gas from British suppliers and also relied on the London sewage system, and any interference with the utilities needed by the British Embassy in Moscow would risk reciprocal action in London. This line of argument was then dropped by the Russians, but they continued to try hard to persuade the Embassy to move.

Many years later Prime Minister Thatcher asked Gorbachev to agree that the United Kingdom should keep the Embassy in Moscow as well as building a new office block in another part of the city centre. Gorbachev was apparently surprised and unprepared. But Mrs Thatcher and he were getting on well and he agreed to her request. We still have the old Embassy in all its splendour opposite the Kremlin and a modern building not far away for offices and some staff accommodation.

Travel

Pascale and I did some exciting travelling in the Soviet Union during this second Moscow posting. We went to the Baltic States, Crimea, Central Asia and the Caucasus. Our travels gave us a glimpse of parts of the Soviet Union in very different regions, from Riga on the Baltic Sea to Frunze (now Bishkek) in Kirghizia on the frontier with China. We learned something of economic conditions and the atmosphere far from Moscow.

Armenia felt more open to the world, partly because Armenians living in the west visited often and sometimes helped to fund restoration of old buildings; and Estonia, with its pre-war experience of democracy, seemed less rigid in a different way. Soviet totalitarianism was everywhere but its style varied somewhat.

We drove to the Caucasus from the north, along the spectacular Georgian Military Highway which I felt I already knew from *A Hero of Our Time* by Lermontov and descriptions by Tolstoy. We stayed a night in a rather charming small hotel near the Highway. When we came to pay there was consternation at the reception desk. The manager was out, and no one else knew which tariff to charge British guests. They showed me their instructions on this complicated matter. These prescribed that Soviet citizens were to be charged the lowest price. Call it X. Visitors from other communist countries were to pay 3 X. Americans and Germans were to be charged 10 X and various other foreigners 7 X. Nothing about British visitors. I suggested that we should pay 8 X and the hotel staff agreed with visible relief. Discrimination and muddle, both illustrated here, were everywhere we went in the Soviet Union.

In our hotel in Tbilisi, the capital of Georgia, men at the next table in the restaurant had a bottle of vodka with a whole lemon in it to give flavour. They invited us to drink with them to Stalin, who was Georgian, now reviled in Soviet propaganda but still popular among Georgians. We declined, as politely as we could. We'll never know whether the vodka contained some knock-out narcotic as well as the conspicuous lemon, but I doubt it because I think the KGB would not have arranged for a husband and wife to be compromised together; the prospect of blackmail would have been slight.

There were apricot trees everywhere in Georgia, with much of the delicious fruit falling from the trees and going to waste. I asked an official what proportion of the apricot crop was exported. He said 5%. In further conversation it transpired that this was the proportion exported from Georgia to the rest of the Soviet Union. None was exported abroad. Another example of the inefficiency of the Soviet economy.

Later that day we visited a vineyard which produced one of the rather good Georgian wines, which were popular in restaurants in the major Soviet cities. In this case 'exporting' was evidently working, but we had a different surprise. When I asked which vintages in recent years were best, the pat reply was that all years are good years under socialism.

In Frunze, the capital of Kirghizia, there was a splendid view from our hotel room: a wide plain and beyond it a range of mountains across the border in China. We were taken to a performance of Kirghizian music. It dragged on and on. Our guide kept saying to Pascale that we must stay till the world-famous star of the celebrated film, *The Red Apple of Kirghizia*, came on stage. Much later this performer appeared. She was short and plump, with Chinese eyes. Nothing wrong with that – except that the guide, sighing with emotion, kept complimenting Pascale: 'You are so, so like her.'

The Dissidents

There was a new and important feature in our lives in Moscow in the mid-1970s. We got to know several of the leading dissidents. They included some notable writers and thinkers. The foremost among them was the nuclear scientist Andrei Sakharov. He was truly courageous and a great man, one of those few people who radiate goodness. I always found him both shy and forceful in conversation, never raising his voice. He was communicating with the West through the western correspondents in Moscow. Often what he said was broadcast back into the Soviet Union, in recordings of his voice in Russian, by the BBC or the Voice of America, so by this means his views were reaching many people in the Soviet Union itself.

The British Embassy until this time had not had contact with active dissidents, because our job was to deal with the people in power and to manage and develop the intergovernmental relationship and the commercial relationship between Britain and the Soviet Union. It was thought that frequenting the opponents of the Soviet state would make that main task harder.

I thought it was wrong to have no contact with the leading dissidents. We could surely learn interesting things from these outstanding people. Moreover, it would be embarrassing for British ministers, if asked in Parliament whether the Embassy in Moscow knew any of the dissidents, now famous in the west, to have to say that we did not. I thought it would be possible for us to have some discreet contacts with dissidents without significant difficulty in our official relationship with the Soviet authorities. So two or three of us in the Embassy began, with the agreement of the FCO, to talk occasionally to Sakharov, Roy Medvedev, Lev Kopelev and other dissidents. Usually Pascale and I saw them at supper in the homes of western correspondents, notably our American friends Alfred and Pie Friendly and Peter and Susan Osnos. This new policy was developed further after 1979 under the Conservative government. The practice worked; our official relationship with the Soviet authorities did not appear to suffer and we benefitted in our understanding of Soviet affairs from the conversations with dissidents.

A Great Art Collector

A couple who enlivened our first stay in Moscow in the early 1960s, and even more when we returned in the 1970s, were George and Zina Costakis. George was a Greek born in Russia, and he worked as an administrator in the Canadian Embassy. He was a passionately dedicated art collector who made a great collection of Russian art of two very different types – religious icons from past centuries and modernist art of the early twentieth century.

The Soviet authorities had banned display of modernist art since 1932. George had bought several thousand works privately from the artists and their families, often searching long and far to find them. His collection included many of the best paintings by the world-famous Russian artists of the early twentieth century, notably Malevich, Chagall, Kandinsky and Lissitsky. Many other modern artists of that same generation, who had not left Russia after the revolution of 1917, were unknown internationally. George collected these artists as well as the ones who were famous outside Russia. In 1961 I introduced him to Camilla Gray, who was visiting Moscow to research this period of Russian art for her book *The Russian Experiment in Art.** Published in 1962, Camilla's

---

* *The Russian Experiment in Art 1863–1922*, by Camilla Gray, Thames and Hudson Ltd, New York, 1962.

book introduced to the world many of the important artists who did not emigrate and whose work Camilla had seen in the Costakis Collection: Liubov Popova, Olga Rosanova, Nadezhda Udaltsova and others.

Pascale and I went to parties at George and Zina's flat and were fond of them both. There were congenial evenings when he played the guitar and she sang. George was passionate about his art collection and wanted to found a museum where it could be cared for and exhibited after his death. But this was unthinkable at that time in the Soviet Union, because the Communist Party approved of socialist-realist art, and the artists in George's collection were not realist but modernist and in many cases their work was abstract. At the same time it was unthinkable that George and his family would be allowed to leave the USSR with this hugely important and valuable collection. So George's longing for a museum for his whole collection could not be realised.

The one alternative idea was for George to give part of the collection to the Soviet state and to seek permission to emigrate with his family and the rest of the collection. George suffered severe KGB harassment; he was under serious stress and his health declined. He decided, after much agonising, to apply to emigrate with Zina and their family. After difficult discussions with the authorities, George wrote formally to the Minister of Culture in October 1976, offering to donate much of his collection to the Soviet state and proposing that he should be allowed to emigrate with his family and take with him the rest of his collection of early twentieth-century Russian art.

There was good art of this kind in the vaults of some Soviet museums but, being out of favour with the authorities, it was not displayed. So why would the Ministry of Culture want more art of this type from the Costakis collection? The main reason, I think, was that this art was admired by experts and collectors in the West and had become extremely valuable. The Ministry must have thought that one day this great school of Russian art might return to favour in the Soviet Union, and they wanted to hold more of it in store for a future change of policy. Some of the official art experts in Moscow privately admired the modernist works and hoped for such a change.

While George was negotiating with the Soviet Ministry of Culture about the deal, he sometimes asked for my personal advice on the next step in the negotiations. One Saturday afternoon he arrived in tears at our flat. I was about to take Julia and Charlotte sledging. They realised when George arrived that I would be tied up for some time. Dusk comes very early in Moscow in winter and they knew that the sledging expedition would not take place. They sobbed and George sobbed even more.

The arrangement under discussion between George and the Ministry of Culture was that he would donate a large number of his twentieth-century works, including the most important ones, to the Soviet State and would take abroad one third by value of his modern collection. The reason for George's tears that afternoon was that the Ministry of Culture had told him that the list of works he wished to take out of Russia was 'optically impossible' because it comprised a larger number of items than was allocated to the Soviet State. It was not surprising that more works were on the list for George to take abroad; they were the less valuable ones and represented one third by value, while the works representing two thirds by value, which were on the list for the Soviet State, included many of the most important and valuable works.

George and I drank mugs of tea and talked intensely about this problem. We found a way of shortening the list of works which he would take, without changing its content. We grouped numbers of drawings and other works by a single artist as sets of works, which would appear as single items on the list.

After more ups and downs, and continued intense stress for George, an agreement was reached which allowed him to take abroad many of the modern works in his collection, while his gift to the Soviet state was much greater by value and included works of the highest quality. In 1977 the Costakis family emigrated with their share to Greece. This arrangement was unprecedented in the Soviet Union and I think George obtained the best deal that was possible for his family.

The art George took to Greece was bought after his death in 1990 by the Greek state and is displayed in the Museum of Contemporary Art in Thessalonica. It has been shown with great success in exhibitions in many countries.

Policy changed in Moscow after the end of the Soviet Union. George's works that remained in Russia are often shown in exhibitions there and displayed as part of the permanent collection of the Tretyakov Gallery. In a major exhibition in 2014–15, marking the centenary of George's birth, over 200 works from his gift were shown at the Tretyakov. The catalogue of this exhibition shows that the agreement between George and the Ministry of Culture, enabling him to emigrate, was based on the amended list of art drawn up by George and me on that tearful Saturday afternoon in 1976.

George's great service to Russian art is that he saved innumerable masterpieces by buying them and caring for them during more than four decades when the authorities disapproved of non-realist art and there were few private collectors. George is now recognised, by the art world of Russia and abroad, as one of the greatest ever collectors of Russian art.

Oddities of Moscow Life

We were lucky to have our own garage behind our house in Moscow. In the diplomatic blocks of flats, where nearly all foreigners had to live, you would see in the car park early on winter mornings scores of cars with their bonnets open and people grovelling with torches in the engine, their bottoms facing skywards. This was because the cars had electric plug-in heaters to prevent the engines freezing, and these had to be unplugged in the dark before the cars could be used to drive to the office. Hundreds of bottoms in this awkward position in the freezing darkness is a scene emblematic of the quaint discomforts of expatriate life in Moscow in the 1970s.

For over half a century, broomball has been a popular feature of the lives in winter of many young westerners in Moscow. On a flooded and frozen tennis court at the British Embassy, players, moving fast, use brooms to propel a ball across the ice. Trainers, not skates, are worn. One Sunday afternoon in the mid-1970s, Sir Terence Garvey, the British Ambassador, found his garage blocked by a visitor's car. He went to the entrance of the broomball court to ask the owner to move the car. A tall and heavy US Marine, a security guard at the US Embassy, was brooming the ball at full speed along the side of the court right by the entrance. To prevent a collision he scooped up Terence in his arms and yelled 'Who the hell are you?' Terence replied politely that he was the Ambassador. The story has it that the Marine never played broomball again.

Pascale and I enjoyed this second stay in Moscow. Life was a bit easier than a dozen years before and the Embassy could achieve more. We were delighted to be returning to London and that the children would have a normal British life for several years. Even for a dedicated traveller like me 'east west, home's best' becomes a compelling feeling after years abroad.

8

HEAD OF ARMS CONTROL AND DISARMAMENT DEPARTMENT, FOREIGN AND COMMONWEALTH OFFICE
1977–1979

I resumed my diary on 9 July 1978, almost 19 years after the previous entry and nine months after our return to London from our second posting in Moscow. I wrote

> I have become a Soviet specialist and am very interested by the politics and culture of Soviet Russia and the oddities of a Westerner's life in Moscow. Having spent five years there, in two periods of 2½ years, and two years on the Soviet desk in the FCO, I can say that I know the subject. I hope soon to move from my present job as head of Arms Control and Disarmament Department to be head of Eastern European and Soviet Department. I hope in a general way to be Ambassador in Moscow one day. Most people in the Diplomatic Service who know the personalities likely to be involved would say I had every chance of that. I believe it too, except that I know my health may spoil before I can reach that level.

I was referring to coeliac disease, which had been diagnosed in 1970 after a dozen years of constant tummy trouble. My gloomy remark turned out to be wrong: I am writing these lines 39 years later. Strict observance of a gluten-free diet and excellent doctors in NHS hospitals have kept me going pretty well, and I was not hampered by my health when in my fifties I held difficult senior jobs with extremely long hours.

Another point from my diary in July 1978 is about Sebastian. That month, at the end of his third term at Eton, he won for the second time a distinction in the end-of-term examinations. I wrote that this was a major achievement, but that was not all: he also came fifth in the whole of his year of some 250 boys and top of all the boys who were not scholars. That, I wrote, was 'an altogether brilliant result. He is a tremendously hard worker, has a gift for producing his best in exams and does well in all subjects. Last term his strengths were English and French. This term they were Latin and History. He is also strong in maths and physics. Judging by this term's results he may get another distinction next term and that would make him an Oppidan Scholar; he may have a brilliant Eton career ahead of him'. I was extremely proud. And my prediction was right. Sebastian did get another distinction the next term and became an Oppidan Scholar. His subsequent career at Eton took him to the very top; he became Captain of the Oppidans, which roughly is joint head of the school.

*****

To be head of an active and prominent department in the FCO was a key stage in a British diplomat's career. The Arms Control and Disarmament Department was both at this time. It was logical for somebody knowing the Soviet Union to do this job. Arms control and disarmament were a big part of East-West relations.

I was pretty much ignorant of the important technical dimension of the subject, but diplomats are always having to learn new things. So again I faced a steep learning curve; and with invaluable help from colleagues in my new department and by hard reading of the files and talking to experts, I tried to scramble up the curve as fast as possible.

I had for the first time a fairly close view of a Foreign Secretary in action. In contacts at work Dr David Owen did not try to be liked. He was 39 and I thought he was saying to himself that many a more experienced Foreign Secretary had been seduced by this efficient nest of mandarins and that he'd show who was boss. I admired his energy, courage and determination. He made good use of some of the best FCO people and was trying hard to settle the great intractable problem of Rhodesia. I thought he would not succeed, since his time as Foreign Secretary was likely to be short, with a general election not far off. He would probably depart having achieved little that was tangible, but to be seen to try really hard, I thought, was an achievement in politics.

There was a widespread view at that time that nuclear arsenals were being built up unnecessarily by both sides in the Cold War. This so-called arms race was seen as a waste of money, which ought to be spent on urgent needs like education and healthcare. It was true that the USA and the USSR had more nuclear missiles than were necessary. Each needed enough to have a 'second strike capability', meaning that, if either was attacked by nuclear missiles, it would still have enough nuclear missiles to retaliate. Each would suffer immense damage and countless casualties. Each would therefore know that launching nuclear war would lead to its own destruction. This key element of deterrence was called 'Mutually Assured Destruction' and it was what prevented the Cold War from ever becoming a hot war.

Mutually Assured Destruction did not require constant development of more advanced nuclear weapons or ever increasing numbers of them. There was scope for limitations and reductions in the numbers and for some curbs on development of new weapons. At the same time each side acutely distrusted the other, and needed to be confident that the other would not cheat by continuing secretly to accumulate nuclear weapons in violation of agreed limits. That is why verification of compliance with limits and reductions was essential, and no agreements could be made without it. Verification could partly be achieved by satellite photography, but the only really reliable means was inspection of weapons production factories and testing sites, including sometimes inspections which need not be notified in advance.

The nuclear arms race was one big reason for the public pressure in the UK and other western countries, and from many states which did not have nuclear weapons, for new moves in arms control. At the same time there were calls, which western governments considered dangerous, for unilateral nuclear disarmament, meaning the destruction of our nuclear arsenals without the Soviet Union having to do the same or in the naïve hope that the Soviet Union would follow suit. This was the fallacy of CND and other campaigners for unilateral abandonment of nuclear defence. If the West had followed their view, the USSR, with its nuclear arsenal still in place, would have been able to threaten nuclear war without fear of retaliation.

That was the background to my job as head of the Arms Control and Disarmament Department. It was a job which involved, for the first time in my life, a serious domestic political angle. Dr Owen saw arms control as a subject which had popular appeal in Britain and could be helpful to the Labour Party and himself electorally.

So my Department was required to be active and positive, and to be seen to work hard for progress in arms control. At the same time we needed to be sure that any proposal we made or supported would not undermine the UK's defence capability. We were still waging the Cold War and a key element of our policy was still the strong western defence stance, including nuclear defence, so that the Soviet Union could not be tempted by aggression, or by threats to use force, because the risks were too high.

We needed to achieve a combination of objectives, finding steps in arms control which would appeal publicly in Britain but which were also acceptable from the point of view of British and western defence. The Foreign Secretary, who was responsible for British policy in arms control, focussed properly on the arms control aspect of this, while the Ministry of Defence was rightly wary of any risk of undermining British defence. I wanted to find proposals which could achieve progress, as desired by my boss, David Owen; but, as someone who knew well that the Soviet Union was still a danger, I wanted also to pay attention to the views of the Ministry of Defence on the security of the UK.

I saw an opportunity for useful work in arms control without risk for British security. A Special Session on Disarmament of the United Nations General Assembly was to start soon after I took up this job. In the enormous forum of the General Assembly it wasn't going to be possible to negotiate specific arms control agreements in all their expert detail. The UN's purpose was rather to increase the pressure for progress in arms control and to give the members of the UN the opportunity to express their views. Dr Owen was determined that Britain should be conspicuously active and positive, and be among the leaders in proposing new steps. The way I tried to meet that requirement was by putting forward a Programme of Action in Arms Control which would be a British proposal for an overall programme for progress in the coming years. It comprised immediate proposals for reducing or limiting weaponry, medium-term proposals and long-term proposals, as well as suggestions for international studies of how some of the arms control proposals should be tackled. This was an attempt to set out a desirable road map for future progress in arms control, rather than a single proposal of substance. It made a good impression in the UN and the Foreign Secretary was content with it as the British contribution to the UN Special Session. The results of the Session were satisfactory for Britain but in some ways disappointing.

Far more of my time was taken up with work on a genuinely important project in arms control. This was a negotiation between the United States, the Soviet Union and the UK on a treaty banning all testing of nuclear weapons. It was rare for the UK to be negotiating with the two superpowers on a subject of wide international importance. This echo of Britain's role as one of the 'Big Three' powers after the Second World War was a matter of importance and pride to our ministers; and Prime Minister Callaghan, as well as Dr Owen, took a close interest and wanted the UK contribution to the talks to be significant and admired.

No new nuclear warhead could be brought into service in defence without being tested in a controlled explosion, to confirm its effectiveness and reliability and its environmental effects. Nuclear tests in the air, under water and in space had already been banned, but underground tests were still permitted. A ban on all tests would place a limit on development of new nuclear warheads and therefore be an important step in arms control. Because nuclear explosions emit harmful radiation, it would also be a valuable environmental move.

This negotiation was very serious and very technical. One of its important elements was to agree verification systems which would give states confidence that no-one would cheat. That involved seismic science. How do seismologists, engaged in monitoring underground explosions to ensure that no-one is conducting secret nuclear tests, tell the difference between a real earthquake and an earthquake artificially provoked in order to mask the reverberations from an underground nuclear test? We in the FCO worked with the UK's defence scientists at Aldermaston and with seismologists and international lawyers and other experts, all sorts of different disciplines coming together in a negotiation where Britain was playing an important role together with the Soviet Union and the United States. Much progress was made and we thought we were coming close to success. My department was beginning to plan the establishment of seismic monitoring stations in various British territories, from the Pitcairn Islands to Saint Helena. (Lord Carrington, when he became Foreign Secretary in 1979, called them windmills, a characteristic dash of banter when an office meeting became stodgy.)

After Ronald Reagan became President, the United States focussed on developing more advanced nuclear weaponry, and the test ban negotiations were set aside. Mrs Thatcher's new government in Britain had no trouble with this US position. This was one of the few examples I witnessed of British foreign policy changing in a specific way when the government changed.

The test ban negotiations were resumed with more participants much later, and a comprehensive test ban treaty was at last agreed and was approved by the UN General Assembly in 1996 after the end of the Cold War. It has not entered into force because some key states, notably the USA, have not ratified it.

The other major subject we handled in the Arms Control Department was the prevention of the spread of nuclear weapons to more countries. It was essential to do everything possible to prevent the spread of nuclear weapons, because their proliferation to more states would greatly increase the risk that nuclear weapons would be used: and that would be an enormous tragedy for mankind, with appalling destruction, huge numbers of deaths and terrible environmental damage.

The paradox here is that nuclear weapons were actually preventing war between the antagonists in the Cold War, because each side knew that the other would be able to respond in kind to a nuclear attack. But other states, if they obtained nuclear weapons, might actually use them if the victim was unable to respond. It was however argued, very logically, that it was unfair and unreasonable for countries which already had nuclear weapons to keep on amassing them while countries without nuclear weapons must undertake never to acquire them. This reproach came from many members of the United Nations.

The logical answer was that the states with nuclear weapons should undertake to limit and reduce the numbers. The Strategic Arms Limitation talks between the United States and the Soviet Union were a partial answer. Our attempt to negotiate a complete ban on nuclear weapons tests was another aspect of the effort. For Britain and France it was difficult to accept reductions in their nuclear weapons because they had only the minimum number necessary for a credible nuclear force, a number far below the nuclear arsenals of the Soviet Union or the United States. The UK was therefore not well placed to advocate reductions in nuclear weapons stocks. This was one reason why the Labour Government in the UK was extremely energetic in working towards a ban on nuclear weapons tests.

During my time as head of the Arms Control and Disarmament Department, I did a good deal of public speaking in the UK. I wanted to explain, to audiences which were sometimes critical, that the British government was truly working hard for progress in arms control, while always safeguarding our defence capability at the level necessary to our contribution to deterring aggression by the Soviet Union. I lectured in Exeter Cathedral, to an audience which I think was generally sympathetic to my remarks. I spoke quite a few times in universities and at meetings of the United Nations Association in various regions of the UK. There I found some agreement but also much criticism on the lines that we should be willing to cut our own arsenal if others did the same and the need for verification should not prevent this. It was unusual for an official to argue publicly for policies which ministers would normally be the ones to advocate and justify; but David

Owen encouraged me, and his Minister of State, Lord Goronwy-Roberts, stressed this public speaking when he praised the Arms Control and Disarmament Department in the House of Lords on 21 February 1979.

My time in the Arms Control and Disarmament Department was exacting, because of the complexity of the work and need to master the technical detail. But it was well worth the effort, because the cause of trying to limit armaments is important substantively and politically and the need to preserve and enhance British security in negotiations on arms control treaties is vital. I experienced some sharp moments in working for David Owen, when he would criticise me for giving too much weight to the views of the Ministry of Defence. In my discussions with the Ministry of Defence there were moments when officials there were even sharper with me, for the opposite reason! This was a demanding job where I learned much.

9

HEAD OF EASTERN EUROPEAN AND SOVIET DEPARTMENT, FOREIGN AND COMMONWEALTH OFFICE
1979–80

I now moved to become head of the Eastern European and Soviet Department of the Foreign and Commonwealth Office. Soviet affairs were my main professional interest. This was my fourth job dealing with my favourite subject. I was pleased, too, to be dealing with strategic matters – the Soviet Union and its activities across the world and in East-West relations; as well as the UK's bilateral relations with the USSR and the other communist countries in Europe. This group included several very interesting countries, Poland above all; I now had my first opportunity to deal with them.

I started the job a few weeks after Mrs Thatcher's Conservative Government took office on 4 May 1979. Soon after I began, Lord Carrington, the new Foreign Secretary, invited Prime Minister Thatcher to the FCO to meet the experts on Soviet affairs. I think his purpose was to show her that the FCO had real expertise and that she could rely on us, as well as listening to the views of independent experts. The two experts attending from the FCO were Rodric Braithwaite and myself. Rodric knew the Soviet Union well. He was to be British Ambassador there when the Cold War ended.

Carrington asked me to speak first in the meeting. He told me beforehand that the Prime Minister was likely to interrupt my remarks; he said I should continue whatever I was saying and not let her break in. I was very conscious that Mrs Thatcher's views on the Soviet Union and on policy towards it were likely to be different from ours in the FCO. This was a challenging moment, and I prepared for it carefully.

I began my talk by describing the difficulties facing the Soviet Union in the political, social, economic and technological fields. Soviet people no longer believed that Marxism-Leninism would deliver a better future. Improvements in their standard of living had for a decade become smaller and smaller each year. Soviet agriculture was a disastrous failure. The West was increasing its economic lead over the Soviet Union.

Mrs Thatcher began at once to interrupt. I kept going and finished my short talk. Lord Carrington said later that she was first astonished, then bemused, and finally impressed.

When I had finished my piece, she asked whether the Soviet Union could survive the difficulties I had described. Rodric and I replied that decline had set in and the seeds of change were there. The Soviet Union was not muddling along; it was muddling downwards. But the repressive system was still effective and would be able for years to keep hold of power.

Mrs Thatcher asked who would lead the Soviet Union after Brezhnev. I expected this. I said that we could see which members of the Soviet leadership would be in the running. They were the few who were members both of the Politburo of the Communist Party, which was the highest authority in the USSR, and of the Secretariat of the Party and thus in executive charge of a major area of policy. A possible successor would also need to be working in Moscow and not in one of the regions of the USSR and he would probably need to be of Russian nationality rather than any of the other ethnic groups in the Soviet population. I said that the speeches of the leaders varied somewhat in the points of policy that each chose to stress and also in style. We could therefore judge the general approach of each of them. I described the few candidates who could be identified at that time, notably Andropov. I did not mention Gorbachev because he was not then a member of the Politburo.

Mrs Thatcher told Lord Carrington after the meeting that he had some good people. She said it was a pleasant surprise that Rodric

Braithwaite and I had given different opinions on some points; she had expected the FCO to have a single view on everything, which its officials would express in unison.

The differences between Mrs Thatcher and the FCO turned out at this meeting and over the ensuing months to be narrower than I had expected. They were considerable in public presentation and sometimes on specific matters of policy. But in the analysis of the nature and plight of the Soviet Union they were similar.

The strategy of the FCO, and indeed of the West, in the Cold War comprised deterrence, to prevent aggression, and détente, to try to open the Soviet Union to influences from outside and increase contacts which would show that the West was far ahead in standard of living as well as freedom. In this approach, arms control and disarmament were a means of limiting the *risks* of deterrence and indeed its cost, but never at the expense of any reduction in the *effectiveness* of deterrence.

Margaret Thatcher did not accept our view that détente was part of a thought-through strategy for prevailing in the Cold War. She saw it as a weak attitude towards the Soviet Union. Our view that deterrence was the essential requirement, without which détente would not be possible, was the same as the view of Robert Conquest, who was Mrs Thatcher's most important independent adviser. He said 'There is nothing the Russians can do so long as we keep our level of arms right.'

I gave a number of lectures to British organisations with the title 'Are the Russians really dangerous?' My conclusion was that the answer was up to us in the West: the Russians could not make dangerous moves so long as we maintained deterrence, which made it impossible for them to risk aggression or a threat of aggression. My conclusion and Conquest's were the same.

* * * * *

In fact, my time in this job turned out to be a period when détente between East and West suffered major setbacks. My role was not what it had been in Moscow and in the Arms Control Department – to try to foster progress in détente between East and West. It was to propose and promote steps towards the Soviet

Union which would demonstrate British disapproval of the Soviet invasion of Afghanistan at the end of 1979; and then in 1980 to analyse the rise of the Solidarity Trade Union in Poland and propose policy on this. Martial Law was imposed in Poland in December 1981. By then I had moved to head the Policy Planning Staff of the FCO, but I remained deeply involved in policy towards the Soviet Union and on Poland.

On 8 December 1979 Lord Carrington as Foreign Secretary sent a major despatch to our Ambassadors abroad. It was a guide to our policy in East-West relations. I had drafted this despatch following much discussion among officials and Ministers in the new Conservative Government. It continued to be the basis of our policy through the negative episodes of the Soviet invasion of Afghanistan later in that December and the declaration of martial law in Poland two years later.

Carrington's despatch argued that the Soviet aim was to defeat the West in a struggle waged by all means short of war. The USSR hoped, with its military strength, to become the dominant factor in Europe. Détente for the Soviet leadership was a tactic to lessen the risk of nuclear confrontation and to obtain technology, credits and grain. In their view détente did not require them to slow their military build-up, relax their internal dictatorship, loosen their grip on Eastern Europe or renounce their freedom to intervene in developing countries.

The Soviet Union, as part of its duel with the West, had challenged the latter to a contest of ideas. The West should win this contest and our answer should be 'take you on'. Our democracy, ensuring that policies rest on public consent, had a powerful advantage of flexibility over the Soviet regime, which could not tolerate any views that differed from its own. Our Alliance, based on common interests, was politically stronger than the Warsaw Pact, which was a Soviet instrument of domination in Eastern Europe. We in the West must manage our own affairs successfully, particularly our economies, if our ideas and our societies were to prevail, not only in East-West terms, but in the competition for influence in the Third World. Here too we were the stronger, for the USSR faced chronic problems of inefficient allocation and use of resources and could not satisfy its consumers. We should work to bring home to developing countries the real nature of the Soviet system, its economic and other failures and its inability or unwillingness to provide development aid in anything like the sums offered by the West.

Lord Carrington continued that East-West contacts were part of our armoury in the contest of ideas. Trade, cultural exchanges and other contacts between the West and the Soviet Union would bring more information about the successes of the West to people in the USSR. A major purpose was to do what we could to undermine Soviet power by encouraging the tendencies towards diversity within the Warsaw Pact, tendencies exemplified by Romania's foreign policy, Hungary's new economic mechanism and Poland's particular brand of pluralism. We had no interest in provoking a crisis in the region, which would again be ended by invasion if the Russians thought it necessary.

* * * * *

The reason why the heyday of détente was over by the time I came to the Eastern European and Soviet Department was the failure of the Soviet Union to fulfil many of the undertakings it had given in the Helsinki Final Act. There had been no easing of the autocracy in the Soviet Union and dissidents were still being persecuted.

Then came the very important event of the Soviet invasion of Afghanistan on Christmas Day 1979. The interventions in East Germany in 1953, Hungary in 1956 and Czechoslovakia in 1968 were illegal acts of brutality which had the purpose of restoring or maintaining the Soviet system in those countries. In Afghanistan the Soviet Union, for the first time since 1945, was invading a country not already under its control. This was bound to cause great concern to the West and to countries to the South of the USSR. It redoubled western dissatisfaction with Soviet behaviour and reversed the process of reducing tension between East and West which the USSR had wanted. It caused the sharpest crisis in East-West relations since the Soviet invasion of Czechoslovakia in 1968.

In November 1979, a month before the Soviet invasion, I circulated a memorandum among FCO colleagues about the way the United Kingdom and the West should react if the invasion took place. I wrote that we could not prevent invasion, but if it happened we should use it to warn the world, and especially developing countries and countries near the Soviet Union, about Moscow's 'cynical imperial behaviour'.

Afghanistan was (and remains) a highly unstable country. There had been a regime which was friendly to the Soviet Union, led by Moscow's protégé Taraki. This regime was overturned in a coup led by Amin, and Taraki was murdered. The Russians did not trust Amin. The large number of Soviet advisers in Afghanistan, from the KGB and the Soviet Armed Forces, had tried to prevent the change of regime and had failed. Amin had many opponents murdered. Soviet influence in Afghanistan virtually ceased to exist. The Soviet Union looked impotent and was determined to recover from the humiliation and regain strong influence over events in Afghanistan.

Moreover, the Soviet leaders detected signs that Amin might start cooperating with the United States. This may have stirred up the old Russian complex about being encircled by hostile states. The Soviet Union faced NATO to the west and south-west, with the US and pro-American Japan to the east. It had bad relations with China to the south-east. The Soviet leaders may have had nightmare visions of the United States establishing influence in Afghanistan on their southern frontier, nearly completing a cordon of unfriendly states around three sides of the Soviet Union. If this was their fear, it was a paranoid reaction but typical of Russian psychology for many, many decades past.

The Soviet leaders decided, against the advice of their generals, to intervene in Afghanistan temporarily with a limited force to replace Amin. This 'limited' invasion was to escalate into a war lasting nine years.

The West had not reacted with concrete measures to the Soviet military interventions in East Germany, Hungary and Czechoslovakia. But this military intervention outside the area of the Warsaw Pact was an important and dangerous departure. It brought Soviet forces nearer to the oil-producing countries of the Middle East. The West knew little of the Soviet motives, beyond the obvious point that Moscow wanted to re-establish its influence in Afghanistan.

The invasion confirmed our view of Soviet policy in Lord Carrington's despatch of three weeks earlier. But an additional dimension was now needed – a policy for containing the new phenomenon of Soviet military interference in the third world.

Much of my work in early 1980 concerned the British and western reactions to the invasion. It was condemned in a resolution at the United Nations, which the UK promoted. The Moslem countries, strongly critical of this invasion of Moslem Afghanistan, supported the resolution.

President Carter, untypically, reacted strongly. He suspended the effort to persuade Congress to ratify the SALT Two agreement with the Soviet Union about curbs on nuclear weapons. He declared an embargo on US grain sales to the USSR. The United States, West Germany, Canada, China and Japan boycotted the Olympic Games in Moscow in summer 1980.

It was clear from the start that the Soviet Union had harmed its international reputation by this invasion, which many countries were bound to condemn. It had created an opportunity for the West to point out the aggressive character of Soviet foreign policy. The US and the UK were leaders in the condemnation. Mrs Thatcher's public comments were stronger than those of other West European leaders. In the FCO I coordinated studies on how to impress on countries to the south of the Soviet Union that they might be at risk if the Soviet Union was allowed to get away with this act of aggression without strong international condemnation.

There were differences among the members of the European Community on how far to go in reacting to the invasion of Afghanistan. Germany wanted to preserve détente and was reluctant to do much. France was reluctant about measures, for instance concerning trade, which would hurt Western Europe as well as the USSR. The British attitude was firmer and the British measures reflected this:

- We stopped contacts at ministerial level with the Soviet authorities.
- We cancelled exchanges of military delegations with the USSR.
- The UK-Soviet Credit Agreement was not renewed.

- We tightened our controls on export of sensitive technology to the USSR.
- We led the Europeans in agreeing not to sell to the Soviet Union food products, including grain, which the US had embargoed in response to the invasion of Afghanistan.
- We pressed in the European Community for an end to subsidised sales of surplus butter, meat and sugar.
- We began confidential discussions with close allies about giving military aid to the Afghan forces which were resisting the Soviet invasion.

Mrs Thatcher urged the British Olympic Committee to boycott the Moscow Games and Parliament favoured this. Some British athletes decided not to participate in the Games, but many others went to Moscow.

On a lighter note, I went with Lord Carrington to Bucharest in March 1980 to put our case to the Romanian leader, the notorious dictator Ceausescu. That January Romania had not joined the other communist countries in voting against the resolution in the United Nations which condemned the invasion of Afghanistan. This abstention was a daring act for an ally of the USSR. Lord Carrington wanted his visit to be a gesture of support for Romania. We also wanted to see whether Ceausescu could be persuaded to go one step further and actually criticise the Soviet invasion. We thought that he might be attracted by our view that the Soviet aggression must be condemned, since Romania, which had disagreements with Moscow, might be a future victim.

This visit sparkled with entertaining moments. Travel with Peter Carrington was always a joy because his sense of humour was constantly in action. The first comic feature in Bucharest was the VIP guest house where we stayed. Its walls were made of glass. The incongruous note was that numerous stuffed heads of boar, stags and elk were hung on the inside of the glass walls. Attached to glass they looked hilariously peculiar from inside the house and even more so from outside. Next, we could not reduce the stifling heat in the guest house because the radiator controls did not work and the windows did not open. We shrugged and laughed.

Then we went to a dinner given in Lord Carrington's honour by the Romanian Foreign minister. The minister's wife was a blonde actress with a flamboyantly low-cut gown. Carrington, sitting next to this vision, looked amused and ostentatiously averted his eyes from the spectacular cleavage.

The next morning he and I went to see Ceausescu. Carrington, incidentally, had a private nickname for the dictator: 'Pull out your fingernails'. I was puzzled when Carrington drew his wristwatch out of his cuff, and kept glancing at it during his conversation with Ceausescu. From time to time Ceausescu gave a start and his face was contorted by a spasm. After the meeting, Peter joked to me that this tic must occur when executions were taking place. He admitted that he had timed Ceausescu's spasms, to find the interval between them. It was always fifteen minutes, according to the Foreign Secretary's watch. I think his motive was amused curiosity.

We were driven next day to Poiana Brasov, a ski resort, along bendy mountain roads. I was sharing the back of a car with a senior official from the Romanian Foreign Ministry. He and I had the task of negotiating the joint press statement which the two Foreign Ministers would issue at the end of the visit. We worked through part of the draft, but the Romanian official became violently sick from the combination of the winding road and his concentration on the draft statement. The work had to be completed in the hotel that evening.

The draft I had prepared for this joint statement was composed of phrases used frequently by Ceausescu to castigate western colonialism and especially US involvement in Vietnam. I used his cliché phrases to condemn the Soviet invasion of Afghanistan. The Romanian Government did not hide from us that they disapproved of the Soviet invasion and feared that it might one day be a precedent for invasion of Romania, if Soviet disapproval of Romania's somewhat different foreign policy became sharper.

It seemed at first that the Romanians might agree to our draft of the joint statement. But we heard just before we left Bucharest that Ceausescu had ruled that Afghanistan should not be mentioned directly. No problem for the Foreign Secretary: the statement was issued without its direct mentions of Afghanistan. We briefed the British press that the words of the statement obviously applied to the current Soviet actions in Afghanistan and the British journalists agreed. The headline in one London paper was 'Carrington coup over Romania's Afghan stance'. The passages borrowed from Ceausescu's statements which the press relished particularly were 'deterioration of the international situation is the result of policies based on force and violation of national independence' and 'international disputes should be settled by peaceful means, by negotiations based on respect for independence.'

When the first resolution about the invasion was passed in the UN, 104 countries joined in condemning Soviet aggression. Even more voted for later resolutions. The Soviet Union must have been surprised and dismayed by the world's condemnation. And there is no doubt that the western sanctions, which went beyond the declarations with which we had criticised the Soviet invasions of Hungary and Czechoslovakia, had surprised the Soviet Union. They were probably one of the factors in the Soviet decision not to invade Poland in 1981.

On 20 May 1980, the Prime Minister held a small meeting at 10 Downing Street about the Soviet invasion of Afghanistan. Lord Carrington was there. I enjoyed the meeting, where Mrs Thatcher said that the FCO papers on Afghanistan, which we had submitted to her, were fascinating and extremely interesting. She had read every word. There was great similarity, she said, between the FCO's views and those of her academic advisers, though the latter knew less about the subject and could not put as much flesh on their ideas as the FCO had done. My feeling was that the FCO's attempt to show Mrs Thatcher that we understood the Soviet Union and favoured firm policies was proving reasonably successful.

In the FCO we were now thinking about measures the West could use in future to reduce the risk of further Soviet adventures. This was the additional feature we considered necessary for our policy on dealing with the USSR.

One approach was to draw up a list of deterrent measures, notably western military deployments and exercises in or near countries where Moscow seemed to be considering invasion. A lesser deterrent option was announcements of sanctions western countries would apply if the Russians committed aggression. We were working on some new sanctions, notably halting export to the Soviet Union of technological products, chosen specifically to hurt the Soviet economy.

We foresaw difficulties, but not insuperable ones. It would be necessary for measures to be taken *before* the Soviet Union acted, so as to have a chance of influencing Moscow. An important requirement would be that the main western countries should act together. This is always a tall order and would be more difficult to achieve when we were acting in advance of the Russians, before any major crisis had actually begun.

A different but complementary approach we thought about was to strengthen countries at risk of Soviet bullying. We might provide training for their armed forces or send military advisers and sometimes military equipment. Economic aid would be a possibility. We should brief the leaders of such countries personally about our assessment of Soviet intentions and capabilities.

We wrote comprehensive papers about these ideas and others, which we submitted as proposals to the Foreign Secretary and then the Prime Minister and other British ministers. The ideas were then discussed with the US, Germany and France and more widely among friendly countries.

Lord Carrington launched the idea of an international conference on Afghanistan, where the interested countries would agree that foreign intervention would cease and Afghan neutrality be endorsed. We officials worked up a full proposal. The purpose was to maintain pressure on the Soviet occupation forces and also to give the Soviet Union a possible way out of Afghanistan if in due course it wanted to end its entanglement in that intractable country.

The proposal of a conference about a new status for Afghanistan was endorsed by the Foreign Ministers of the European Community. It was welcomed by the United States and many other countries including neutral ones. In July 1981 Lord Carrington put it to Gromyko, the Soviet Foreign Minister, who described it as unrealistic. He claimed that Pakistan and Iran were intervening in Afghanistan, and their interventions must cease before the Soviet Union could consider the departure of its troops.

10

POLAND'S HISTORIC DRAMA

The most important event during my time in the Eastern European and Soviet Department was the rise of the Solidarity trade union in Poland in 1980. I continued to work on this subject after I moved to head the Policy Planning staff in 1982.

Solidarity began with strikes in the shipyards in Gdansk (Danzig) and then spread to become a national movement. A free trade union, not under the control of the Communist Party, was clearly incompatible with the Soviet model of power, where all activity must be controlled by the Party.

This posed a greater threat to the Soviet hold on Eastern and Central Europe than the events in East Germany in 1953 or Hungary in 1956 or Czechoslovakia in 1968, when the Soviet army had intervened with force to crush movements for change. I thought that Moscow, if it still intended to insist on the Soviet system throughout the Warsaw Pact, must put an end to Solidarity in some way and, if necessary, by invasion. I made this prediction at a meeting of western officials dealing with Poland. My own boss, Julian Bullard, thought I was too pessimistic, and the others at our meeting agreed with him.

After the collapse of communism in Europe much information became available, including secret Polish and Soviet documents. There is fascinating material on the website of the Wilson Center in Washington. This shows that the Soviet leaders were appalled by the rise of Solidarity and realised that it might become a threat to the communist party's monopoly of power in Poland. Moscow also realised that the communist regimes in other countries in eastern and central Europe, and in the Soviet Union, could then be threatened too. The situation was recognised as more dangerous for the communist regimes than the resistance crushed by Soviet forces in East Germany, Hungary and Czechoslovakia in the past.

In 1980 the Polish Communist regime made major concessions. They recognised the right to strike and permitted the establishment of free trade unions, and in November Solidarity became legal. This made legal a situation totally incompatible with the Marxist-Leninist principle that the Communist Party must control and determine everything that mattered. I did not see how the Soviet Union could tolerate this violation of its ideology and its doctrine on how power should be exercised and above all the threat to its power in Poland. By autumn 1981 Solidarity had become a political force on a national scale. In Moscow the need to crush Solidarity must now have become even more imperative than before.

In 1980, Soviet Marshal Kulikov, Commander-in-Chief of Warsaw Pact forces, was leading the preparation of full plans for the invasion of Poland by fifteen Soviet, two Czechoslovak and one East German Divisions. The Soviet Politburo reviewed the plans. The intended date was 8 December 1980. On 5 December Kania, then Polish leader, pleaded at a summit meeting of Warsaw Pact leaders for the invasion plan to be cancelled. The Soviet leaders were somewhat reassured by his claim that the Polish authorities could deal with the threat from Solidarity. Kania made the same plea personally to Brezhnev, who concurred, and the invasion plan, which the Soviet leaders had not yet formally approved, was shelved.

The papers at the Wilson Center show that General Jaruzelski, then Prime Minister of Poland, began planning Martial Law in February 1981. In March, however, the Polish leaders decided that the Communist Party, the army and the police were too weak to impose and operate martial law. Too many members of these organisations could not be relied on to participate in enforcing it.

The minutes of meetings of the Soviet Politburo, among the papers on the website of the Wilson Center, reveal more of this story:

Soviet Politburo meeting 29 October 1980
The idea of a state of emergency in Poland (meaning Martial Law) is discussed. Brezhnev calls the Polish situation 'a raging counter-revolution'. There are many complaints at this meeting and later ones about the inaction of the Polish leaders in the face of Solidarity.

Soviet Politburo 22 January 1981
The Politburo is told that the Polish leaders reject the Soviet recommendation for Martial Law. Gromyko, the Foreign Minister, says 'It is impossible to overstate the danger posed by Solidarity' but other members of the Politburo are inclined to be reassured by Kania's presentation on 5 December.

Soviet Politburo 2 April 1981
Brezhnev says: 'we are all deeply alarmed; the Polish leaders just talk, they don't act. The Soviet leaders must tell the Poles to declare Martial Law and explain what it involves.'

Soviet Politburo 7 April 1981
Gloom all round. The Polish Communist Party is seen as weaker than the Church and Solidarity. Kania and Jaruzelski, the Polish leaders, lack the determination to crush Solidarity, but there are no alternative leaders.

Soviet Politburo 9 April 1981
Asked for their views about the possibility of Soviet invasion, the Polish leaders have said (at a secret meeting between Andropov, head of the KGB, and Jaruzelski on 3 April) that invasion is absolutely impossible. They have also said that Martial Law is impossible.

Soviet Politburo 13 April 1981
The view of the meeting is that Solidarity is now able to take power and is restrained mainly by fear of invasion. (Note: this

implies that the threat of invasion should be maintained as long as possible, even if it is bluff).

Soviet Politburo 23 April 1981
Policy discussion which shows alarm but suggests no serious moves. Neither invasion nor Martial Law is mentioned.

Brezhnev meets Kania and Jaruzelski 14 August 1981. He tells the Poles 'Any hope of defending Socialism by means of persuasion, without resorting to other means ... is an illusion. Sooner or later, the communists will have to square off directly against the enemy ... This had better not occur too late.'

Brezhnev/Kania telephone conversation 15 September 1981. Brezhnev excitedly asks 'If Poland is ruled by Solidarity, who will guarantee the inviolability of our vital lines of communication?' (Through Poland to the huge Soviet army stationed in East Germany.)

Soviet Politburo 29 October 1981
Andropov states that the decision not to invade Poland has been taken.

Polish Politburo 5 December 1981
The Polish leaders reach a 'consensus' on imposing Martial Law.

Soviet Politburo 10 December 1981
(Three days before the declaration of Martial Law in Warsaw.) The meeting is informed that Jaruzelski (now Polish party leader) has said that, if Polish forces are unable to cope with resistance to Martial Law, he hopes for Soviet help, up to and including the introduction of armed forces. Andropov says 'we cannot introduce troops into Poland. That is the proper position, and we must adhere to it until the end. Even if Poland falls under the control of Solidarity, that's the way it will be ... And if the capitalist countries pounce on the Soviet Union, and you know they have already reached agreement on a variety of economic and political sanctions,

that will be very burdensome for us. We must be concerned above all with our own country and about the strengthening of the Soviet Union.' There is no opposition in the meeting to the view expressed by several Politburo members that the Soviet Union should not invade Poland. Gromyko expresses the general view that the restoration of order in Poland is the responsibility of the Polish Communist Party. Suslov (the hard-line chief ideologist) says that the Soviet Union 'has done a great deal of work for peace ... This has enabled all peace-loving countries to understand that the Soviet Union staunchly and consistently upholds a policy of peace. That is why it is now impossible for us to change the policy we have adopted towards Poland ... There can be no talk at all of introducing troops ... Invasion would be a catastrophe.'

These documents show that some of the Soviet leaders decided in October 1981 at the latest against invading Poland. The rest of the Politburo was told on 29 October. For at least a year before Martial Law was declared the Soviet leaders had been pressing the Polish leaders to impose it. The Polish decision on Martial Law was taken after the Soviet decision not to invade. So Jaruzelski was lying when he said later that he introduced Martial Law in order to forestall Soviet invasion. Moreover, he appealed to the USSR, just before declaring Martial Law, to invade if the Polish authorities could not enforce it.

On 13 December 1981 Martial Law was imposed and then Solidarity was banned. The Soviet Union immediately declared its approval of Martial Law. (It is worth noting, however, that another key principle of the Marxist-Leninist state was that the Communist Party would always control the armed forces. So for the Party to pass power to the military was a humiliating necessity for the Soviet Union, an admission that the Party in Poland could not run the country and the army must be given the leading role.)

Martial Law did turn the clock back. The change in Poland was reversed. Brezhnev told the Soviet Politburo that counter-revolution had been crushed. He was wrong. The reversal was not total: Martial Law did not eliminate Solidarity or the huge influence of the Catholic Church. In spring 1982 the general view in western governments was that Martial Law had calmed the Polish situation and that Jaruzelski would probably stay in power for quite a time. Solidarity was apparently cowed.

It soon became clear, however, that beneath the quiet surface there was resentment and restiveness, among factory workers and many others. On 3 May 1982 there were demonstrations across the country, apparently co-ordinated in secret by Solidarity working underground.

Meanwhile the Polish economy continued to decline, and a collapse seemed increasingly likely. The Government in London wrestled with a quandary about whether to give economic support to Poland. We had an interest in the avoidance of economic collapse, which would mean that Poland's large debts owed to Britain would not be paid for years and perhaps never. It might well precipitate Soviet invasion. On the other hand it was clearly the Soviet Union that should be supporting the Polish economy and we did not wish to provide funds which would reduce the amount needed from Moscow. That could be seen as subsidising Soviet power over Poland just when the Poles had been making clear by supporting Solidarity that Soviet control was the last thing they wanted. We were also conscious that the British public would expect the government to be involved in helping a European country which might be about to suffer famine. After the declaration of Martial Law I recommended that the UK should concentrate on humanitarian aid, especially food, to help the Polish people who were facing shortages of necessities.

* * * * *

During the 1980s Solidarity became more visibly active. In 1989 the Polish leaders lifted the ban on its activity and felt bound to negotiate with it. The negotiations were followed by a semi-free election, another step which flatly contradicted Marxist-Leninist doctrine. Solidarity won a stunning victory. In August 1989 it was leading a coalition government in Warsaw and in December 1990 Lech Walesa, the leader of Solidarity, became President of Poland.

Meanwhile Gorbachev introduced in the Soviet Union in 1988 his reforms known as Perestroika and Glasnost (reconstruction and openness). This development showed that there would be change in the Soviet Union itself. It led, together with the dawn of democracy in Poland, to transformation in the other countries of Central and Eastern Europe. The Berlin Wall was opened in November 1989. East and West Germany were unified in October 1990. The Soviet Union abolished the Communist Party and then the USSR itself. It introduced many freedoms. It lost large territories.

These great events swept away communism in Europe and ended the Cold War. Europe became a safer continent.

*****

So what were the real reasons why the Soviet leaders decided not to invade Poland in 1980–81? In 1980 they were making detailed plans for invasion, but then decided against it. They urged the Polish leaders to impose Martial Law but they were not sure that it would succeed. What they were sure about was that invasion would be a catastrophe. The leaders were aware that Solidarity might come to power in Poland. They nevertheless decided that the disadvantages of invasion outweighed the need to ensure that Soviet domination in Poland was preserved.

This decision was a total reversal of Moscow's policy in the face of less potent anti-Soviet movements in communist countries in Europe in the past. It turned out to be the first major stride on the road to the collapse of Soviet power in central and eastern Europe and of the Soviet Union itself.

The main reason for not invading Poland given by Andropov in the Politburo on 10 December 1981 was that harmful western sanctions would follow. US exports of grain to the Soviet Union had been halted in response to the invasion of Afghanistan. President Reagan had lifted that embargo in April 1981. If the USSR had invaded Poland, supplies of grain might well have been stopped again. But the Soviet Union at this time was not dependant on US grain. In fact, its purchases were falling because grain could be imported from other producer countries at lower prices than the US required. It seems clear therefore that Andropov was referring in the Politburo to a wider range of Western sanctions, and his words quoted above suggest this.

Suslov's remarks to the same Politburo meeting display concern that invasion would destroy the Soviet reputation in the world for upholding peace. He was no doubt thinking that the Soviet war in Afghanistan was already harming the image of the USSR in the developing world. Two invasions at once would have looked very belligerent and would indeed have severely harmed the Soviet reputation. In addition, the Soviet leaders knew that the Polish army, or much of it, would fight and Soviet soldiers would be killed. A bloodbath in Poland would be a disaster.

These reasons must have been important in the fateful decision not to invade Poland. Yet the Soviet leaders knew the decision was dangerous and momentous. I think there may have been another, deeper reason. The leaders, facing intractable economic problems at home and no longer believing in the political philosophy they still professed, may have lost the self-confidence to defend their interests by military means if necessary. Their willpower had faltered; they had lost their nerve. That may have been the main reason for this hugely positive turning point in the history of Europe.

The Soviet Union welcomed and supported Poland's declaration of Martial Law. It was obvious that Moscow had played a major role in the decision. In its reactions, the West held the Soviet Union responsible. President Reagan took several immediate steps to show American condemnation. These included the suspension of licences for export of high technology to the USSR and tighter controls on the export of oil and gas equipment.

Mrs Thatcher wanted the UK to react firmly. I coordinated the selection of our measures towards the Soviet Union. They included tighter restrictions on travel by Soviet diplomats in the UK, reduced activity under four bilateral agreements on technical cooperation, termination of the British-Soviet maritime agreement and new restrictions on Soviet fishing around Britain. Our purposes were to achieve a reasonably united Western response and thus prevent the Soviet Union's crisis in Poland provoking a crisis of Western unity; to respond to the abhorrence in Western public opinion at Soviet sponsorship of the clampdown in Poland; and to add somewhat to the factors that might weigh in Moscow against expansionism and for restraint in foreign policy in future. Our analysis in the FCO was that the Western reactions demonstrated two useful things: that the West held Moscow accountable for developments in Poland and that such Soviet actions had a significant effect on East-West relations. Press articles and public statements in the Soviet Union suggested that this message had been registered and that the Russians were disappointed at the degree of unity that the NATO countries displayed.

II

HEAD OF POLICY PLANNING, FCO, THE FALKLANDS WAR 1980–82

My colleagues in the Planning Staff of the FCO were a small group of bright people with varied expertise. We had the tasks of ... well really anything the Permanent Under-Secretary, the top official, assigned to us. The PUS at this time was Sir Michael Palliser, a man of charm as well as high ability. We were the FCO's in-house think tank, a ginger group for producing new ideas and challenging existing policies. Our direct access to the Foreign Secretary, and even more often to the PUS, was intended to enhance our influence. We had these categories of work:

- devising and presenting new policy ideas, as requested by the PUS or the Foreign Secretary or on our own initiative; from long-term planning papers on policy in East-West relations to specific subjects like the Cyprus problem.
- to intervene in the FCO's policy-making process in any field, whenever we wished to criticise or make suggestions. Our interventions were always copied to the PUS, an example of the way we could exert influence. The departments in whose business we meddled were never angry; they argued their case when they disagreed with us. I recall energetic discussion but no row.

- to draft the speeches of the Foreign Secretary, and some by the Prime Minister and also other FCO Ministers and the PUS. This included Lord Carrington's major declaration on deterrence and arms control in his Churchill Memorial Lecture and Francis Pym's speeches in the House of Commons during the Falklands crisis.
- crisis management; the head of the Planning Staff was vice chairman of the FCO's Crisis Management Group set up to deal with each crisis as it arose. The chairman of the group was usually the Deputy Under-Secretary (the level below the PUS) who was responsible for the field of work where the crisis had arisen. The main example in my time in the Planning Staff was the Falklands crisis; the imposition of martial law in Poland and the Iraqi invasion of Kuwait were other big examples.
- to be the main link between the FCO and academics and institutions concerned with foreign policy. This was fun. I met many clever and entertaining people and attended many conferences, always seeking ideas which the FCO should consider and trying to convince the academics of the views of the Office.

I also had a highly confidential role. The Foreign Ministers of Britain, the United States, West Germany and France held private consultations from time to time on difficult subjects of policy. To back up those meetings there were meetings of two senior officials from each of the four countries. The fig-leaf used to justify these important meetings, when news of one of them leaked, was that they existed for discussing matters concerning Berlin, where these four countries had particular responsibility. Discussion of Berlin crises had indeed been the origin of these meetings and Berlin was still discussed, but for many years the meetings had also been used to discuss other important or difficult matters. The British representative at official level was the Political Director of the FCO, the immensely able and agreeable Julian Bullard, who was a role model to my generation of British diplomats. I was the other British representative. In my time the Quad, as this four power group was called, discussed policy towards the Soviet Union, Poland, the Soviet invasion of Afghanistan, and the Falkland Islands among other things.

The Falklands War

I had never dealt with the Falklands or indeed with South America in my work. On the day of the invasion, I was at an Anglo-German conference in Cambridge. I was telephoned by the FCO and asked to return and see the Permanent Under-Secretary. Michael Palliser asked me to coordinate the work of the Office on the Falklands crisis.

Lord Carrington, as Foreign and Commonwealth Secretary, was constitutionally and politically the Minister responsible for the Falkland Islands. The top officials in the FCO tried to persuade him that he should not resign, for he was needed even more in the crisis that had just begun. He nevertheless decided that he should take responsibility. In his memoirs he makes clear why: 'The nation feels that there has been a disgrace. Someone must have been to blame. The disgrace must be purged. The person to purge it should be the minister in charge. That was me.'* His resignation was the honourable act of an honourable man. We officials were deeply upset to lose a first class Foreign and Commonwealth Secretary.

I began work in my office immediately after my conversation with Michael Palliser. The first thing I did was to consider what actions were possible in the new situation of Argentine military occupation of the Falklands. The two main possibilities were a war to liberate the islands and a negotiation to try to persuade Argentina to withdraw in the face of wide condemnation from other countries of this act of aggression. Both these actions were already in discussion by our Ministers. Were any other options available? Any which might avoid the loss of lives and indeed the high expenditure which a war would bring?

To answer my question I needed to think widely. There seemed to be two kinds of possibility. One would be to devise a solution to the question of the future of the Falklands which would be acceptable to the Islanders and yet would satisfy Argentina's obsessive yearning for sovereignty.

There have been a few places in the world where sovereignty has been shared between two countries. But none of the precedents seemed at all likely to work, or to appeal to the Falkland Islanders

---

* Lord Carrington, *Reflect on things Past*, William Collins 1988, page 370.

at any time and certainly not when they were experiencing how unscrupulous and aggressive Argentina could be.

Looking purely logically at the situation I also thought that it might be feasible to pay each Falkland Islander a sum sufficient to enable them to move to another English-speaking territory and there resume their way of life as sheep farmers. New Zealand sprang to mind as a possible place for such a plan.

This blue sky thinking was an attempt to enable ministers to consider all possibilities and not only the obvious ones. Such thinking is a normal duty of officials. But I did not think that any of my far-fetched ideas should or would be taken seriously. I did not put them to ministers because the War Cabinet decided immediately both to send forces to liberate the Falklands and to use the six weeks until the forces reached the Falklands to try by negotiation to persuade Argentina to withdraw without a war.

As coordinator of the FCO's work I played an active role in the Crisis Management team of the FCO and sometimes attended Margaret Thatcher's War Cabinet, where she and a handful of selected ministers, senior officials and military leaders directed British policy and actions in the crisis. I kept myself informed about all the work of the FCO concerning the crisis, to ensure that all our actions were compatible with each other and with the UK's overall policy and especially with our military intentions.

I worked twelve or more hours a day for the next six weeks. This work pattern was partly caused by the time difference between London and the UN in New York. The reports of debates and negotiations from Tony Parsons, our highly effective Ambassador at the UN, left New York late in the evening there and reached the FCO an hour or so later, which was about 6 am the next morning. I needed to read them, discuss them with colleagues and draft a paper suggesting our next steps for the War Cabinet which met at the start of the working day in London. Often that paper was accompanied by the draft of new instructions for Tony Parsons, which the War Cabinet might discuss. Then the instructions were sent by telegram to Parsons, in time for the morning's work in New York.

Colleagues in the FCO had meanwhile read in the night the reports from our embassies in many capitals on their discussions about the Falklands with the governments there. These reports were discussed within the FCO and often with the Ministry of Defence and other Government Departments. Instructions to our embassies were drafted and if necessary submitted for approval to the Foreign Secretary or another FCO Minister. We spent long hours on all this reading, drafting and consulting and there were many, many meetings where our policy was developed. And constantly in this punishing schedule, each of us had to think carefully about what adjustment of policy and what actions to suggest at the next meeting. I think all the officials involved found the work essential, absorbing and exhausting.

There was at first sharp recrimination in Parliament and the media about who had been responsible for allowing the disaster of the invasion to happen. It fell to me to draft Francis Pym's first speech in the House of Commons as Foreign Secretary, on 7 April. His keynote was 'We must look forward in confidence, not backward in anger.'

Pym said the Security Council of the United Nations promptly and decisively endorsed the British view of the invasion of the islands. It adopted – the very day after the invasion – a resolution put forward by Britain. That resolution demanded an immediate cessation of hostilities and an immediate withdrawal of all Argentine forces, and it called on the governments of Argentina and the United Kingdom to seek a diplomatic solution to their differences and to respect the United Nations Charter. Britain immediately accepted the injunction to seek a diplomatic solution and observe the Charter.

The new Foreign Secretary's speech achieved its purpose: it turned the House of Commons toward the tasks ahead and away from the recrimination that had dominated its debate on the day after the invasion.

Another important part of the FCO's work was to persuade members of the European Community to impose sanctions on Argentina as the aggressor and to keep the sanctions in place until Argentina withdrew from the Islands. We also put our case for sanctions to members of the Commonwealth. We generally managed to persuade the members of these two very different organisations to apply sanctions against Argentina.

A particularly important case was France. There were fairly close ties between France and Argentina, and France had supplied Argentina's Exocet missiles, which posed a serious threat to our Navy in the area of the Falklands. But France was also a former colonial power with some overseas territories still, and therefore could understand and indeed admire Britain's reaction to Argentina's invasion. President Mitterrand probably also had in mind that French support for us in the Falklands crisis would be a signal to any country with designs on a French overseas territory that a military response would be likely.

Margaret Thatcher and François Mitterrand were very different people, but each respected some things about the other and there was a rapport between them. He telephoned her to express support soon after the invasion of the Falklands. She persuaded him to refuse to supply Argentina with any more equipment for the Exocet missiles. He also gave us the radar guidance codes for the missiles.

*****

The reason for the UK's immediate and crucially important decision to despatch a military force to the South Atlantic was that it was unthinkable to leave British territories in the hands of an aggressor. Unthinkable, indeed, to leave the Falkland Islanders to suffer under a hostile invader which also was a military dictatorship. To fail to exercise our right under the UN Charter of self-defence against aggression would have been to condone aggression. Many doubted the feasibility of winning a war on the other side of the world, but Mrs Thatcher was delighted that the Navy advised her that it could be done.

While our force crossed the world, we made our attempt to persuade Argentina by negotiation to withdraw peacefully from the Islands. This was my main activity in the crisis. I was glad to be in the thick of the diplomacy.

The core of my role was to think about our aims and tactics in the negotiation with Argentina and to consult with others in the FCO and other government departments about our ideas, which then were submitted to the Foreign Secretary and the War Cabinet.

This work involved concentration and mental effort, which were interrupted by endless telephone calls, day and night, and many meetings every day to discuss the proposals. This combination of hard thinking and constant interruption is characteristic of work in a crisis. I managed to keep it up for many weeks, and so did many colleagues. We were hugely motivated to make a contribution in the crisis, and adrenalin as well as determination compensated for the lack of sleep.

The government and Mrs Thatcher herself took the negotiations seriously and worked hard for weeks to achieve progress. In the first phase of negotiations, the US Secretary of State, General Alexander Haig, was the intermediary, with involvement for part of the time of the President of Peru. I was glad that Haig took on this task. It was a good choice from our point of view because of the close US-UK relationship and the power of the US in the western hemisphere.

It quickly became clear that there would be three main subjects in an immediate negotiation with Argentina. The first would be a cease-fire and withdrawal within a stated time of the Argentine forces and the British force. The second would be an interim administration of the Falkland Islands. The third would be a negotiation about the future of the Islands.

A British territory had been the victim of aggression and illegal occupation, but it was the UK which devoted major effort to the negotiations at many levels from the Prime Minister downwards. We wanted, and Mrs Thatcher herself terribly wanted, to avoid the loss of young lives in a battle for the islands. Our lesser purpose was that we wanted the world to see that we were negotiating seriously, in case the diplomatic effort should fail and we might be left with no choice but to liberate the islands by military means.

Argentina's purpose was to achieve its longstanding aim of gaining sovereignty over the Islands. We made, after careful consultation, the substantial concession of saying that sovereignty could be part of negotiations about the future of the Islands. Argentina insisted intransigently that it must be agreed before negotiations that they would endorse Argentina's claim to sovereignty.

The UK could not possibly accept this. How could Britain hand to Argentina the sovereignty which it was trying to seize by aggression? How could the Islanders be asked in these circumstances to accept the thing they most strongly opposed? The Foreign Secretary summed up our position in the House of Commons on 13 May: 'We accept that negotiations about the future of the islands can exclude no possible outcome but equally we insist that they must determine none. Nothing excluded, nothing prejudged. That is a reasonable position and one on which we shall not compromise.'

We were willing to accept other points, not least the withdrawal of our forces if Argentina's left the islands, and the replacement of the British Governor of the Falklands by representatives of three other countries. David Gillmore, who was the senior FCO official dealing with the defence aspects of the crisis, said later 'Christopher Mallaby ... who was Head of Planning Staff, used to present a new plan every morning before 8 o'clock. He was quite remarkable in producing imaginative new ideas. But none of them ever turned out to be acceptable to Argentina.'

On 5 May, the UK and Haig agreed on a proposal to be put by the President of Peru to the military regime in Argentina. The latter rejected our plan. Haig's impression was that the Argentine regime was unreliable and incompetent. The contrast between the aggressor who was clearly not trying in the negotiations, and the victim of aggression who was trying hard, was obvious to all concerned at the UN.

On 8 May the UN Secretary General, Perez de Cuellar from Peru, began his attempt to broker an agreement between the UK and Argentina. He is an able and impressive diplomat, and he tried hard to make progress. At no point did it seem that he would be biased, as a Latin American, in favour of Argentina in the effort to reach an agreement. Argentina continued to be totally intransigent in the negotiation and to show no inclination to reach agreement. The British force was coming nearer to the Falklands and a growing number of delegations at the UN were anxious to pass a resolution calling for a ceasefire, to avert hostilities.

We in the FCO Planning Staff reviewed British policy in the negotiations. Our assessment, when preparing advice for Francis Pym before a meeting of the War Cabinet on 14 May, was that it was still not quite certain whether Argentina's objective in the negotiations was really to negotiate or merely to gain time while the weather worsened around the Falklands, making operations harder for our forces when they arrived. In fact this point in our assessment was too cautious. We became sure very soon after this that Argentina was not seeking agreement but was playing for time in the hope of holding on to the Islands. Argentina was also trying to put itself in a good public position to blame Britain if the talks failed. The War Cabinet's view remained that a settlement would be preferable to war, and that military action following a breakdown of negotiations that would be blamed on Argentina was preferable to action following a breakdown that could be blamed on the UK.

Mrs Thatcher held an important meeting at Chequers on 16 May. Tony Parsons and our Ambassador in Washington, Nicko Henderson, participated. The meeting decided that the UK would put forward a document stating its position, which would be put to Argentina with a deadline of 48 hours for agreement. Perez de Cuellar agreed to present this British document to Argentina. The latter produced a blatantly unacceptable counter-proposal, probably hoping to provoke the UK to break off the talks. Perez de Cuellar thought the Argentine proposal unreasonable and self-destructive.

Argentina must have realised, as the British forces came near to the Falklands, that our counter attack might well succeed in expelling their forces. On 10 May, ten days before the British forces were ready to land, Argentina made the apparently important concession of ceasing to insist that future negotiations about the Islands must be preceded by agreement that the Argentine claim to sovereignty would be accepted. But this apparent concession was short-lived. On 18 May Argentina reverted to its earlier views. On 20 May Perez de Cuellar put his own proposal to the UK and Argentina. It was close in substance and largely in wording to the UK position.

Francis Pym on my advice suggested to the War Cabinet that we should accept Perez de Cuellar's proposal on condition that Argentina accepted it within a deadline of a few hours. This move would show that Britain had gone on trying to reach a negotiated settlement until the last minute. I also argued that this would cost us nothing because Argentina would not accept the Secretary General's proposal. Parsons thought Argentina might accept it as a basis for yet more discussion, in order to delay action by the British force.

The Prime Minister rejected Pym's suggestion. She said that our soldiers were about to land on the Falklands and there could be no question of delaying the landings. It would be confusing and demoralising for them to hear that we had accepted this proposal just when they faced the fighting. I immediately realised that Mrs Thatcher's point about our soldiers was right. Parsons told the Secretary General that the time for negotiation had passed, expressing this message carefully and with appreciation of the efforts that Perez de Cuellar had made.

Argentina did not respond to the Secretary General's paper. Perez de Cuellar told Argentina that he now had no choice but to discontinue his attempt to negotiate.

On 21 May the British military landing in the Falklands went ahead successfully. Our forces began the difficult task of expelling Argentina from the islands and putting an end to aggression. During the fighting some of the UK's friends at the UN became increasingly insistent that hostilities and casualties must cease and negotiation must resume. There was renewed pressure on the UK, from the United States among many others. Anti-colonial sentiment among UN members was evident in the discussions.

But there was no sign that Argentina would end its illegal occupation of the Falklands except by losing the war. The British forces on the Islands were advancing and that outcome looked increasingly certain. The Security Council met again and the UK and the US blocked a resolution calling for a cease-fire by using our vetoes.

The war, though short, was tough, partly because of the terrain and the weather. Every soldier killed is a tragedy and the British casualties were 255. I think Margaret Thatcher thought of them frequently forever afterwards. Thank goodness the number was fewer than the Ministry of Defence in London had predicted. Argentina lost 649 lives. Three Falklands civilians were killed.

On the evening of 14 June I arrived home from the FCO late for supper. I switched on the television in our children's playroom to watch the 10 o'clock news. Argentina had surrendered. I wept in my relief and joy.

* * * * *

I believe that the victory had a valuable effect on the mood of Britain. For several years there had been a mood of pessimism, and the self-confidence of the British had weakened. One reason was that our economy had persistently performed poorly, and much less well than those of France and especially Germany. Repeated strikes and work stoppages had added to the sombre mood. Some of the media had suggested that the UK had begun a period of decline.

If the government had made no attempt to deal with aggression against a British territory, there would have been severely critical comparisons between this inaction and our courage in greater crises in the past and especially our essential role in the war against Nazi Germany. The unhappy national mood would have become even more morose. Had we decided to fight but not succeeded in liberating the Falklands, the mood of self-doubt would have deepened even more.

As it was, the courage, skill and triumph of our armed forces in the Falklands and the resolution of Mrs Thatcher and her government boosted our national morale. The economic success which soon became apparent in the United Kingdom did even more to raise confidence and restore pride. The ensuing period of prosperity put an end to the talk of decline. The victory in the Falklands and above all the transformation of Britain's economic performance are the achievements that made Margaret Thatcher great.

* * * * *

After the war two of the major repercussions were that the military dictatorship in Buenos Aires was deposed and the British defence arrangements for deterring aggression against the islands were strengthened. The economy of the islands was developed and diversified. Sheep farming had been the one significant activity. Now, the UK established an Exclusive Economic Zone around the Falklands, and licenses were henceforth required for the ships of other countries to fish there. Fisheries came to represent 50–60% of the economy. Tourism became a useful source of income. So did exploration for oil under the sea around the islands, an activity which continues today. Argentina still claims sovereignty. The UK avoids discussion of this; we and the islanders can hardly be expected to consider it after the Argentine aggression in 1982.

Dealing with the Soviet Union

The most important and comprehensive policy study we wrote in my time in the Planning Staff was about how the West should handle relations with the Soviet Union in the wake of its invasion of Afghanistan. Our paper proposed a wide range of measures to strengthen countries where the Soviet Union might try to intervene by force or other means in order to gain predominant influence. The novelty of our paper was partly that we proposed a systematic approach by the western countries, with suggestions about the role each should play. The measures we discussed included the creation of an international rapid deployment force, which might deter Soviet invasion, especially if it was deployed or conducted training exercises in or near a country where invasion was likely to be under consideration in Moscow. We proposed a study to identify the countries where the Soviet Union might seek dominance and we suggested measures to boost those countries, by aid and military training and other means, to strengthen them against Soviet blandishments.

I briefed Malcolm Rutherford, a distinguished journalist on the *Financial Times*, about this thinking, and he wrote a long article in November 1980. I was surprised when it appeared, because Malcolm wrote that a likely forum for discussing our paper with allies would be the Quadripartite Group, which dealt ostensibly with Berlin. I had not mentioned this to Malcolm but he had guessed that this secret forum would be chosen. That was a small embarrassment for me since Malcolm's guess was correct and other countries participating in the Quad might be cross that I had apparently leaked its current agenda. This was a lesson to me that briefing a serious and expert journalist could lead to revelations about things I had not said!

Drafting Speeches

Of all the speeches I have drafted, I think the one that reads best today is the Churchill Memorial Lecture delivered by Lord Carrington in Luxembourg on 27 October 1981. I had much help from colleagues, notably John Weston, then head of the Defence Department of the FCO. Carrington's lecture is a classic, complete and comprehensible statement of the case for deterrence as a means of preventing war and a careful and convincing rebuttal of those who advocated unilateral disarmament by the West. Here is one passage:

> The purpose of deterrence is to influence the calculations of anyone who might consider an attack, or the threat of an attack, against us; to influence them before any such attack is ever launched; and to influence them decisively. Planning for this means thinking through the possible reasoning of an adversary ... It rests on blocking off in advance a variety of possible moves in an opponent's mind... To do this is not to have a war fighting strategy or to plan for nuclear war ... it is to ensure that, even if an adversary believed in limited nuclear war, as Soviet writings sometimes suggest, he could not expect actually to engage in one without losses out of all proportion to the desired gains ... NATO, then, is there to deter a possible adversary from starting a war, by making sure that the risk will always be too high.

It was a pleasure to draft speeches for Lord Carrington, an extremely amusing as well as distinguished man. He required that draft speeches should always include a large amount – perhaps one third of the text – of what he called levity. That meant not only jokes but also amusing touches like anecdotes or popular sayings. I acquired a collection of dictionaries of quotations, which were useful. But one early example showed me that suitable levity could be hard to find.

Lord Carrington was to make a speech after a lunch of a large group of senior British businessmen. He wanted to tell them what British embassies abroad can do to help British exporters. That was close to my heart and rather easy to write, because of my experience of export promotion in New York. But what jokes could I include? I asked several friends in business whether they knew of good jokes about business or exporting. The only good suggestion came from my Cambridge friend David Williams. On leaving Cambridge in 1959 David had been inspired by Prime Minister Macmillan's slogan 'exporting is fun'. He got a job with a major British engineering firm and was assigned to oversee the construction of a steel-rolling mill in Romania. He needed a new passport. In those days the application form asked for your profession. David did not think of himself as a businessman or a company director, so he wrote what he thought he was, an exporter. When the passport arrived his profession was given as ex-porter.

I was pleased with this little story about a former porter, which seemed both funny and appropriate to the occasion. When Lord Carrington saw my draft speech he rejected my joke, saying that it was far too complicated for an audience of business people after a boozy lunch. That stuff about a hyphen would be too much for them to appreciate. He invited me to come with him to the lunch, to see how he presented the speech. On the way he pulled a scruffy army notebook out of his coat pocket, consulted it, looked pleased and returned the notebook to his pocket. He used the draft speech very much as it was, but when he came to the place where my joke had been, he replaced it by the following from his notebook. A British exporter is visiting clients in France. There is a gap in his programme at midday. He goes to the nearest bistro to have lunch and, having little French, does the simplest thing of ordering the set menu. The first course is soup. When it arrives, there is a fly struggling on the surface. The businessman calls back the waiter and complains in his patchy French 'Enlevez le mouche'. The waiter replies with shocked disapproval, 'Non, non Monsieur – *la* mouche.' To which the businessman exclaims 'Fantastic eyesight, these Frenchmen!' This brought the house down.

Another example of Carrington's requirement for levity came when he was giving a lecture at an American university. I supplied a couple of examples to show that Winston Churchill was right to say that the British and the Americans are divided by a common language. The remark 'I'm mad about my flat' means to an Englishman 'I'm crazy about my apartment' but to an American it means 'I'm furious about my puncture'. Pascale had an experience of that kind when we were living in New York. She remembered late one afternoon that we had people for dinner. She rushed to the meat department of a famous store and breathlessly asked the butcher to sell her a joint. The man paled and then said he could not supply that substance; he was a butcher not a pusher, thank you very much Ma'am!

Drafting speeches for Margaret Thatcher was exacting. Michael Alexander, her foreign affairs Private Secretary at that time, and I would talk about a forthcoming speech and what content to suggest. When we had agreed, I would do a first draft and Michael would amend it to bring it closer to the Prime Minister's style. Sometimes we went through this process several times. Then Michael would submit the draft to the Prime Minister, who had been in touch with the work all the way.

A day or two before the speech was to be made, a small group of officials – usually Robert Armstrong, Michael Alexander and I – would join Mrs Thatcher in her private sitting room upstairs in 10 Downing Street at about 7pm, and start working through the speech.

Margaret Thatcher was very, very rigorous. She wanted every sentence to be justified. You are saying this, do you really mean this exactly? Show me why it's true. Wouldn't it be truer to say that instead? There would be several minutes of quite strong argument about a sentence that was a line and a half or two lines long. And then on to the next sentence. The discussion was amicable but tough.

There were no domestic staff at Number 10 in the evenings. When it was time for supper, the Prime Minister herself would fetch a shepherd's pie from the oven. We would sit round the kitchen table for a brief meal. We had a glass of whisky before the meal and after it we worked again on the speech and could have more drinks if we wanted. On one occasion the discussion went on very late, and tomorrow's newspapers were delivered. There was a break for 20 minutes while the Prime Minister read the daily summary of the press which her press secretary, Bernard Ingham, had prepared. Then we went back to the speech. The hardest moment for me was to resume this exacting work after my concentration had been suspended during the interval.

For five years in London I had enjoyed fascinating work at the heart of the process of making foreign policy. I was ready to go abroad again. We moved to Bonn, where I was to be one of the two deputies of the Ambassador.

12

CABINET OFFICE, THE ANGLO-IRISH AGREEMENT 1985–88

Pascale and I spent two and a half years in Bonn, which are covered in Chapter 13. Then we returned to London where I was lent by the FCO to be one of the Deputy Secretaries in the Cabinet Office. They formed the level immediately below Sir Robert Armstrong, who was the head of the Cabinet Office and Cabinet Secretary and also Head of the Civil Service. What I most enjoyed during this time was the close experience of how the British Government at the top level really works and how ministers and senior officials interact day by day.

The Cabinet Office is a department which has the important function of promoting efficient decision-making by the government and ensuring that new policy is effectively developed, coordinated and implemented. The Cabinet Office also leads and coordinates the Government's handling of crises, whether natural disasters, terrorist incidents or international crises.

The Cabinet Office in my day was not under the direct control of a minister but was led by Robert Armstrong. Nor was it the Prime Minister's own department like the White House in the US or the Federal Chancellor's Office in Germany, which directly serve the President or the Chancellor and are often as important in creating policy as the ministers in the government. We did a great deal of work for the Prime Minister and were greatly influenced by her views but we also did much work for other ministers who chaired committees of the Cabinet.

These numerous committees of ministers were there to reach decisions on subjects of interest to several departments. Below them was a range of Cabinet committees at senior official level, which tried to reach agreement among departments before ministers took the decisions.

I attended ministerial committees when the subject was in my field, sitting next to the chairman, who was often the Prime Minister, and commenting on points of fact or answering questions during the discussion. Then I would write the minutes of the meeting, recording the decisions reached and which Department was to take the actions agreed.

It was more impressive than daunting to participate in a meeting chaired by Margaret Thatcher – on one condition. She had an insatiable appetite for facts. Brevity was not what she cared about in a brief; she wanted comprehensive information. I knew I must be even more fully informed than her. I therefore prepared extremely carefully.

It has been said that Mrs Thatcher made up her mind before meetings and drove the discussion to the decision which she had already reached. But on subjects which were new to her, or on new developments in a subject she knew, she took account of the comments of ministers and the advice from officials in the meeting. On subjects she already knew well, she did sometimes insist on a view she had reached before the discussion began.

With her ministerial colleagues Mrs Thatcher could be harsh. When she considered a minister, even a senior one, to be unclear or soft – 'wet' as she would say – she could be crushing and disdainful in her put-downs. There was sometimes a bit of this even with ministers whom she considered loyal to her personally.

In my experience the Prime Minister was considerate to officials. It was said that she disliked the FCO, which was true as a generalisation. But she liked and approved of some of the senior diplomats. For instance Tony Parsons, who was Ambassador at the United Nations at the time of the Falklands war and later her foreign affairs adviser; Antony Acland, who was head of the FCO from 1982; and her private secretaries who were seconded from the FCO, above all Charles Powell.

One example of the tender heart beneath her dynamic energy came after Mrs Thatcher left the Government. When she visited Indonesia, our Ambassador, Sir Roger Carrick, took her to visit the Commonwealth war cemetery in Jakarta, where she saw my father's grave. Roger Carrick told me that she wept quietly for some time. Roger thought – rightly I am sure – that the cemetery reminded her of the British servicemen who had died several years earlier in the Falklands war and her tears were especially for them.

The main responsibility of my small but capable team in the Cabinet Office was the coordination of policy-making in the fields of foreign affairs, defence and Northern Ireland. My function was to manage the making of policy in matters in my field where several government departments had an interest and especially where they disagreed.

I found that the senior officials were able people working conscientiously to produce recommendations for ministers in the national interest. Ministers were in control, and the relationship between them and the officials was mutually respectful and usually considerate.

I chaired some of the Cabinet committees of officials. The discussion was always polite but real arguments were common and the atmosphere could become chilly. The officials defended the particular interests of their own departments but wanted whenever possible to reach a joint recommendation on policy. It was preferable for officials to agree, but not at the price of producing a watered-down compromise and therefore a weak proposal. So I worked, as chairman of many meetings of senior officials, for a single clear and specific recommendation. If that proved impossible my staff would write a paper setting out the different views of the various departments and suggesting options, which a meeting of ministers would then consider.

Sometimes a department which thought a clear conclusion would not be favourable to its interests would drag its feet and try by inertia to avoid progress towards decisions. I tried to galvanise the foot-draggers, applying what I called vicarious willpower.

The argument 'we've always done it this way' was a danger signal. It could be a sign that the speaker had no substantive arguments for the case he or she was making. My usual reaction was to say that a longstanding practice might well be ripe for review, to see whether it was still the best way of doing things.

A less serious risk was that senior officials might occasionally devote inordinate time to lesser matters where agreement was hard to achieve. One example concerned the British Antarctic Survey, a research activity with a relatively low budget that had been funded by several departments with an interest in the research. One of them announced that it would no longer contribute to the budget. The others wanted the research to continue but did not say so, for fear of being asked to pay more. I asked each point blank in private whether they wanted the research to end; if they did not care, we could solve the problem by recommending that the activity should cease. We then agreed in the committee that we all wanted the research to go on. Next we resumed discussion of which departments should contribute to funding the research. I suggested various arrangements, and finally got agreement. The Permanent Secretary of one of the departments complained to Robert Armstrong that he was being forced by me to meet bills he could not afford. Robert asked me to give up the effort to reach agreement on this narrow matter. He arranged a rapid fix among Permanent Secretaries, who proved more flexible than their senior staff.

Some policy matters went to Cabinet for discussion and decision. When this happened in my field I wrote the Prime Minister's brief for the meeting, suggesting what outcome would be best. I also drafted the minutes of Cabinet discussions in my field. I submitted the drafts to Robert Armstrong, who had immense experience of this process and always produced efficient and elegant results. This work mattered because the minutes had to record clearly the decisions the Cabinet had taken. Sometimes the Prime Minister did not actually sum up at the end of a discussion or state directly what decisions were being made. The minutes then had to state the conclusions and decisions which the Prime Minister had obviously intended although she had not actually said so, and to say which department of government was to take action on each decision. In my time the minutes of Cabinet meetings were never challenged by a minister.

My staff were responsible for the operation of the Cabinet Office Briefing Room, known as COBR, pronounced cobra, which was the government's headquarters for managing crises. I was involved in meetings about various sorts of crisis. I was also much involved in exercises in COBR to practise and test the government's decision-making procedures and communications in a major crisis. This was usually a simulation of an international crisis which culminates in a decision by the Prime Minister on whether the UK should use nuclear weapons. My strange role was to play the Prime Minister as she chairs meetings through days of mounting crisis and ultimately must decide the terrible nuclear question.

Mrs Thatcher did not make as much use of ministerial committees of the Cabinet as some prime ministers have done. I therefore had less work on this front than some of my predecessors. Another function, too, was less active than usual: advising the Prime Minister on policy on the subjects I was covering. The main reason for this was that Charles Powell, the Prime Minister's Private Secretary for foreign affairs, was extremely influential and effective.

I did lead the production of some long-term policy papers. For instance, in May 1986 I chaired a group of officials who produced for the Cabinet a paper on the future of South Africa after apartheid. It is interesting that the senior officials from the ministries concerned with South Africa came up with an assessment which turned out to be too pessimistic, for we saw only a 5% chance of a peaceful transition to black majority rule, which of course was the best outcome and the one that actually came about in 1994. Mrs Thatcher and other ministers were influenced by this paper.

I also undertook particular policy projects, usually allocated to me by Robert Armstrong. The first of these came just after my arrival in the Cabinet Office.

The Anglo-Irish Agreement of 1985

The negotiations on an agreement between the UK and the Republic of Ireland on matters concerning Northern Ireland had begun some months before I joined them in April 1985. The agreement was signed on 15 November 1985. Between those dates this was my main activity.

The fundamental fact underlying the problem of Northern Ireland is that the Catholic community is the majority in the island of Ireland but is a minority in Northern Ireland, while the Protestant community is the majority in the north and a minority in Ireland as a whole. The Protestant majority in the north, represented by the Unionist parties, was totally determined to remain within the United Kingdom. The extreme nationalist Catholic organisation, the Irish Republican Army or IRA, was carrying out terrorist atrocities in Northern Ireland and in England and elsewhere.

The British aims in the Anglo-Irish negotiations were:

- to obtain greater cooperation from the Irish Republic in countering terrorism.
- by allowing the Irish Republic a consultative voice on certain fields of policy in Northern Ireland, to show the Catholics there that violence was not needed in order to make their views heard, and to reduce their bitterness in the face of their inability as a minority to win a share in power through elections.
- to show the United States that we were trying to achieve progress in Northern Ireland.
- to obtain the repeal of articles 2 and 3 of the Constitution of the Republic of Ireland which claimed that Northern Ireland was part of the Republic.

The Republic of Ireland wanted:

- an Anglo-Irish joint body with a say in decisions on economic and social policy in Northern Ireland.
- representation of the Catholic community, and participation of judges and police from the Republic, in the police and the courts in Northern Ireland.

The UK was not willing to concede joint authority in Northern Ireland or participation by the Irish Republic in decision-making there. The Irish Republic was not willing to remove articles 2 and 3 of its Constitution. But the Agreement, quoted below, had very satisfactory provisions on the future of Northern Ireland.

I had never worked on the Irish question. Robert Armstrong included me in the British negotiating team to help him in the work, especially drafting the planned agreement and his reports to the Prime Minister after each session of the negotiations. It was difficult for me to work on a new step in Irish affairs without knowledge of the long history which deeply influences the relationship between England and Ireland today. I did a good deal of background reading but all through the negotiation I felt that I was a beginner in a complicated subject; which indeed I was.

The Irish team in the negotiations were talented and dedicated officials. Dermot Nally, head of the delegation, and Michael Lillis stood out as exceptionally thoughtful and impressive. The atmosphere in the negotiations was positive and all of us wanted if possible to reach a useful agreement. This was an achievement in itself, given the bitterness of the relationship between London and Dublin in many periods past. On our side Robert Armstrong was a wise and determined leader. I was also impressed by David Goodall. He had been my predecessor in the Cabinet Office and was now a Deputy Under-Secretary in the Foreign Office. He played a leading role in conceiving the idea of the negotiation and throughout the negotiations themselves. I think that Robert Armstrong and David Goodall both cared personally about doing something positive for the relationship between the UK and Ireland and for Northern Ireland, after London's sometimes callous behaviour in the past.

The Prime Minister's instincts were Unionist. Her Methodist background was one reason. The IRA attacks on Unionists were another important one. She had herself survived an assassination attempt by the IRA, in the Brighton bombing the previous year.

The Anglo-Irish agreement was a highly unusual, imaginative and even daring idea: a neighbouring country was given by treaty an advisory say on some areas of policy in part of the United Kingdom. I think this was far out of line with Mrs Thatcher's feelings as a British patriot. But she wanted to make progress in Northern Ireland, especially in combatting terrorism. Other ways of achieving this had not borne fruit. She listened to the advice of one or two ministers and of Robert Armstrong. She authorised the attempt to negotiate and then our positions all through the negotiations. She was in control.

It was a help that Mrs Thatcher liked Garret FitzGerald, her Irish opposite number. I think she found him attractive. I met him several times during the negotiations, including one long private conversation. I found him clever and approachable: and obviously a good man.

A major feature of the Agreement concerned the future of Northern Ireland. The UK and the Irish Republic agreed

> ...to affirm that any change in the status of Northern Ireland would only come about with the consent of a majority of the people of Northern Ireland; to recognise that the present wish of a majority of the people of Northern Ireland is for no change in the status of Northern Ireland; to declare that, if in the future a majority of the people of Northern Ireland clearly wish for and formally consent to the establishment of a united Ireland, they will introduce and support in the respective parliaments legislation to give effect to that wish.

So the Irish Republic recognised that Northern Ireland wished to remain in the United Kingdom and the British said that they would accept the creation of a united Ireland if a majority of the people in the North one day wanted this.

In the preamble at the start of the agreement there were some important points. The two governments recognised

> ...the need for continuing efforts to reconcile and to acknowledge the rights of the two major traditions that exist in Ireland, represented on the one hand by those who wish for no change in the present status of Northern Ireland and on the other hand by those who aspire to a sovereign united Ireland achieved by peaceful means and through agreement. [The two governments reaffirmed] their total rejection of any attempts to promote political objectives by violence or the threat of violence and their determination to work together to ensure that those who adopt or support such methods do not succeed.

The Agreement set up a British-Irish Intergovernmental Conference for regular discussion of political matters, security matters, legal matters including the administration of justice; and the promotion of cross-border co-operation. This meant consultation, not joint decisions. The United Kingdom Government accepted that the Irish Government would put forward views and proposals on matters relating to Northern Ireland within the field of activity of the Conference 'in so far as those matters are not the responsibility of a devolved administration in Northern Ireland'. This last clause meant that if any of these matters were devolved to a government in Northern Ireland which had widespread acceptance in the community, discussion of them in the Intergovernmental Conference would cease.

The Agreement was not revealed to the Unionists in Northern Ireland until the last moment. The reason was that the Unionists, when informed of the previous major attempt to make progress on the subject of Northern Ireland, had destroyed that agreement. The decision not to inform the Unionists this time was risky and controversial; Margaret Thatcher was convinced that no other course was possible.

When the agreement was discussed in Cabinet before it was concluded, one senior minister expressed grave doubts. But there were no resignations at that level. Ian Gow, the Prime Minister's former Parliamentary Private Secretary and now a minister at the Treasury, did resign. The IRA saw him as an enemy. Tragically, he was assassinated in 1990.

The Agreement probably dented the assumption of the Unionists that they could always call the tune in dealing with the British Government about Northern Ireland. It began the decline of America's ignorant sympathy for the IRA and blindness to its frequent use of terror. It improved relations between London and Dublin. The result for cooperation with the Irish Republic in combatting terrorism, which for the Prime Minister was the main aim of the whole negotiation, was disappointing.

In the Agreement each side obtained much less than it had wanted. It was the most that the two could agree on at that time. The Agreement was a significant event. It was a brave innovation by Margaret Thatcher. It paved the way towards the far more important agreements about Northern Ireland in the next few years. For me it was a privilege to be involved in a successful attempt to make progress on an intractable problem that was to contribute to later agreements which brought a halt to violence.

Security Matters

Another function of the Cabinet Office was to coordinate the work of the intelligence services and the use by government of the information they produced. When the government learned of the intention of Peter Wright, a former member of the Security Service, to publish a book about his alleged exploits in that secret work, the coordination of the Government's response fell to the Cabinet Office. Robert Armstrong asked me to undertake this work.

Before leaving the Cabinet Office that evening I asked our archivist to send me the files about past cases of public servants publishing books about their work. The archivist had a sense of humour: the file on top of the pile on my desk the next morning was entitled 'The Mallaby Affair'. It was about my uncle, Sir George Mallaby, who in 1965 had published a book called *From My Level*, which consisted of pen portraits of ministers, civil servants and others with whom he had worked as a senior official. This book was considered by some to be inappropriate, on the grounds that retired officials should not publish opinions about their former political masters. It contained no confidential information and I assume it was not thought to be a breach of security. The then head of the Civil Service issued an instruction that certain officials working closely with ministers should not keep diaries. That must be one of the most unenforceable instructions in the history of the public service.

On retirement after a long but not distinguished career in the Security Service, Peter Wright had been furious about what he regarded as an inadequate pension. He may have written *Spycatcher* as revenge. He was obsessed by various far-fetched theories about Soviet spies in high places in the British Government. One of his theories was that Sir Roger Hollis, a former Director General of the Security Service, had been a Soviet spy. A high-level enquiry had concluded that there was no evidence that Hollis had been a spy. Wright also alleged that Prime Minister Harold Wilson had been a spy, an idea which was never credible.

Wright prepared to publish *Spycatcher* in Australia, where he was living in retirement. The British Government applied to the courts in Sydney to ban publication. The Australian Courts ruled against the British Government. The legal proceedings in Australia, where Robert Armstrong spoke for the UK government, stimulated wide interest in the book, and it sold in large numbers.

I spent many hours with the Security Service and Government lawyers, working on points raised in the court in Sydney and preparing material for Robert, with whom I spoke every evening. Ministers were interested and involved, and the media were avid with curiosity.

When the Government went to court in London to block publication in Britain, I thought there was no chance of success because copies of *Spycatcher* were by then arriving from Australia in travellers' luggage and an injunction to prevent publication would not have prevented availability of the book. But the Government had one valuable success. The English courts upheld the duty of confidentiality on the part of public servants. So we won on the principle but lost the specific case against *Spycatcher*.

After that episode, the Government decided to review the Official Secrets Act, to see whether it could be made less strict on some matters and more effective on matters arising from the *Spycatcher* case. Robert Armstrong chaired a committee of Permanent Secretaries to consider this. I supported him in that work, drafting papers and making suggestions. By the time I left the Cabinet Office in 1988, the scope of the changes we would want in the Official Secrets Act was clear. The amended Act was passed in the following year.

I shall not attempt here to explain every change made in the Act in 1989. Briefly, we narrowed the scope of the previous offence of wrongful disclosure. We defined more clearly the obligations of government employees. We chose just six categories of information which must not be disclosed without permission. These included security and intelligence, defence and international relations. The 1989 Act gave definitions of damaging disclosure for each of the six types of information. It placed certain obligations on former public servants. And it said that people outside government may not disclose information received from a public servant who did not have permission to disclose it.

I learned from these experiences of intelligence matters. The work was necessary, but I did not enjoy it.

I greatly enjoyed other aspects of my work in the Cabinet Office. Especially working closely with Robert Armstrong, who is one of the wisest, most impressive and most considerate colleagues I have known. I was also glad to have come to know many of the ministers in Mrs Thatcher's Government and to have worked often with the Prime Minister. That experience was valuable when I resumed my diplomatic career as Ambassador in Germany and then in France.

13

GERMANY BEFORE THE TRANSFORMATION

Pascale and I moved to Bonn in March 1988. We stayed nearly five years. I found that I could be more effective each year, with growing experience and contacts, and I was glad to remain that long.

I was appointed Ambassador to the Federal Republic of Germany – West Germany. In 1990, about halfway through our time, East and West Germany were unified and I became Ambassador to united Germany. So I was the last British Ambassador to West Germany and the first to united Germany.

The Ambassador's Work
After I left the FCO, my grandchildren pursued me with questions about what diplomats really do. They had a point: many people have only the vaguest idea of the work of Ambassadors. Many may doubt that the work justifies the costs of diplomacy to the taxpayer. So what did I do in Germany?

A British Ambassador's purpose in life is to advance British interests and win support for British policies. That's what the salary is for. As Ambassador in Germany you must ensure that the German government understands the British position on all subjects that interest both; and do all you can to influence German policy on these matters. You must know everything significant that is happening in Germany, in politics, the economy, business and other important fields. You must help British firms to sell in

Germany; and must promote cooperation, for instance cultural or scientific or academic, between the two countries where that will do good for British interests.

An Ambassador must satisfy several markets. First of all, the British Government which is your employer. That means not only the FCO but also the many other government departments which the embassy serves. Secondly, you must lead and motivate the staff. Each plays a necessary part in the operations of the embassy. So ensuring that they are happy and work hard is a high priority. The third market that the Ambassador must impress is the German people of influence: in politics of course, and the people who matter in many other fields in Germany, not only in the capital but in the other cities. This is a big task. You must know the regional governments, the leaders of industry and banking and the main figures in the media. That means a great deal of travel across Germany, often several days a week.

The parties and the public functions which the Ambassador attends are an instrument in this work. Since they are frequent, it is important to keep the alcohol intake occasional and low, if you want to stay healthy and avoid the awful fate of laying down your liver for your country. These events are not particularly amusing, but they are useful. In surroundings more relaxed than an office, a chat with a minister or other decision-maker enables you to get to know them better, and that will make it easier to cooperate with them and to try to influence them in future. For instance, when you've had a drink and a laugh with someone, you feel more free to telephone them on urgent business at uncivilised times like evenings and weekends. Conversations at receptions often provide the opportunity to explain a British point of view to one of the German decision-makers, or to ask questions which will help the embassy to understand the reasons behind a German policy.

My diary for 1988 shows that I worked on average 72 hours a week. This number was to increase greatly when German unification came into sight in 1989. In 1988 over half my working hours were spent on office work, and 20% at parties including the many we hosted. The next largest activity was meetings with German ministries and politicians; then calls on firms and contacts with the press.

For example, in the second week of January 1989, some of the things I did were:

One-on-one business meeting with the Federal Chancellor's Diplomatic Adviser

Meeting with the German Deputy Minister of Defence to rebut public complaints about the noise made by aircraft of the Royal Air Force stationed in Germany

Three meetings with German journalists including one long on-the-record interview

Dinner given by the German Foreign Minister for the departing US Ambassador

New Year reception given by the German President

Reception given by the German Defence Minister

Lecture on the Thatcher government's policies to the training school of the German Diplomatic Service

Lecture to the Bonn Rotary Club on 'Britain as a partner for Germany'

A light-hearted speech to the German Cambridge Society.

A typical week-day in Bonn in 1988 would go like this. After reading the German newspapers, my first event would be breakfast with a German politician or senior journalist, to advocate British policies and to obtain information and hear expert opinions, so as to understand German policies and politics more thoroughly. Then I would be driven to the embassy, working on papers or by telephone, as I always did when travelling by road or rail. On arrival at the embassy offices, I check the arrangements in my programme for the day, dictate to a secretary an account of key points from my discussion at breakfast, and then scan the FCO telegrams which have come in overnight. There might be 60 telegrams to scan, comprising some 90 pages, about half requiring a careful read. Some would be instructions from the FCO for the embassy to raise a particular matter with the German government and deploy particular arguments. Many of these instructions concern matters in discussion in the European Community.

In taking action on these instructions, the ideal technique, if there is time, is to talk first to the German ministries which are most likely to agree with the British position. We can then take account of their views when we speak to the ministries which we think we might be able to persuade. We speak last to the ministries least likely to agree with us. If we can win the agreement of most German ministries, the ones least likely to accept our views may be influenced towards us by the risk of isolation in the government. This is a laborious process requiring tact and care, which we adapt case by case. It is designed to give us the best chance of persuading Germany to agree with us, but it is not certain to work.

Some of the telegrams we receive are reports from other British embassies, mainly in Europe, about the policy of those governments on subjects which my embassy is also handling. Some are reports sent the previous afternoon by my own embassy; a few of these I have written or approved but most have been sent without my direct involvement.

At 9.45 comes the embassy's morning meeting, known irreverently as Morning Prayers, which lasts about half an hour. I chair it twice a week. The regular participants are mainly the heads of the sections which comprise the embassy. They are an able and dedicated team, all contributing to the performance of the embassy and of the Ambassador. The meeting decides who among the staff will deal with the various instructions received that morning from London. I take action on some of these. The meeting discusses the main events of the previous day in Germany and the main stories and commentaries in that morning's German press, which everyone is expected to have scanned beforehand. The meeting decides what reports we should send to London that day or prepare for sending in the coming days.

The mention of instructions about matters in discussion in the European Community exemplifies a difference between the diplomacy of the UK compared to Germany and France at the time I was in Bonn and Paris. We used our bilateral embassies in Europe to put British views to governments. To make this possible, our embassies were kept informed of the myriad details of daily negotiations in Brussels. French and German Ambassadors were not kept informed in detail and therefore could not discuss such subjects in an operational way with governments.

My embassy would find out or deduce which aspects of a particular issue mattered most to Germany. We might then report that for political reasons Germany had no room for compromise on such and such points, while on such and such others Germany could give ground. Whenever possible we would suggest to London an arrangement which would suit both Britain and Germany.

Morning Prayers having set the scene for the day, the Ambassador spends the bulk of the morning in two or three meetings and on desk work in the office. One of the meetings might be with a visitor from Britain – perhaps an industrialist or banker who wants advice about the state of the German economy or likely decisions by the German government. Another would be a call on a German minister, to conduct specific business on FCO instructions. A third might be an internal embassy meeting to decide how to handle a new issue or to review the draft of some major report in preparation.

At lunch, the Ambassador talks business. You might give a lunch for the British journalists in Bonn, to brief them on your current preoccupations and purposes and hear their comments on developments in Germany. Or you might host a lunch for a visiting British delegation from government or business or the Trades Unions, with German guests from the same field of activity. Or you might lunch one-on-one with a German politician or industrialist, a senior official or the editor of one of the newspapers, or a television commentator on international affairs. In the afternoon, your programme will be like the morning's – several meetings and office work between. In the early evening, the Ambassador may attend a reception or give one for a British company seeking to expand its sales in Germany or for a visiting British minister or a delegation of MPs. Later, you may give a dinner for a similar purpose, when you will make a short speech. Or you may give a full length, 40-minute speech in German in Bonn or further away, or a television interview to explain British policy on whatever subject is active on that day.

When all that is over, around 1030 or 11 pm, you go through at home the papers in your overnight box of work. Reading the papers, taking decisions and writing instructions should be done by midnight.

As Douglas Hurd wrote in his memoirs 'The pell-mell of modern diplomacy has to be lived through to be understood.'[*]

* * * * *

I had a special role, shared with the American and French Ambassadors in Bonn. These three allies and the Soviet Union, as victors in the war, had Reserved Rights and Responsibilities in relation to the so-called German Question and Berlin. The German Question was the question of Germany's ultimate shape and status – whether the country should remain divided or be reunified and where its final frontiers would be. These Reserved Rights in effect were limitations on the sovereignty of the two German states, pending solution of the German Question. The three Western Ambassadors in Bonn and the Soviet Ambassador in East Berlin were responsible for any work which needed doing in the field of the Reserved Rights and Responsibilities. The German Question did not involve much work until change started in East Germany; and then unification came into sight, when it dominated my life for a year.

My responsibility relating to Berlin brought much enjoyable activity. The elected City Government, which ran the affairs of West Berlin, liked the Allied presence there to be visible, as a reassurance to Berliners that their security was not in danger despite the isolation of the city. I was glad to go often to Berlin, making speeches and appearing on public occasions.

I supervised the work of our Mission in Berlin, which was similar to the work I was involved in when Pascale and I lived there in the late 1960s, described in Chapter 4. I kept in close touch with the city authorities. The Generals who successively commanded the British garrison, Patrick Brooking and Robert Corbett, were impressive and helpful and I saw them often. Our team of diplomats was ably led by my friend Michael Burton. As in the 1960s, the US, the UK and France were careful to ensure that the post-war status of Berlin was not undermined by current developments, for it was the legal basis of our military presence.

---

[*] Douglas Hurd, *Memoirs*, Little, Brown 2003, page 377.

This was still a crucial part of western policy in the Cold War, because the Allies' military presence made it impossible for the Soviet Union to attack West Berlin without risking a world war.

The responsibilities of the three western Allies in Berlin concerned mainly the efficient operation of air, road and waterway travel between West Germany and West Berlin across East Germany, on which we were always ready to intervene with the Soviet Embassy in East Berlin if there were difficulties. We also discussed with the West Berlin government the city's relations with East Germany and East Berlin. The Allies still became involved in dealing with any dispute or incident between West Berlin and East Germany, including the tragically frequent shootings at the Wall of East Germans trying to escape to the west.

*****

I had spent two and a half years in the Bonn Embassy in the early eighties, as the Ambassador's deputy for political affairs. I therefore knew the politics of the Federal Republic well and many of the personalities, including the Federal Chancellor, Helmut Kohl, and the Foreign Minister, Hans-Dietrich Genscher.

So the learning curve for my work as Ambassador, beginning only three years later, was already behind me when I arrived in 1988. The events of my first stay had included the creation of the coalition government of the CDU-CSU on the centre–right of politics and the Liberal FDP, a coalition which continued in office beyond my time as Ambassador. I had also experienced the bitter controversy in Germany about the stationing there of US medium-range nuclear missiles, which Kohl, like the British Government, considered necessary for the maintenance of NATO's deterrence of the use of force or the threat of force by the Soviet Union. In a demonstration of political will, Kohl had led the government and parliament to agree that the missiles be stationed in the Federal Republic. I had also observed the emergence of the Green Party as a force in politics and had got to know several of the leaders.

During our stay in Bonn in the early 1980s I had also learned to understand a subject which till then I had found puzzling. I had sometimes thought that the Bonn government was too generous in providing funds to East Germany, thus easing the difficulties of the communist regime. In a series of fascinating conversations with Hermann von Richthofen, then in the Federal Chancellor's Office, I learned about the motives and the interests of West Germany in sometimes dealing generously with East Germany.

West Germany had been engaged since 1969 in an innovative and important policy of increasing contacts with the communist countries in Eastern Europe. Bonn wanted to include East Germany in this Eastern Policy or *Ostpolitik*. One consideration was that the Germans in the East were still suffering as a result of Nazism and the war, because the Soviet occupation of the area had prevented the prosperity and the freedom which West Germany had since enjoyed for decades. The use of West German money to alleviate the difficulties of life for East Germans was seen as a moral duty, and concessions which would ease the lives of East Germans in other ways could be obtained from the regime in return for the financial support. The East German public learned from West German television that the West Germans were helping them. The attitudes of East Germans, when change began in 1989, were surely influenced by this background. There were also advantages for Bonn in making the East German regime dependant to some extent on West German funds.

Hermann von Richthofen was later German Ambassador in London, when I was Ambassador in Bonn. He and Christa and Pascale and I have been fond friends for over 30 years.

An Overdressed Ambassador among Ladies Déshabillées

I was told before leaving London that I would need a diplomatic uniform, because the British Army and Air Force in Germany would expect me to wear it at their military parades and other major events. I had never owned, or wanted to own, a diplomat's uniform. Indeed it had seemed to me to belong not in modern Britain but in Gilbert and Sullivan's comic opera, the Pirates of Penzance. I decided, now that I was said to need the uniform, to swallow my scruples and enjoy this new experience.

The FCO offered me an allowance to buy a new made-to-measure uniform. I thought money could be saved for the taxpayer if I could find a retiring Ambassador who would pass his uniform to me. Sir John Graham, who was about to retire as Ambassador at NATO, gave me his uniform, complete with cocked hat and ceremonial sword, as well as the dark blue tail coat and trousers with gold braid everywhere. It was not quite right for me in size. In fact, there was a conspicuous gap between the front of the tail coat and the top of the trousers. A tailor in Savile Row, the expert on diplomatic uniforms, told me that Johnny Graham's uniform could not be altered to fit. I suggested that the front of the tail coat should be extended downwards to meet the trousers. No, said the tailor; that would be obvious and ungainly. Then I suggested that the trousers should be extended upwards. The tailor said that my waist would then appear to be under my arm pits. I insisted and after an argument the tailor agreed to extend the tailcoat downwards and the trousers upwards to close the chasm.

My mother, as mothers will, wanted a photograph of me in this new finery. I looked in the telephone directory for photographers. The first three were horribly expensive. The fourth, which was in Pimlico, offered a better price. I travelled to Pimlico by Underground, carrying my uniform complete with sword in a bag. As I went down the escalator at Green Park Underground, the sword slipped out of its scabbard and clattered down the escalator in front of me. I knew something about the counter-terrorism legislation in force in Britain and that brandishing a sword on the Underground would certainly be illegal. I galloped after the sword and caught it before the bottom of the escalator. I arrived at the photographer's studio feeling hot and bothered.

I was shown into a cubicle to change into the uniform. I had never before undertaken this complicated process, and there was a risk that I might put buttons into the wrong holes or attach a gold braid cord in the wrong way. A few minutes after I started I looked up and saw that the photographs by this photographer displayed on the walls were all of naked ladies. I was taken aback but decided to complete the job rather than creeping away and finding another photographer. The photographs were satisfactory and my mother displayed one in her apartment at Hampton Court until she died. What I never discovered was whether the photographer added to his nude display one example of his art which did not show a naked lady.

I wore the uniform for the ceremony when I presented to the Federal President my credentials as Ambassador in West Germany; and for several parades of the British forces in Germany each year. As Ambassador in France, my next and final diplomatic job, I wore it only occasionally.

Daily Life

Our official residence in Bonn was a large villa in art nouveau style, beside the Rhine in Bad Godesberg. The interior was light and airy and we had spectacular views over the river. The muffled chug of barges going north and south was soothing and agreeable. We had a terrace beside the river, where I amused myself by training the wisteria to frame the view. There were good walks along the Rhine in both directions and in the hills on the other side.

A British Army Colonel, who came to stay, evidently wished to let us know during breakfast that he had recognised the style of architecture. He declared, 'What a lovely house, my favourite style – typical nouveau riche.'

Security was a major concern. We knew that the Irish Republican Army (IRA) were interested in me as a target for assassination. Two or three times we were warned by our security people that the IRA might be planning an attack for the coming weekend. There was only one way to approach our house by car, a winding village lane where a terrorist could have hidden or a bomb been planted. When we were warned, we went away for the weekend, sometimes to Pascale's family in Paris.

Our protection against a terrorist attack included security guards at our house and bullet-proof windows and alarm systems. I had three young German policemen as bodyguards, who usually carried their guns conspicuously. It was a peculiar experience to be followed by armed bodyguards through the exhibitions of contemporary art which we liked to visit. They were nonplussed by the art, tried to look interested and only looked miserably embarrassed.

Another awkward situation arose when I went fishing for trout in the River Ahr, an hour from home. There are many stories of fly-fishermen hooking not trout but trees or even cows by mistake. The first time I went fishing with the bodyguards, I waded in my long boots to the middle of the small river and started casting a trout fly upstream. The policemen lumbered into the water without boots, got soaked to the waist and took up position behind me. When I realised where they were, I stopped fishing and pointed out to them that my trout fly, as I propelled it backwards in the air in order to cast forwards, might well catch them in the face. We splashed our way to the river bank and negotiated an arrangement: they agreed that I should go fishing without them, on several tedious conditions. I should never use my own car or an embassy car. I should never fish at weekends, the obvious time for terrorists to think I would be at the river. The police were doing their duty, to ensure that the danger of a terrorist attack was reduced as far as possible. Our arrangement was a nuisance for me, but well worth it because I got my fishing and there were no terrorist attacks.

The bodyguards were sometimes helpful in unexpected ways. Once Pascale and I went with Julia and Charlotte to the opera in Cologne. When we reached the theatre, I realised that I had forgotten to bring our tickets. Since our policemen always sat behind us in theatres and cinemas, I knew that our four empty seats would be just in front of theirs. Problem solved!

Another security precaution was that I always had seat 1A on flights. The crew were trained to keep an eye on the person sitting there. One weekend in 1988, I attended a small meeting called by Geoffrey Howe, the Foreign Secretary, at his official country house, Chevening in Kent. On the Sunday afternoon I went to Gatwick Airport to fly back to Bonn. In the departure lounge I bought several bulky Sunday papers. I spread them out on a table and began to read. When my flight was called, I scooped up this pile and went on board. Sitting in seat 1A, I found a luridly conspicuous porn magazine among the newsprint. How it got there I never knew. I thought I'd simply leave it under my seat, but the crew would have realised that it had been left there by the British Ambassador. I took it home to Bonn, for disposal there. Hopeless! The cleaner next morning would have found it in the bin in my study. Same problem with disposing of this awful publication in my office at the embassy. On Monday evening, desperate to be rid of this embarrassment, I took the magazine furtively under my jacket to the Kenyan Ambassador's reception, in a restaurant, for his country's National Day. I asked my bodyguards to wait outside the Gents, and binned the offending magazine there. Relief!

* * * * *

Pascale's and my visits to Berlin, staying in our charming house in the Grünewald forest, were welcome as a contrast to life in Bonn. Bonn was the site of government and Parliament and the main theatre of German politics, and therefore vastly important in my work. Berlin is an exciting city full of things to see and do. It was a pleasure for Pascale and me to spend time there again, and it reminded us of our happy period there twenty years earlier.

Sebastian and Emily, when on holiday from their work or studies in England, often came to stay with us. They especially enjoyed West Berlin, which for us had the unique interest of being an island of democracy within communist Europe. We visited East Berlin, the seat of government of East Germany. It was dull and drab but less so than Moscow at that time; and there were world-class museums.

When we arrived in Germany, Sebastian was 23 and had begun his work as a journalist at *The Economist* in London. Emily, now 20, was at Royal Holloway College, London University, enjoying her study of French literature under a brilliant professor. Julia at 16 was at school at Bryanston and was soon to go to university at Oxford. Charlotte was 15 and was soon to move from St George's School at Ascot to Bryanston. Sebastian, then Emily, got married in England while we were in Germany. Each invited the future spouse to stay with us in Berlin.

* * * * *

As Ambassador I maintained close contact with the Commanders in Chief of the British Army and the Royal Air Force in West Germany, and the embassy advised them on their relations with German authorities, from the Federal Government to local mayors; for instance, on environmental matters, especially complaints from local communities about our military exercises or the noise made by our aircraft flying over Germany. This flying was part of the training of the Royal Air Force pilots and thus of our arrangements for deterring Soviet aggression; in explaining this to Germans I called it the Sound of Freedom.

Many of our soldiers in Germany went away for a few weeks to fight in the expulsion of Saddam Hussein's invaders from Kuwait in 1990. There was a full programme of events to comfort and occupy the soldiers' wives, who remained in Germany. My role in this was to chat with the German wives of British soldiers, some of them very young. I asked one group whether things were okay for them. They beamed and said all was fine, and several said joyfully '*Wir haben die Lady Di gesehen*'. We have seen Lady Di, with Di pronounced Dee. I told the Princess of Wales that her meeting with a group of young German wives had made them happy even when their husbands were away fighting.

* * * * *

In the many public speeches I made in Germany, European affairs were a frequent theme. When the Maastricht agreement was being negotiated I thought that the British objections to a single currency were unanswerable. How could it be sensible to have a single currency with one interest rate and one exchange rate for countries with different levels of development and rates of growth? How could a low interest rate that suited a country which needed to boost growth be right also for a country which was growing fast and faced the risk of inflation? I often explained these criticisms in my speeches. Business audiences understood my strictures, but some others, including politicians enthusiastic about the EU, did not want to know about economic objections; they wanted the single currency because they wanted progress in building a united Europe. (At this time the Federal Government had doubts about the single currency and the Bundesbank was dead against it. Mitterrand later persuaded Kohl to commit to it, in return for French agreement to German unification, as described below.)

A Major Analysis, Soon Overtaken by Events
In April 1989, I sent the FCO a comprehensive assessment of West Germany as an ally. Much of this was about the German Question.

I began by saying that it would be hard to find any responsible observer, German or foreign, in West Germany who saw any prospect of the Federal Republic leaving the NATO Alliance or of an early move to achieve unification.

I sketched out in this report some of the history of the unification question. The aim of unification was written into the Constitutional Law when the West German Federal Republic was formed in 1949, but the implication was that it was a long-term objective. A strong, democratic Federal Republic, profiting from the western connection, would meanwhile be better able to influence the question of Germany's future. That remained the general view. Opinion polls showed that a majority, even among the young, still thought of the Germans as one people. But in 1987, 72% of West Germans were found not to expect unification in the foreseeable future. It was still an aspiration of many people, but definitely not a policy.

I continued that the Federal Republic was the one successful democracy in German history, and had by now achieved security and peace for a period longer than the tragic stretch from 1914 to 1945. It had achieved great prosperity, building Europe's largest and the world's third largest economy. It had gained self-respect and much international respect.

That despatch described accurately the scene and the general view in West Germany in spring 1989. Change was underway in Poland but the dramatic and immensely positive changes in Germany and the rest of central Europe that lay ahead were not then in sight. My despatch, like the views of Germany's politicians and the media, was rapidly overtaken by events.

Change in East Germany

Within weeks, we in the Embassy in Bonn were reporting to the FCO on the likely effects on the Communist regime in East Germany, and on Germany as a whole, of the changes that had now begun in some other communist countries in Europe. The great transformation was beginning. It was a privilege for me, as well as very rewarding, to be there at this important time, when Germany was unified and the Cold War ended and with it the Soviet threat to Britain and the western world.

Our assessment in the embassy was that East Germany was bound to change. How could change be avoided, with democratic reform taking place among East Germany's eastern neighbours and even the USSR itself changing under Gorbachev? Not to speak of the magnetic attraction of the tremendously successful, bigger Germany next door and West Berlin flourishing in the middle of East Germany. We also foresaw that when reform started, it might go very fast, since the East German regime would have no reason to exist once Marxism-Leninism, which had always been the justification for this separate German state, was discredited as a total failure.

On 11 September 1989 I wrote to the FCO that discussion of the German Question had welled up in West Germany. The reasons included the democratic change in Poland and Hungary and the wave of emigrants from East to West Germany and the drama of the escapes by East Germans through Hungary. Marxism-Leninism had lost all credibility. You could see why Germans were asking themselves whether this rapid change could bring reform in East Germany; and whether it could even make reunification or some kind of federation possible one day. Reunification was still only a hope but there was suddenly more interest in it and people were beginning to wonder whether it could become more than a hope. Politicians and experts did not expect it to become a goal of active policy in the foreseeable future.

At this point the official West German view of the situation in East Germany saw growing public frustration there but the regime's policy set against reform. Almost all West German politicians saw little chance of change in that situation, or of major disruption of public order, for several years. There was disagreement about the wishes of East Germans for the future. The current rush of emigration was proof that the East Germans wanted to live like the West Germans. Some in Bonn deduced from this that the East Germans wanted unification. Others thought that the East Germans would prefer a system retaining some characteristics – for instance no giant private firms – of their present system and for the foreseeable future a separate East German state. No-one now saw any chance that unification, if it did come one day, would be on any basis other than Western democracy.

There were many demonstrations in East Germany. In one in Leipzig on 9 October there were probably 100,000 people on the streets, marching peaceably. Armed police and other security personnel, perhaps 10,000 of them, were standing by for action against the demonstration, if the order was given. The local party leader in charge tried to get a decision on whether to use force from the party leadership in Berlin. Having got no reply, he ordered the security forces to use force only defensively. This meant that force would not be used to halt or break up the demonstration. The bosses in East Berlin had chosen not to authorise the use of force against this vast demonstration. The fate of Communist East Germany was probably sealed that day.

The change in East Germany accelerated over the next two months. In the most important countries in Eastern Europe, the Soviet grip was loosening and in Poland democracy was already victorious. In a speech in Strasbourg on 6 July Gorbachev said that interference in the internal affairs of allies or any country was impermissible. Gorbachev meant that change in the communist countries in Europe was their own affair and the Soviet Union would not intervene. This abolished the Brezhnev Doctrine. Gorbachev had told the leaders of the Warsaw Pact countries when he became Soviet party leader in March 1985 that this would henceforth be Soviet policy.

Gorbachev, when visiting East Berlin on 7–9 October, told the leaders of the communist parties, 'If a [communist] party pretends that nothing special is going on, if it does not react to the demands of reality, it is doomed.' He made the same point several times in different words. The Soviet leader was not only trying to reform the system in the USSR itself but was also encouraging change in the other communist countries in Europe.

The drama in Germany had begun. I wrote at length to the FCO on 8 November, describing the changing views in West Germany and suggesting British policy on the questions that lay ahead. Little did I know that the change was about to accelerate more dramatically than I or anyone could have imagined.

Above left: The author's father in 1935 on honeymoon.

Above right: The author and his father, 1938.

Below: The author and parents, 1938.

Above left: The author's mother and Antony and Sue, 1950.

Above right: The author and his grandfather, 1952.

Below: Antony and Sue at Camberley, 1952.

The author as a
2nd lieutenant in the 9th
Lancers, 1955.

Wedding, Paris, 16
September 1961.

Author on the frozen Moscow River, 1962.

Pascale on the frozen Moscow River, 1962.

Pascale and the
Cadillac, 1963.

Above: Kolya Karetnikov, Russian composer and friend of the author, 1991.

Right: Volodya Lindenberg, Russian-German physician and writer and friend of the author.

Below right: The children at Kuskovo near Moscow, 1975.

The interior of the Berlin house, 1989–92.

The Berlin house dining room.

The four ambassadors after their meeting in Berlin on 11.12.89. From left: Vernon Walters, USA; the author, UK; Vyacheslav Kochemassov, USSR; and Serge Boidevaix, France. (Courtesy of the PA Picture Alliance)

The view across the Rhine from our Bonn house, 1988–92.

The Bonn Embassy exterior, 1988–92.

Lord Carrington teasing the author.

Right: The author on the terrace of the Berlin house.

Below: The author and Chancellor Helmut Kohl, 1992. (Courtesy of Michael von Lingen)

Left: Charlotte on the Berlin Wall, 1990.

Below left: Emily, 1988.

Below right: Sebastian, 1993.

Right: Leaving for Paris through the unfinished Channel Tunnel, January 1993. (COI photograph licensed under the Open Government Licence version 2.0')

Below: The Embassy dining room, Paris, ready for our dinner for Mary Soames, 11 September 1993.

Backgammon with
Charlotte, Paris 1994.

Fiftieth anniversary
of the Allied landings
in southern France,
with US Ambassador
Pamela Harriman.

Charlotte, 1994, Paris.

With Simone Veil, French minister and politician, 1994.

The author and Pascale with writer and political figure Maurice Druon at his home near Saint Emilion.

The front of Paris
Embassy.

Reception in the Paris
Embassy garden.

The author and his daughter Julia in the
Paris Embassy in 1994.

Above left: The author speaking in Paris Embassy, 1995.

Above right: Granddaughter Sarah, Paris 1995.

Below: Farewell call on President Jacques Chirac, 3 July 1996.

Above: The author relaxing, 2007.

Left: Pascale, 2010.

14

THE FALL OF THE BERLIN WALL AND THE RUSH TO GERMAN UNITY; AN 'ALARMING' AMBASSADOR'S ACCOUNT

The Berlin Wall was opened the very next day, 9 November 1989, a great date in the history of freedom. It was also one of the most positive muddles in history, the result of confusion among the East German leaders, who were not clear about what they were deciding and did not keep each other informed.

The decision was important to the Soviet Union but it was not consulted. Moscow had only seen an earlier version of the new regulations on travel abroad by East Germans, which was much less radical and made no change regarding Berlin. The decision on 9 November was to allow people to leave for West Germany with less justification than before and less documentation. Schabowski, the member of the East German leadership who announced the decision in a disastrously inept press conference, was confused and visibly rattled. He kept pausing to squint at a note of the leadership's decision, which he had received only after his press conference began. Schabowski said that the new decision on freedom of travel applied to travel to West Berlin, but did not answer the final question, from Daniel Johnson of the *Daily Telegraph*, who asked whether the Wall itself was included.

Schabowski said that the decision would take effect immediately, although the leadership had decided to implement this huge change nine hours later, at 4am. He declared that East Germans would need permits to cross to the west. This meant that the authorities intended to decide who would be allowed to leave the country. But this critical point was never put into effect.

East Berliners rushed to the Bornholmerstrasse checkpoint at the Wall and other checkpoints. The frontier guards had no new instructions. The crowd of East Berliners built up fast. They became impatient and chanted 'Open the door' with increasing anger. The guards asked their bosses for authority to open the gate. The bosses declined. After further agonised hesitation the guards at Bornholmerstrasse opened the gate without authority at 11.30 pm. After going through, some people began immediately to dismantle parts of the Wall.

Some nine million East Germans visited West Berlin in the next seven days, more than half the number of the population. Most returned home, and this was a relief not only to the East German government but also to the West German authorities because difficulties over accommodating immigrants were looming.

In 1948, when Stalin blockaded west Berlin, the then Mayor, Ernst Reuter, made a passionate appeal for the world's attention: 'Ye peoples of the world, look upon this city.' Shock and sympathy were the world's reaction then. Now, 41 years later, the peoples again looked upon Berlin. Delight and celebration were the reaction this time. Television in many countries showed the scenes of joy as the Wall was opened and east Berliners swarmed through and then began to demolish that notorious instrument of totalitarian repression.

* * * * *

That evening in Bonn I came home from a meeting and Pascale told me the Wall was open. I was astonished, and jokingly asked her how many drinks she'd had. I telephoned Robert Corbett, the General commanding our garrison in Berlin, to get the latest news. He and I agreed that Pascale and I would come to Berlin as soon as possible.

We flew in a small British Army helicopter from Bonn to Berlin very early on 11 November 1989, about 33 hours after the Wall was opened. We wore heavy coats over our town clothes, which we would need for official engagements in Berlin later in the day. The flight, which we shared only with the army pilot, was noisy and uncomfortable but short.

It was dark and very cold when we landed beside the Berlin Wall on the western side. There were crowds of people. I assumed they would be westerners who, like us, had come to see history happening. It took me a few minutes to realise that most were East Germans. The mood seemed to be happiness and awe; there was no open excitement yet. Many easterners could not believe that this sudden change would last; they were far from confident that the Wall would remain open. I had about a dozen enjoyable conversations with East Germans. I asked several why they were spending their visit to West Berlin just walking along the western side of the Wall. The typical reply was 'seeing the Wall from this side makes me really believe that I am out.'

I am proud to say that the British Army in Berlin had set up a tea stand by the open Wall, so the first experience of East Germans, as they poured through to freedom, was a free cup of British army tea – strong, sweet and scalding – to help against the intense cold. The soldiers of the Royal Welch Fusiliers dished out the tea rapidly so that the queues of shivering East Berliners did not wait long.

* * * * *

From the Wall I was driven in a police car to the Town Hall of Schöneberg in West Berlin which was the office of the Governing Mayor, Walter Momper of the SPD, a roly-poly charmer whom I knew well. My local police driver, thrilled by the night's events, drove me at breakneck speed with siren screaming. We dashed across red lights galore. I too was exhilarated.

I was glad on this momentous day to revisit the Schöneberger Rathaus. I revelled in the contrast between the dramatic breakthrough now and the daily detail of Berlin business when I worked in that building in the late sixties as the British representative in the constant consultations between the western Allies and the city government (Chapter 4).

After my nerve-racking drive from the Wall, I was early for my meeting with Momper and the American and French Ambassadors from Bonn. So I joined a queue of East Germans who were waiting outside a bank for their 'welcome money'. Each was given DM 100, about £30, to spend while visiting West Berlin. I asked several neighbours in the queue what they would buy. The first answer was tropical fruit. On western television they had seen that bananas and tangerines were part of everyday life in West Germany and West Berlin. They were determined to enjoy this symbol of the higher standard of living in the West. The second thing that people said they were going to buy was toys. That surprised me because the toyshops of East Germany were rather well stocked, compared with other shops there. What this showed of course was that children in East Germany watched western television like their parents, and therefore knew and wanted the latest western toys. West German TV had a huge influence on public opinion in East Germany. The regime allowed the people to watch it, and even made the technical arrangements to ensure that it was received in areas where reception would otherwise have been difficult. The communists did this because they thought western TV helped to keep the people content. This was a naïve miscalculation, for the people realised more and more that their standard of living was well below that of West Germany.

While I was waiting in the Mayor's anteroom for our meeting to begin, Schabowski of the East German communist leadership, who had made the inept announcement of the opening of the Wall, telephoned Momper to say that two or three members of the newly appointed leadership of the communist party had resigned because they disagreed with the decision not to use force against demonstrations. Momper relayed this to me with a big smile. This news was an extremely welcome indication that the police and the East German army would not resort to force. We also thought it improbable that the Soviet forces in East Germany (which at 380,000 were larger than United States Forces in all Europe) would use force against demonstrations. Then on 10 November, the day after the Wall was opened, Gorbachev, in a gesture which no earlier Soviet leader would have dreamt of making, welcomed the opening of the Wall and told the US that he wanted a peaceful transition. This confirmed that the change in Germany was likely to be achieved without bloodshed.

The meeting of the three Ambassadors with Momper was full of satisfaction. The Mayor was calm. The main theme was the prospects in East Germany. He listened to our comments, which were tentative; like everyone else we had more questions than answers. My own view at this early point in the great story now beginning was that the fall of the Wall made real change in East Germany inevitable. The division of Germany and Berlin would now erode in daily life as contacts multiplied.

That evening Pascale and I travelled through the Wall to East Berlin. At Checkpoint Charlie my official car was checked as usual by Soviet soldiers. This felt amusingly incongruous: hordes of East Berliners were streaming back after a day in West Berlin and were not controlled because they were far too numerous for the frontier police to check.

We then went to a concert in the British Embassy in East Berlin, where we were to meet some of the church leaders and others who were critics of the East German regime. That was the first time I met Manfred Stolpe, a senior official of the Evangelical Church in East Germany, who after unification was to become Prime Minster of Brandenburg, the region round Berlin, and Transport Minister in the German Government. He told me much later that he and other opponents of the regime greatly valued the concerts at the British Embassy in East Berlin, because the music masked their conversations and they could confer together without being overheard by Stasi microphones. That was an accolade for Nigel Broomfield, our Ambassador, whose concerts had aided the democratic opposition against the dictatorship.

On my return to Bonn I telephoned Charles Powell, the Prime Minister's Private Secretary, and then Stephen Wall, Private Secretary to Douglas Hurd. I suggested to Powell that the Prime Minister might enjoy a visit to Berlin to see history and freedom in the making. Powell said Mrs Thatcher could not come, without explaining why. The Foreign Secretary agreed to come as soon as possible. His aim, I think, was to see what was happening at first hand and to show Britain's sympathy with the reformers in East Germany.

Douglas was anyway visiting Bonn on 15 November, and we went on to Berlin the next day. I warned him that there would be throngs of journalists, for he was the first Western Minister to visit Berlin since the opening of the Wall. As we got out of the car on Potsdamer Platz, journalists surrounded the Foreign Secretary, perhaps eight deep on all sides. They formed a tight block of people like a massive rugby scrum, which moved quickly eastwards and through the checkpoint at the Wall into East Berlin. Douglas Hurd escaped from the scrum of journalists and cameras, shook hands with an East German border guard and returned to West Berlin. This incident was both moving and comic. Douglas reported to the Prime Minister that the role of the Western allies continued to provide a sense of stability in West Berlin. The Berliners were glad of this reassurance in the rush of change.

* * * * *

I focussed now on the role I should play as the process of change accelerated. As well as reporting events and prospects in Germany, I intended to advise the British Government how the major elements of the change in Germany might work out and how, in British interests, they should; and how we should use our influence and our continuing Rights and Responsibilities relating to the German Question and Berlin to maximise the chances of the results we wanted.

At this point major change was afoot in East Germany, and even more in Poland and Hungary; and Gorbachev was attempting reform in the Soviet Union itself. It was probable that communism was doomed in East Germany. The regime had been forced to open the Wall. A totalitarian regime which cannot maintain total control cannot survive without major changes.

In West Germany people now saw the possibility of sufficient change in East Germany to allow significant change in the structure of the relationship between the two Germanys. West Germans expected real reform in East Germany, but doubted that it would be enough to stop the demonstrations there and the rush of emigration. There was concern that there could be not only instability in East Germany but even a breakdown in public order. There was a strong feeling that evolution in East Germany, not rapid change, would suit West German interests but did not seem likely.

The view in West Germany was that Gorbachev had evidently decided reform would be less dangerous to East Germany's stability than no reform. But there was also a feeling that the Russians would be more strongly opposed to a political transformation there than in Poland or Hungary and would seek to insist on maintaining East Germany as a separate state. This was because East Germany, the linchpin of the Warsaw Pact, was essential to the continuation of the Soviet Union's power in Central and Eastern Europe.

I did not yet think that unification was certain to be the outcome of the current change. Knowing Mrs Thatcher's acute sensitivity on this point, I did not want to predict that unification was going to happen before that was clear.

I wrote to the FCO about the extremely important question of the possible forms of a new relationship between East and West Germany, a question which had not yet entered the debate in the politics of West Germany. One conceivable outcome might be a separate but fundamentally reformed East Germany, still communist but much less autocratic. This is roughly what Gorbachev wanted in the Soviet Union. I did not think an outcome like this would last in East Germany. The justification for a separate East Germany, apart from Soviet power itself, had always been the ideology of Marxism-Leninism, which now was totally discredited. This left the possibility of the Soviet Union maintaining power against the wishes of a majority of the population of East Germany, an arrangement which would not be likely to endure.

A more likely outcome would be two democratic German states, cooperating closely and increasingly. Or there might be two German democracies in a federative structure with numerous joint policies. I concluded that there were reasons for expecting unification to be the final outcome, perhaps after some years of lesser stages such as increasingly close and extensive cooperation.

You could see that various developments might bring unification close. The people of East Germany might see it as the shortest and safest route to democracy and prosperity. If reform movements and demonstrations called for unification as a means of guaranteeing freedom, would a political party or a leader in West Germany issue a ringing appeal for a drive for unification? West German opinion might be swept by a wave of emotion supporting the appeal. And would the people of East Germany feel confident that a reformed system, if achieved there, would last if the country remained separate?

Then I raised another important question, which was to be a theme of my writing for months: the future military alignment of Germany and its parts. For the foreseeable future it would remain critical to the West that the Federal Republic should be in NATO and that Allied forces, above all American, should be stationed there, probably in reduced numbers. The Federal Government and the great majority of West Germans in responsible positions were saying that their country would remain firmly aligned to the West and that neutrality was not an option. I was less confident: I thought that a public debate about neutrality could occur in due course. It was probable that the Soviet Union would try to make neutrality the condition of unification. There were people in the SPD opposition in West Germany and possibly one or two in the Federal Government who might be tempted. But if, as might be the case, the Soviet Union was acting from a position of weakness, in the face of the loss through change in East Germany of its domination in Central Europe, I could imagine that West Germany, with things clearly going its way, might find such an offer as resistible as it had in 1952 when Stalin tried the same ploy – unification in return for neutrality.

I encouraged the FCO to do some serious thinking about the future. We should consider what future structures of the two Germanys would be feasible and desirable. If it came to reunification, what conditions would we want? What would be the implications for our economic interests and for the European Community and above all for NATO? We should make a plan to do all we could, if possible with the United States and France, to influence events so that the arrangement that would suit us best could be promoted.

I argued repeatedly to the FCO that the British Government must make clear publicly that we welcomed the changes in East

Germany, recognised the right of the Germans to choose their own future in self-determination and were willing to support reunification in democracy if that was the clearly stated wish of the German people. This recommendation was important because Britain's standing and influence in Germany in the future would be prejudiced if we were thought to oppose change in Germany now.

* * * * *

A woman in East Berlin borrowed a book from the American library in West Berlin in summer 1961, just before the Wall was built. She returned it on 12 November 1989. The fine for late return of the book was waived.

During these weeks of change I had several informal chats with Hans-Dietrich Genscher, the Foreign Minister. I think he must have realised that I personally favoured unification, although I did not say so because of Mrs Thatcher's views. He was a fascinating figure, astonishingly ubiquitous, dashing around the globe incessantly. His mental and political agility could give the impression that he was obsessed with tactics, ever artful and not always reliable. Some people in London considered him slippery. That was a superficial impression. There was a strongly positive side. I wrote in my diary 'The fact is that he is extremely popular, produces many new policies, is always making speeches and wins arguments against the CDU, the larger coalition partner. And all this he manages despite having a history of heart problems and, it seems, rather precarious health. He is a fantastic operator and a phenomenally effective Foreign Minister.'

Unification in Sight

Another significant change came on 19 November. A new slogan appeared during a demonstration in Leipzig. The main slogan till then had been 'We are the people,' meaning that the demonstrators and not the communist regime represented the people. Now one word in that slogan changed. The new slogan was 'We are one people', which was a call for unification.

The Federal Chancellor, Helmut Kohl, was the most important of the German leaders in this story. He did not glitter but he had golden qualities. Ponderous and provincial, he was easy to underestimate. He seemed ordinary and warm, approachable and homely. People could identify with him. He had a big heart and was formidable in his public appeal and his determination. His comforting confidence and his simplifying sense of what matters could make him seem less effective than he really was.

Kohl was a genial generalist, not a master of complex detail; a problem solver, not an ideologue, or a radical, or a visionary. Nor was he an intellectual, despite his passion for history. He did not like working with files. He would learn about subjects, and take decisions, in long chats with his close advisers.

He had an impressive record of winning elections. His election slogan in 1983, 'This Chancellor creates confidence,' was effective because it rang true to the voters at the time. He was to remain Chancellor longer than any incumbent since Bismarck. I had many conversations with him and followed his political activity for many years. I found him sensible and agreeable. There was nothing to dislike.

Kohl had two main aims. He wanted to give West Germans the feeling that their achievements since the Second World War gave them the right to self-respect again. And he wanted Germany to be embedded permanently in the European Community as well as NATO, so that other countries would recognize that there could be no appalling aberrations like the horrors of Nazism.

* * * * *

On 28 November 1989 Kohl made an important speech. For the first time, unification was moved from the realms of aspiration and made the aim of a staged programme of policy. Kohl did not say how long this process would take. I think his purpose was to present unification as the goal of the changes now under way, so as to lead opinion and put other possible futures, such as two German democracies, into the shade. Dissident politicians in East Germany were brewing ideas of this kind, and Kohl wanted to occupy the high ground.

After Kohl had spoken, his diplomatic adviser, Horst Teltschik, briefed the US and French Ambassadors and me. Teltschik presented Kohl's speech as an attempt to put German unity at the end of a lengthy process and thus to head off calls for early unity. I wrote to the FCO that the major innovation in Kohl's 10-point programme – the suggestion of confederative structures between East and West Germany – need not alter present alliances and should not be harmful. But Kohl's decision to set out a programme culminating in unity, without consulting the US, the UK or France, the powers with special rights regarding the German Question (or indeed his coalition partner), was a sign of the speed with which the debate was moving. And Teltschik volunteered that Kohl's vision of a lengthy process before unity might be overtaken by other views before long. I noted in my diary that until this moment there had been no significant force in German politics whose current aims included unification; and now the big aim of the government itself was unity.

Horst Teltschik is a man of great ability, charm and energy with whom I had a close and productive business relationship. He played a central role in the achievement of German unity. We became friends. His 50th birthday in June 1990 brought me together with Kohl in a relaxed and happy private party. Pascale and I brought a birthday cake with 50 candles, which I bore into the party at the moment when coincidentally the Federal Chancellor arrived. During the dinner, Kohl made a speech including the quip that he had never expected to see the British Ambassador helping as a waiter. He would commend me to 'Margaret'. No, he said, he had better not do that, since a commendation from him to Mrs Thatcher might ruin my career. He called me a treasure of an Ambassador.

The approach of German unification was gaining speed. On 5 December I commented to London that Kohl's remark to NATO the previous day that unification was not on the agenda would no longer be endorsed by many people in Bonn. I think he talked like that in order to calm West Germany's Allies in NATO, without himself agreeing with the remark. The major uncertainties at this time included the Soviet Union's position and the wishes of the people of East Germany. Both now seemed to be shifting in the direction of possible unification. I advised that the UK should prepare to cope with the possibility of fast movement towards unification, in case events, notably on the streets of East Germany, produced it. In this report I showed clearly that I now expected unification, and it could come soon.

I argued that the sheer size of the Soviet Union, the expansionist history of Russia, the risk that a truculent and reactionary leadership could one day have its finger on the Soviet nuclear trigger, and also the risk of years of uncertainty in Eastern Europe, made it imperative to maintain the Western security system including a lasting American military presence in Europe. I hoped that NATO would be adapted, not replaced. That was a major aim, and we should not lose sight of the possibility of a united Germany belonging to the Alliance. But NATO and German unity might be difficult to reconcile. I was wondering whether the Soviet Union would accept that East Germany should not only leave the Warsaw Pact, condemning that organisation to futility or collapse, but also should move across and join NATO, the Western Alliance which Moscow had long seen as its bitter enemy.

I also suggested that we should consider an additional buttress for freedom, security and peace in Europe after the Cold War, a new Helsinki Final Act which would be legally binding (which the existing Final Act was not – see Chapter 7). The states of Europe and the US and Canada would undertake to abide by principles embodying democracy, rule of law, the market economy, respect for human rights, condemnation of aggression and so on. Some new elements would be added, such as a procedure for the peaceful settlement of disputes between states. This kind of thinking was advanced by leaders from east and west, especially Gorbachev.

I now held a series of meetings with political leaders from the SPD, including Vogel, the party leader, and Willy Brandt, the grand old man of social democracy in Germany, as well as another meeting with Seiters, the Minister covering the changes in Germany, and the US and French Ambassadors. As a result I sent a rather dramatic report to London on 7 December 1989. The view in political circles and the Government in Bonn was now that the East German regime and the Communist Party were collapsing and the people were calling increasingly for unity. All authority could fade away within weeks. It was more a question of the death of institutions than of chaos with public order breaking down.

Things might not move that fast, but the major lesson of recent events was that the pace of change had accelerated and was still accelerating. It was probable that 60–80 per cent of the people of East Germany now wanted unity, and the main reason was that they had become convinced that their own leaders could not cope and that reform could not be achieved in a separate East Germany.

* * * * *

On 8 December the Soviet Union proposed, in the light of the 'emerging, extremely acute situation' in East Germany and around it, that the Soviet Ambassador in East Berlin and the US, British and French ones in Bonn, as the representatives in Germany of the Four Powers with Reserved Rights in relation to the German Question, should hold a meeting in Berlin at the earliest opportunity. They wanted 'by the very fact of such a meeting' to demonstrate the continuing responsibility of the Four Powers in German affairs. While the Soviet Union favoured an exchange of views on the German situation as a whole, they suggested that, if the western powers preferred, the declared subject of the meeting could be confined to a discussion of Berlin questions, in particular some recent proposals by President Reagan about Berlin. The proposed venue was the building of the former Allied Control Council, where the Four Powers had held their meetings after the war and had negotiated the Quadripartite Agreement on Berlin in 1971 (Chapter 5). Despite considerable reservations on the part of the West German government, the three western governments agreed that the meeting should take place on 11 December. Our main reason was that we wanted to keep open our channels of communication to the Soviet authorities in East Germany. We knew that they were worried about the situation there, fearing in particular that the families of Soviet soldiers could be hurt in demonstrations. We did not want to make them even more jittery.

I said in a BBC interview before the meeting that the western participants would talk only about Berlin, and the BBC commented that this was clearly a front for discussion of German affairs more widely. It was not. The three Western Ambassadors spoke only about the outstanding western initiative concerning West Berlin.

The Soviet Ambassador did speak of wider issues but the Western participants did not respond. The meeting was amicable but inconclusive.

The photograph of the four Ambassadors on the balcony of the Allied Control Council building caused considerable resentment in Germany, and was described by the US Ambassador as 'the worst picture of the year'. The reason was that the photograph might give the impression that the Four Powers were trying to take the lead in deciding the outcome of the changes in Germany, without the participation of the two German states. The West German President, Richard von Weizsäcker, was one of those who sharply disapproved of the photograph. I explained to him the reason why we agreed to the meeting, namely to keep open lines of communication with the Russians when they were jittery, and told him that we had spoken only about the outstanding Berlin initiative.

This episode had no substantive importance but refusal to hold the meeting would probably have made the Russians even more anxious; and holding it did remind Germans of Allied Rights with regard to the German Question, which the media had shown every sign of overlooking.

15

DIFFERENCES WITH PRIME MINISTER THATCHER; GERMAN UNIFICATION ACHIEVED

In my opinion Mrs Thatcher was the greatest British leader since Winston Churchill. His achievement was the greatest possible: he made a vast personal contribution to the preservation of liberty itself. Her achievement was less great but still immense: she led the policies that transformed the British economy. Having lagged behind France and especially Germany in economic growth for decades, the United Kingdom became at least as successful as them. In the 23 years from 1982 to 2005, German growth was higher than ours in only four – 1984 and 1989–92. From 1993 to 2005, UK growth was higher than German every year.

Mrs Thatcher also made a significant contribution to the last phase of the Cold War. She had always been a champion of NATO and its deterrence of Soviet aggression. Now, she was the first western leader to see that Gorbachev was different from his predecessors and her inspired cultivation of dialogue with him was a success. The Iron Lady contributed to the melting of the Iron Curtain.

When I was Ambassador in Germany and France there was keen interest in Mrs Thatcher's economic reforms. Germany, like many other countries, later carried out reforms influenced by hers. Her achievement brought prestige and admiration for Britain. I am personally grateful for one particular side effect: Britain's economic success strengthened my hand in my ambassadorial role. I am also grateful to Mrs Thatcher for a different reason: it was she who took the decision to make me Ambassador in West Germany.

Mrs Thatcher distrusted Germany because of the two world wars. The Second World War had coincided with her teenage years, a time when all of us are likely to be impressed by significant experiences, which for many become an influence for life. She therefore did not at all like the idea of German unification. This was not the general feeling of her generation of politicians in Britain. For instance, three members of her first cabinet – Willie Whitelaw, Peter Carrington and Francis Pym – had fought in the war and won the Military Cross for bravery and now were not opposed to German Unification. I do not think Margaret Thatcher's attitude was a considered view. Rather it was a gut feeling which dated from the Second World War.

This feeling based on Germany's appalling behaviour in the war was entirely justified if one looked at the Nazi period alone. But it ignored important contemporary considerations:

- The Federal Republic in West Germany, far from being bitter and vengeful like interwar Germany, was a mature democracy, comfortable with itself, stable and efficient. It was extraordinarily successful economically. It was the most successful of all states in post-war Europe.
- The Federal Republic was deeply integrated in the structures of the West, through NATO and the European Community; and this greatly reduced any chance of Germany going wrong again.
- The Federal Republic was acutely conscious of Germany's crimes in the Nazi period and therefore cautious in foreign policy and determined to avoid actions which could cause concern to other countries. In German schools this attitude was dinned constantly into the minds of children, and the resulting conviction was shared by the population in general.
- Britain had been declaring for decades its commitment to the aim of a reunified, democratic Germany and indeed was legally bound by a Treaty to this undertaking. Unification in freedom had now become a clear prospect. How could we renege?

- The Germany which would be united, consisting of West and East Germany and Berlin, was one third smaller than Germany in 1938. The German territories to the east of East Germany had been lost as a result of the Second World War.

As well as these arguments about Germany itself, there was a much wider strategic consideration which was the basis of United States enthusiasm for unification. Unification of Germany in freedom, by putting an end to East Germany, would strike away the linchpin of the Warsaw Pact and make certain the end of Soviet domination in central Europe. It would ensure the end of the Cold War, with a peaceful victory for the West. That would remove the greatest threat to the United Kingdom's security for the last forty years.

I knew from the start of the changes in Germany that Mrs Thatcher did not like the idea of unification. She sought to persuade other national leaders that change in Germany must not take place too fast or bring instability in Europe, and that unification was not at present desirable. She tried this with Reagan, Mitterrand and Gorbachev, among others. She also made public statements on these lines, which made the German media see her as an opponent of German unity, which indeed she was. A notable example was her remark at a NATO Summit meeting on 4 December 1989 that reunification should not take place for ten or fifteen years, which was widely reported and criticised in Germany. Even more resented was Mrs Thatcher's comprehensively negative interview about Germany in the *Wall Street Journal* on 25 January 1990.

Here is part of it:

Central Europe is full of minorities. It was the Helsinki Accord which said we do not violate one another's boundaries, we do not, and thirty-five nations signed that, we change them only by agreement. And this is what I am saying to you the whole time. You can only have that agreement against a background of stability and security, that is why your NATO is important because it has given stability and security ... we hope to be able to keep that stability and security because otherwise the history of Europe, if it were ever to be repeated, is appalling ...

Now you talk about a resurgence of nationalism. Nationalism
has never died, never ... The European ideal did not begin
with the Community. The European ideal is not the property
of the Community. We should never have had the European
ideal had Europe been a monolithic, united, political unit,
as was China, as was the Ottoman Empire, as has been the
Soviet Empire.

At the end of November 1989, Margaret Thatcher wrote on a
report of mine, with evident disapproval, 'Christopher Mallaby
seems to *welcome* reunification.' As an admirer of the Prime
Minister, who of course was my ultimate boss, I was concerned
by the major difference between her strongly negative feelings
about German unification and my positive views. My wish and
my duty as Ambassador were to continue to put my assessments of
events in Germany and my suggestions on UK policy clearly to the
Government in London, while avoiding public statements which
could be taken as opposing Mrs Thatcher's views. I did not feel
that my position as Ambassador was in danger and I was confident
that the Foreign Secretary and other Ministers shared my general
view. I was in an awkward situation and I did not like it, but I was
sure that I was right about German unification and I was clear
about what I must do.

There was an argument between the Prime Minister and me at the
beginning of 1990. On 5 January I repeated my recommendation
that the UK should adopt a more positive public line on the
possibility of unification. Four days later the Prime Minister's
office commented crossly to the Foreign Secretary's office that
Mrs Thatcher thought my message showed a lack of understanding
of our policy which she found 'alarming'.

This flurry was significant for me because of what it showed.
Mrs Thatcher disliked my suggestions for a more positive public
line because her own feelings about what was happening in
Germany were not positive at all. She was right that developments
were moving very fast and that the Bonn Government was not
consulting its allies as much as we had a right to expect. But
the real difference between Mrs Thatcher's attitude and mine
was that she did not favour unification because of deep feelings

of distrust for Germany which derived from the past; and I was convinced that she was ignoring important contemporary facts. She was unimpressed by the argument which most motivated me – that unification would accelerate and make certain the end of communism in central and Eastern Europe and would bring the liberation of millions of Europeans from Soviet domination.

* * * * *

As unification became increasingly likely I thought the right policy for the UK was to push Germany hard for closer consultation and to argue for less rapid change, if a slower pace was feasible. The speed of events was caused mainly by the demonstrations in East Germany, not by the West German government, and the United States favoured rapid progress towards unification for the reasons about liberation of Central and Eastern Europe, which were the main factor for me.

I wanted the UK to take a public position that would increase our clout in the international discussions about the current changes, and this meant that we should say we would support unification if that was what the German people chose. I was by now convinced that unification would become certain before long. To oppose it would then be futile. I hoped that my acute differences with the Prime Minister would then dissolve. Meanwhile I remained determined to continue to report developments in Germany accurately and frankly, while suggesting a more positive British public line when I saw an opportunity. I continued to make many suggestions about UK policy on the various elements and many ramifications of German unification.

A Sunday Walk in East Berlin

I visited East Berlin with Emily, now 22, on 7 January 1990. Exploring the back streets on this Sunday morning, we met a middle-aged man sweeping the street outside his block of flats. To start a conversation I asked him about life in his part of East Berlin. He said that 40 years of incompetence and nastiness were enough. 'Look what those people have ruined' he said, pointing to the rash of holes in the street and on the front of his home.

When I asked him about the possibility of unification, he said 'We want Helmut Kohl but we don't want Beate Uhse'. Beate Uhse is a chain of sex shops in West Germany. I think this view was common among East Germans. They wanted unity but they did not want the seedier aspects of western life or the crime. They may have derived an exaggerated impression of these things from western TV.

Emily and I walked to the Wall through the Brandenburg Gate from the eastern side. A few graffiti had appeared. An incongruous inscription, presumably the work of a British visitor, condemned an unpopular policy of the Thatcher government by declaring in enormous red letters, high up under the central arch of the Gate, 'f*** the Poll Tax!'

Confederation and Transition

By early January 1990, the SPD opposition in the Federal Parliament had adopted the idea of a confederation of the two German states. Kohl disliked this proposition, because it would give East Germany some form of continued existence. I thought that the idea of confederation had attractions. But it would be complicated and unwieldy. There would be three levels of government: a confederal government covering both parts of Germany; an East German and a West German government; and thirdly the Länder governments of the regions, with the important powers they exercised in West Germany already. Moreover, the normal idea of a confederation gives responsibility for foreign policy and defence to the top level of government, whereas it seemed probable then that in a confederal Germany the west would be in NATO and the east would not. That implied that some important aspects of Germany's external relations would be handled by the Confederation and others by East and West Germany. So I thought that this contrivance was too complicated to be the lasting answer to the German question.

In the last weeks of 1989 and the first of 1990 the discussions about Germany among the governments most concerned had become numerous and disorganised. Kohl was moving fast towards unification. Soviet policy seemed incomplete and contradictory, but there was an adamant position against East Germany being in NATO and in favour of united Germany being neutral.

In East Germany the regime was descending into impotence, while the people saw unification increasingly as the quickest and most reliable route to freedom and prosperity.

I wanted the British Government to make a proposal which would not be opposed to unification and would be logical and helpful. This would help us to play our role as the debate about unification developed. My suggestion was that the UK should advocate an agreed transition period from the moment when German unity became certain until it took place. This was an idea which so far had not surfaced in the Bonn government or the public discussion of unification. I thought that it should appeal to Mrs Thatcher because a period of transition would be an opportunity for detailed discussion in relative stability. When I asked leading German politicians whether a transition period would be necessary, they replied that it obviously would be. Given the multitude of matters that would have to be agreed, I thought that a transition period might last five years, perhaps a bit longer.

This suggestion was taken up by Douglas Hurd, who advocated it as an important idea in a memorandum to the Prime Minister on 16 January 1990. Mrs Thatcher put it to Mitterrand four days later. At the beginning of February Hurd thought that the idea was catching on.

My own relationship with Kohl was friendly. We talked quite often. I had a long meeting with him on 25 January 1990 in his office in Bonn. He was confident, energetic and, as ever, talkative. He dwelt on the need for greater European integration, arguing that the more German sovereignty was fused in the European Community, the less there should be articles in the London newspapers about a supposed Fourth Reich. In other words, further integration of Europe would make German unification more acceptable. Kohl argued at length that the economic weight of a united Germany would be in the west and the south west, in the old Federal Republic. Even an economic miracle in East Germany would never make it as important economically as the southern part of West Germany.

When I asked how one could reconcile German unity with the continued effectiveness of NATO, Kohl said that he could not yet answer this question. But it would become easier to answer over time. Kohl said that he wanted to work closely with the United States, Britain and France over unification. He wanted our real, not nominal, agreement. But, he implied, the Germans themselves must be allowed to decide the outcome without any veto for others.

I steered the conversation to the question of timing. I laid out my idea about a transition period, and asked the Chancellor what he thought. Kohl did not respond to this. On the timing of unification, he said it was possible that the date of 1 January 1995 might be when Germany would move from close co-operation between the two parts of Germany to unity in a Federation like West Germany now. His prediction was delivered rather theatrically, as a personal confidence, because 1995 might seem very early for German unification. He asked me, half joking, not to tell Mrs Thatcher, who would be horrified by this date. This was indeed a dramatic thing to say, in comparison with what Kohl and everyone else had expected only a few weeks earlier. But it was soon overtaken by further acceleration of events.

* * * * *

On 26 January, the day after my talk with the Chancellor, I had an hour's private conversation about the German Question with President von Weizsäcker in his Berlin residence, Schloss Bellevue. His views were more moderate than Kohl's, reflecting his more subtle intellect and more elegant style. He wanted the huge changes to take place at a less hectic speed and with more consideration for the feelings of East Germans who might not want everything they knew to be swept away. He was thoughtful, cautious and humorous as ever; the most sincere person possible. He was one of the most likeable men I ever knew and one of the best public speakers. I knew that his father had been the senior official of the German Foreign Ministry in the Nazi period and had been convicted in the Nuremberg trials of complicity in the deportation of French Jews to the death camps. Richard von Weizsäcker always maintained that his father's conviction had been unjustified. I am sure that his father's role was one of the reasons for his constant emphasis on the need for the Federal Republic always to have in mind the horrors of Nazism in its relations with other countries which had suffered then; and in its relations with Israel.

That evening I went to a dinner he gave at Schloss Bellevue in a very traditional dining room with ultra-modern pictures. One of Weizsäcker's staff remarked to me with a smile that the President's taste in art was moving dangerously leftwards. Weizsäcker overhead this and responded with banter, not annoyance. He managed in conversation to move comfortably between philosophical discussion (about Hegel with the Swedish agriculture Minister) to light-hearted chat (with me about the quaint elements in Anglo-German trade – my example of one million dead ducks sold by British farmers to Chinese restaurants in west Germany in 1988).

* * * * *

An ambassador must continue his other work when up to his neck in one major subject. On the morning after my meetings with the German President I went with John Gummer, the British Minister of Agriculture, to a promotion of British food at the famous Berlin department store, Ka-De-We. We were greeted on arrival by two giant Scottish bagpipers. They led us, blaring their music, to the lifts, and went on blaring while we ascended to the next floor, deafening us at point-blank range. In the British food promotion, the pipers set off like galloping elephants across the store, scattering shoppers to left and right with the force of their music and their bulk. I sent the pipers away after five minutes, with many thanks; they had certainly done their job of drawing attention to our food promotion!

Gummer and I began to admire the products on display: 50 malt whiskies, 60 British cheeses, several English wines, 40 British teas, endless shortbread, jams and so on. We kept on being handed liquids and foods to taste and being photographed and filmed for television. Our problem was that there was nowhere to put down an unfinished glass of whisky or a slice of smoked salmon, after one had consumed as much as possible. So I stuffed biscuits and cream cakes into my pockets, to dispose of later at home.

* * * * *

My idea of a period of transition until the day of German unity continued to be raised by Thatcher and Hurd in meetings with other national leaders. The Prime Minister spoke of it in the House of Commons on 6 February 1990. But the internal situation in East Germany had deteriorated rapidly, to the point where collapse of the political institutions and the economy and renewed mass emigration seemed quite likely. East Germany was heavily indebted and might become insolvent. This critical situation made the Americans as well as Kohl determined to accelerate the progress towards unification, in order to reduce the time available for collapse.

The transition idea had run for a month, when it gave our Prime Minister a useful suggestion to contribute to the international discussion of German unification. This had helped at a time when the UK needed to be more active. But now the idea was no longer what was needed, and a bigger and better idea was being discussed.

The New Negotiating Forum

On 13 February 1990 there was agreement on the creation of a new forum to negotiate on the international aspects of German unification. The members were the two German states, the United States, the Soviet Union, Britain and France. This forum came to be called 2+4. The internal aspects of unification would continue to be handled by the two Germanys together, with the West German government keeping the United States, Britain and France fully informed.

I was delighted. German officials had been resisting involvement of the four powers with Rights and Responsibilities in the negotiation on unification. I had participated in several conversations where West German representatives had said their government was 'adamant' on this point. Yet the four powers could not stand aside from the changes in Germany and Europe, which were sure to affect their interests and on which they had the right, by Treaty, to be involved in decisions. The right answer to this tangle was clearly to have a negotiation of the two German states and the four powers together. Douglas Hurd told the Cabinet in London that the UK had played a major part in creating the 2+4 forum.

The agreement on the new forum changed the scene. It was a relief to me and many others that we now knew how the negotiations would take place and we could prepare the British positions on each important point. Mrs Thatcher commented that there was an opportunity for real consultation. She had reason to hope that Kohl would not again make major moves on policy without consulting the US, Britain and France. Her other main concern, the tremendous speed of movement towards German unification, was not removed: the speed of events in East Germany continued to be breath-taking.

Mrs Thatcher's views after the agreement on the new forum are clear from this extract from the record of her meeting the next day with the West German Foreign Minister:

The Prime Minister said that it was very important that Germany should understand the anxieties of others about unification. She tended to speak up more openly than others. But she could assure Herr Genscher that the anxieties she expressed were widely shared in Europe. Her basic concern was that the German government seemed entirely preoccupied with German unification and had not given sufficient attention to consultation with Germany's allies about its wider consequences. As a result the rest of us were feeling ignored or excluded, and problems were being dealt with piecemeal. We had played our full part in preserving Europe's and Germany's security for over 40 years. We had kept to our commitment under the Brussels Treaty to keep substantial forces in Germany, even though it might have suited our interests better to organise our defence differently. She was determined that German unification should not have the effect of undermining the stability and security which Europe enjoyed. Had the Germans been ready to accept from the beginning that the consequences of unification should be discussed [with the US, Britain and France], there need have been no problem. As it was, we were simply told that such vital matters as the future of NATO would be settled in due course. We understood the emotion which unification generated in Germany: the Germans, for their part, should show more sensitivity to the no less genuine emotions of others. The agreement now reached to establish a forum of the Berlin Four plus the two Germanys was an important step forward. But it was a pity it had taken so long.

The most important roles in the 2+4 negotiations were played by West Germany, by far the more powerful of the two German states; the Soviet Union, which had to recognise that it must give up an enormous interest, its power over central and eastern Europe, which it saw as the prize for its huge part in defeating Nazi Germany; and above all, by the United States, which was now the sole superpower and saw German unification as the way to end the Cold War and the Soviet threat and bring freedom to central and eastern Europe. The US Secretary of State, James Baker, was impressively active and effective.

Among the other three participants in 2+4, the United Kingdom played the most important role. This role was less important than it could have been, if Mrs Thatcher had chosen to make use of her fruitful dialogue with Gorbachev and her high standing in Washington to influence the decisions on the international aspects of German unification. Our role in the negotiations was however greater than it appeared in public to be. Why? Because several public statements by Mrs Thatcher gave the strong impression that Britain was against unification. These statements did not stop in February 1990, when unification became certain and the West was on the point of winning the Cold War. Indeed she continued to oppose unification after Gorbachev had accepted it, and he was losing an empire.

So the UK was helpful and contributed some key proposals in the privacy of the 2+4 negotiations but public statements by the Prime Minister seemed to oppose unification. We helped but we looked unhelpful. Not good diplomacy!

*****

One of the many reasons for the continued speed of movement towards unification was that it was Kohl's way of reducing the risk of an acute crisis in East Germany with dangerous consequences for stability there and in the region. Another major concern of the British government including the Prime Minister, and of the United States, was that the immense change taking place might weaken or even endanger Gorbachev's position as leader in the Soviet Union. Unification of Germany in democracy was the last thing the Soviet Union had wanted. Gorbachev realised that the Soviet Union could not stop unification in the face of the collapse of communism in central Europe which he, in an act of statesmanship and realism, had decided not to oppose by military force.

Gorbachev's attitude to unification was quite likely to cause hard-line members of the Soviet leadership to act against him. Western governments were conscious that his removal, if it happened before unification, would probably lead to a reversal of Soviet policy, with refusal to accept unification and an attempt to halt the democratic change in other countries of central Europe. There would have been a dramatic crisis and probably bloodshed in parts of Eastern Europe.

Some voices in the West continued to argue plausibly for slower progress towards unification, so as to reduce the risk for Gorbachev. But it is probable that the speed of progress made it harder for Gorbachev's opponents to arrange a coup. Had they done so, the new dawn which Europe enjoyed in 1989–90 might have been a new chaos instead. Gorbachev was in fact deposed on Christmas Day 1991, when unification had been achieved and freedom had spread across central Europe.

* * * * *

On 16 February 1990, I sent a letter to the FCO about many policy questions which now needed to be considered. I wrote that I was sure Kohl intended that Germany's eastern frontier should be recognised definitively by united Germany. (And the West German Parliament settled this question very soon, on 2 March, as described below.)

I then made detailed comments on Germany and NATO. As well as reinforcing the views I had been advancing since November, I stressed two points which I had not made before. First, the US would certainly insist on keeping some nuclear weapons in

Germany, as protection for their forces which would remain there. So the western participants in 2+4 would need to reject firmly any Soviet proposal for the removal of all nuclear weapons from German soil. My second point was that the period when Soviet troops would remain in East Germany should not exceed a handful of years, since a longer Soviet military presence might give rise to calls from the political left in united Germany for the departure of all foreign forces including American and British.

In emphasising the importance of NATO I was remembering times in the early eighties and before, when senior people in the SPD were critical of nuclear deterrence. I also doubted at this point that Foreign Minister Genscher was firm about the need for all Germany to be in NATO, the most difficult feature of the whole negotiation on unification. He was talking about arrangements where West Germany would be in NATO but East Germany would not. He passionately wanted German unity, and was influenced by his upbringing in the East German town of Halle. I wondered whether he would compromise a bit too much for British liking on the western security aspects of the subject in order to achieve unity.

On 22 February I returned to my insistent theme of Britain's standing in Germany. I warned that our reputation was at its lowest for years. That applied not only in Bonn but in other cities. Politicians and media were bitterly criticising Britain and the Prime Minister personally, and that included those on the right of centre who had admired Britain's economic achievements in the 1980s. The reason was our perceived attitude to German unification. From November to January we had been thought reticent on unification and, when we did say anything, to be keen to stress delay. We were compared unfavourably with France and especially the USA and now with the Soviet Union. Because we were so mistrusted, the parts of Mrs Thatcher's statements which concerned the necessary framework for German unity got all the attention in Germany and were seen as attempts to set conditions and to warn the world against the Germans. This mattered, I wrote, because it destroyed our influence in Bonn.

I recommended a public statement by Hurd which would support self-determination and the spread of democracy in Europe and demonstrate that we had new and constructive ideas for the international aspects of German unity. An early statement demonstrating flexibility and goodwill should help us to play our role to the full in this time of major change.

I was taking a risk in writing so emphatically, given Mrs Thatcher's annoyance at my earlier recommendations about our public position. I sent off that message from Bonn at 11am London time on 22 February 1990. Douglas Hurd made a major speech in the House of Commons that afternoon. It was a comprehensive review of the great developments taking place in Europe, including German unification. The content and tone were new and much more positive about Germany. Hurd welcomed the prospect of unification, saying 'We can be glad, as friends of the new and democratic Germany, that the years of painful division are coming to an end.' He said that the UK had not wanted to be obstructive about the change in Germany but had been concerned about the speed of change. Now, with the agreement on 2+4, we had achieved our aim; we had the forum we needed for responsible and orderly discussion. The speech included many points which I had made in my policy recommendations to the FCO.

Douglas Hurd evidently did not see my message until 26 February, four days after I had sent it. He commented that his speech had meanwhile covered most of my points. Indeed it had; I was grateful and relieved. Douglas Hurd had managed for some weeks to maintain constructive dialogues with Kohl and Genscher, despite what the Prime Minister was saying in public. Now Hurd was saying positive things in public and this would help our standing in Germany.

On 1 March I had a brief talk with the Prime Minister in 10 Downing Street. She was friendly and attentive. She said she knew I did not like what she had been saying in public about Germany. I suggested that the Government should speak in public about the constructive suggestions we were making about the international aspects of German unity.

* * * * *

I was glad when the Federal German Parliament on 2 March made a declaration that Germany had no claims on Polish territory. Kohl told Mrs Thatcher that the West and East German parliaments would make a joint declaration on the inviolability of the German-Polish frontier, and that there would be a treaty on this soon after unification. I had been reporting for many weeks that Kohl would confirm this important point, which bothered Mrs Thatcher and others. It marked the definitive acceptance by Germany of the loss of the third of pre-war Germany which now lies beyond the frontier with Poland.

In my diary on 3 March I noted that one key thing for Britain to watch was that the terms of German unification 'in a few months' should ensure the constitution of the united Germany contained nothing to indicate that there were any parts of Germany beyond its frontiers. Article 23 of the West German Basic Law, or Constitution, which did bear that implication, must be removed. This was done in the wake of 2+4.

I also wrote in my diary about the wider scene.

> The present generation has enjoyed a period in which East-West tension was endemic but East-West war (except by the remote contingency of an accident) was unthinkable for both sides. Our responsibility now is to bequeath a Europe in which another world war remains 100 per cent, not 90 per cent, unthinkable, while tension, now reduced, remains as low as possible between East and West.

I wrote that no-one knew who would succeed Gorbachev or who would succeed his successor. It could be a truculent nationalist with dreams of re-establishing the Soviet Union as a superpower.

> The Soviet Union may become smaller. Its capacity for surprise attack by conventional means is diminishing and will diminish further. But it will retain nuclear weapons. We simply must make the threat of aggression impossible. That requires, in the last analysis, two things. Germany must be in NATO and United States forces must be stationed in Germany. Both points appear to be agreed in the West but the Russians are arguing for German neutrality. They may

come off that, realising that the best way to prevent Germany ever becoming dangerous again is to have US forces there.

In East Germany on 18 March the parties in favour of unification won an election by a large margin. This clear expression of the wishes of the people strengthened Kohl in his drive for unity.

* * * * *

On 23 March I had a talk with Teltschik. He said that there had been a marked improvement in the image of the UK in Germany in recent weeks. One major reason was a message the Prime Minister had sent to Kohl when the Federal Parliament made its declaration on Germany's eastern frontier, mentioned above. I am sure that Douglas Hurd's speech also contributed to this new view. The climate between London and Bonn suddenly seemed good again.

Sadly the bright interval lasted only a few hours. In an interview in the influential German weekly magazine *Der Spiegel*, Mrs Thatcher declared: 'you know what happened with previous assurances [about Germany's eastern frontier], they were overturned by the German courts, and I heard Helmut Kohl say: "no I guarantee nothing. I do not recognise the current frontier". I heard it myself in Strasbourg after the dinner' (at the European Council on 8 December 1989).

Having got wind of this interview before it was published, I telephoned Bernard Ingham, the Prime Minister's Press Secretary, to try to have this remark amended. It was highly unlikely that Kohl would have used the words attributed to him and anyway it had now been decided that united Germany would accept the current frontier. My conversation was in vain; it was too late to change the Prime Minister's interview in *Der Spiegel*.

Teltschik asked me to call that afternoon. He said that the Chancellor was shocked and astonished at the Prime Minister's remarks. Kohl had never refused to recognise the eastern frontier. The only question had been *when* that frontier should be formally recognised. The Chancellor had said in the conversation in Strasbourg that the frontier could be formally recognised only by a united Germany.

Teltschik concluded that this episode had affected the climate between London and Bonn; it was a most unhappy development.

This incident was a nuisance, since it occurred just after progress to restore the British-German relationship had at last been made and just before a British-German summit on 30 March.

* * * * *

I often attended meetings of Thatcher and Kohl between 1988 and 1992. I think they had some respect for each other but were not at all at ease together. He admired her intellect and her effectiveness, and especially her success in economic policy. But he felt that she underrated him and he was intimidated by her emphatic style and powerful personality. She found him 'so German', which from her was not a compliment. I think she meant he was heavy and humourless. She suspected obstinacy and a lack of subtlety and thought that Kohl was sometimes devious. Their attitudes to Europe were completely different: he the enthusiast and true believer in the European cause, she focussed single-mindedly on the pursuit of British interests. They were both great leaders of their countries and they had many overlapping interests. They sometimes tried hard to get on well and occasionally succeeded, but much more often the chemistry just would not work. It was a pity that the German and British leaders could not get on at a time when Germany was becoming even more important to Britain than before.

In fact, the ensuing British-German summit was one of the rare occasions when Kohl and Thatcher succeeded in getting on well. At the dinner beforehand the Prime Minister spoke quite positively about unification. The journalists thought the atmosphere between the two leaders at the dinner was chilly, but I was sitting next to Kohl, and I know that he was in rather good form. The private meetings between the leaders went well. Kohl and Thatcher covered the main points about unification without disagreement, notably the German-Polish frontier and united Germany's membership of NATO. The press conference at the end of the meetings was a real success, not least because Kohl had an uncontrollable fit of giggles at two of Mrs Thatcher's replies to journalists and heaved mountainously with mirth.

Two Plus Four Gets Going

In the 2+4 forum we were likely to face major difficulties from the Soviet Union, for instance on NATO and neutrality for Germany. We were tough on these key western interests but we also wanted to introduce ideas which would make things as easy as possible for Gorbachev in his own country.

I attended the first meeting of 2+4 in Bonn on 5 May. The atmosphere was serious and positive. The key point was a surprise from the Soviet Foreign Minister. Shevardnadze argued that negotiation on the international aspects of unification should continue after West and East Germany were unified and that Four Power Rights should remain in place until a new security system could be established in Europe. Genscher seemed attracted by Shevardnadze's idea. Kohl declared against it. I suppose that the UK might have welcomed parts of this suggestion a few weeks earlier. But now the US and the UK were against. Our reasons were that delay would be dangerous because there could be a change of policy in Moscow and because stability was desperately needed in central Europe. To keep limitations on German sovereignty by maintaining Allied rights would cause resentment in Germany. We had an opportunity to wrap up the German Question quickly through unification; we were determined to seize it.

By now my difference with Mrs Thatcher had become much less significant. She had been reassured by the agreement on the 2+4 forum, and then Kohl had agreed that Germany's eastern frontier would be definitively recognised. Increasingly, she left the subject of Germany to Douglas Hurd. Reunification was certain and the UK was having its say. I was relieved to have weathered my disagreement with this great Prime Minister without serious mishap.

On 25 May I commented that Kohl remained intent on moving as fast as possible towards unification. His reasons included his conviction that East Germany needed to be under competent West German management as soon as possible, in order to handle the total economic transformation. He was also worried that Gorbachev's position was weakening and that getting Soviet acquiescence in Western intentions regarding unification could be even harder with a successor in the Kremlin. I wrote that the political temperature in West Germany was being increased by the spreading realisation that the task of transforming the East German economy was enormous and could cause even greater hardship and crisis there than had been expected. There was a feeling of vertigo in politics. I did not expect this to deflect Kohl and Genscher from their present course. But it demonstrated that they were playing for high stakes and it increased the domestic cost of any apparent setback.

I also attended the second 2+4 meeting in East Berlin on 22 June. The atmosphere was not bad. But Shevardnadze put forward a long paper which was unexpectedly hard-line and inflexible. The Soviet delegation confided that their tough paper came from the Communist Party leadership and should be seen against the background that a Party Congress would take place shortly. That suggested that the Soviet Union might be more flexible after the Congress was over in mid-July.

At strong US insistence, a NATO summit meeting in London on 6 July proposed to the members of the Warsaw Pact 'a joint declaration in which we solemnly state that we are no longer adversaries'. NATO undertook, once Soviet stationed forces had withdrawn and there had been decisions in arms control, to make important substantive changes in its doctrine about the role of nuclear weapons in war, making them 'truly weapons of last resort'. NATO also foresaw further development of CSCE including some new functions and institutional strengthening.

The immediate aim of this radical statement by NATO was to help Gorbachev against attacks on his policies at his Party Congress, and this essential aim was achieved. The London Declaration was also used by Gorbachev on other occasions to help to justify Soviet acquiescence in the unification of Germany and the many other setbacks suffered by Moscow in the transformation of Europe. It was a gesture to Gorbachev, designed to help him politically and to enable him to accept western positions on the key outstanding questions the 2+4 negotiations, above all a united Germany's membership of NATO.

* * * * *

The breakthrough came on 14–16 July, when Kohl met Gorbachev in Moscow and Stavropol, the latter's home town in the south of the Soviet Union. Gorbachev accepted that united Germany would be in NATO. This was the biggest difficulty in the negotiations and agreement was the key breakthrough. I think the US President and his Secretary of State had convinced Gorbachev and Shevardnadze earlier in the summer that the US would insist on united Germany being in NATO. Gorbachev's immense concession was a grand example of political realism. East Germany was an essential part of the Warsaw Pact; its departure condemned that organisation to irrelevance. East Germany would now join the Western alliance, whose purpose had always been to prevent the spread of Soviet power in Europe.

It was agreed at Stavropol that some Soviet forces would remain for three or four years in eastern Germany and the Western garrisons in West Berlin would remain there for the same period. Gorbachev also agreed that Four Power Rights would end on unification and the NATO defence guarantee would apply to all Germany from unification, though no foreign forces or nuclear weapons would be moved into the former East Germany. The exact interpretation of this last point was to cause difficulty till the end of the 2+4 negotiations but was settled at the last minute.

A View from the Top in Moscow

I want to interject at this point a summary of how one of the Soviet Union's top diplomats saw what was happening in mid-1990. This is derived from *In Confidence*,[*] the memoirs of Anatoly Dobrynin, who for many years had been Soviet Ambassador in Washington and at this time was advising Gorbachev in Moscow. Dobrynin writes that Gorbachev wanted to obtain a new security system in Europe as the price for agreeing to German unification. This new system would have replaced NATO and the Warsaw Pact. Dobrynin thought that Gorbachev could have got this and with it a continuing role and voice for the Soviet Union in European security and in Europe's affairs more generally. Gorbachev should have made a detailed plan and conducted a tough and unhurried

---

[*] Anatoly Dobrynin, *In Confidence*, Times Books, New York 1995.

negotiation. But he was outwitted by the West. He did not insist on a new security system and threw away his key cards – acceptance of Germany's unification and membership of NATO – without any serious gains.

Dobrynin in his memoirs does not explain why he thought Gorbachev acted in this way. He merely says that the latter was making policy without the advice of colleagues and officials and that he hoped to strengthen his weak position in the Soviet leadership by success in foreign policy.

I do not believe that Gorbachev would have hoped to gain kudos in Moscow by making immense concessions to the West. On the contrary, the way to bid for kudos would have been to obtain some new European security arrangement in which the USSR would have had a prominent role. Gorbachev had frequently mentioned this idea in general terms since he presented it as 'the Common European Home' in 1987. In 1988 and 1989 he elaborated, saying that the new structure would be tied to the Helsinki Final Act and would replace NATO and the Warsaw Pact; and would advance economic integration across Europe. Its four elements would be collective security based on a doctrine of restraint rather than deterrence, full economic integration across Europe, environmental protection and respect for human rights in every country. Gorbachev and his Foreign Minister, Shevardnadze, went on mentioning this idea in general terms and, as noted above, Shevardnadze suggested in the first meeting of the 2 +4 talks that negotiations on a new security system in Europe should continue after German unification. In October 1989 Gorbachev's influential aide Georgy Shakhnazarov wrote a detailed paper on this, suggesting a staged programme of military measures on both sides culminating in liquidation of the Warsaw Pact and NATO by 1995.[*]

Gorbachev never put a definite or formal proposal to the US or NATO. This is surprising because the West, and notably the US, was willing to think about further developing CSCE, the organisation which had grown out of the Helsinki Final Act.

---

[*] *Masterpieces of History: The Peaceful End of the Cold War in Europe*, National Security Archive Fund 2010, page 22.

Mrs Thatcher told Gorbachev in Moscow on 8 June 1990 that CSCE should be the forum which brought the Soviet Union fully into discussion about the future of Europe. The West would not have considered replacing NATO but Soviet and western ideas on CSCE and on economic cooperation might have been made compatible and the idea of a Common European Home might have had a future in a different form.

I think Gorbachev was improvising hastily in policy on Germany, in the face of the great political and economic problems which confronted him at home. He may have been influenced by the failure of Soviet ideology, which had been a real driver of the policies of Stalin and Khrushchev and the basis of their confidence that the USSR was the vanguard of a new and better world. The leaders and many of the people had ceased to believe in the ideology by the mid-1970s. The acute crisis that gripped the economy in the 1980s confirmed the failure of the system, and the Soviet Union desperately needed western goods and money.

All through the story, Gorbachev's conviction had been that his radical reforms could be carried out within the Soviet system, altering it greatly but preserving the framework. That was now proving wrong, and the need to go much further with reform was beyond Gorbachev's intentions and abilities. This courageous leader who had started the immensely positive changes in the USSR was unable to carry them further.

* * * * *

There was a flurry in London in mid-July. The *Spectator* magazine published an interview with Nicholas Ridley, the Secretary of State for Trade and Industry. He was quoted as saying the European Union was a German racket designed to take over the whole of Europe, and giving up sovereignty to it was as bad as giving it up to Hitler. Ridley resigned on 14 July and the Prime Minister told the House of Commons that his comments did not represent the government's views or hers. I think this was the only sign that any British minister other than Mrs Thatcher herself was opposed to German unification.

I was at Charlotte's school, Bryanston in Dorset, on the day Ridley resigned. I spoke at the school's annual parents' day. Then I went into hospital in London for an operation to remove my gall bladder, which went well. I returned to my post in Bonn a month later.

Just after the Ridley affair, there was another flurry. The German weekly *Der Spiegel* and then the British press published a leaked memorandum by Charles Powell, the Prime Minister's Private Secretary, describing a seminar of experts on Germany held at the Prime Minister's country home, Chequers, on 24 March. When this seminar was being arranged, I telephoned Charles Powell and said that I hoped to participate. The Prime Minister should have her own expert on Germany at this discussion, as well as the outside experts. Charles said flatly that I should not come. I was annoyed.

After Charles Powell's account of the seminar was leaked in July, several of the participants complained publicly that his description was highly misleading. It was condescending and critical towards Germany. There was a great deal of criticism in the German media. Fritz Stern, in his memorable book *Five Germanys I Have Known**[*] wrote that Powell's account 'made it sound as if the [participating] "experts" had shared in bashing Germany. [It] read like the record of a conclave of anti-Germanists, which of course was the very opposite of what it had actually been ... All of us were annoyed by the false impression created by this account and concerned lest our German friends believe it.'

After the German reactions to Powell's account of the Chequers meeting, I was relieved that I had not participated.

2+4 *Succeeds*

While I was away recuperating from my operation much progress was made on the details of the agreement on Germany, and when I returned the date of 3 October had been agreed for unification. There had been many problems in East Germany but collapse of the state was avoided.

The UK had put forward an idea which came from Pauline Neville-Jones and Jeremy Hill in my embassy. There was a risk

---

[*] Fritz Stern, *Five Germanys I have known*, Farrer, Strauss and Giroux 2006.

that there might be a change of leader in Moscow after signature of the 2+4 agreement but before the agreement came into force. A new leadership in the USSR might then have refused to ratify the agreement and the Four Power rights regarding the German question would have stayed in place until it did. That would have given the Soviet Union continued rights regarding Germany for an unforeseeable period. The British suggestion was that Allied Rights should be suspended on signature of the agreement and extinguished when the agreement came into force on ratification. This arrangement, a novelty in international law, was agreed by all in 2+4 and was included in the agreement which was the result.

Another British contribution in 2+4 was that our thinking on many of the international elements and repercussions of German unification, especially early in the story, was more developed than the thinking of the other governments. This enabled preparation of western positions for 2+4 to move more quickly. Moreover, our detailed work on the wording of the provisions for the agreement was a helpful contribution to the success of 2+4 and to the western governments' ability to meet the tight deadlines which were required in the negotiation because of the speed of events in East Germany.

An example of British skill with words came when the Americans suggested that the agreement following 2+4 should list all the Allied Rights and Responsibilities which the agreement would terminate. Instead of that laborious approach, which might have led to argument and delay, the British suggested that the agreement should say simply that the Four Powers 'hereby terminate their rights and responsibilities relating to Berlin and Germany as a whole'. That was agreed.

Another British contribution came at the end of 2+4. There was controversy about what the agreement should say on movement of non-German NATO forces into eastern Germany after the Soviet forces left. All had agreed that all Germany would be in NATO. It was the British who argued strongly on the essential point that the Alliance must have the means, if ever necessary, to fulfil its responsibility for the security of East Germany. In other words, the former East Germany should have the rights of all other areas in NATO and not be a sole exception with less security than the others. Bitter argument about this was settled at the last minute by an American suggestion that movements of NATO forces into the former East Germany should be decided by the government of united Germany.

The final meeting of the 2+4 negotiation was held in Moscow on 12 September 1990. The Treaty on Final Settlement with Respect to Germany was signed. It met entirely the requirements of the western participants. Soviet acceptance of this agreement would have been unthinkable before Gorbachev. It showed that he had fully realised the weakness of the USSR and had made the correct deduction that he could not oppose the wishes of the people of East and West Germany and the other western participants in the negotiation.

The West tried to give Gorbachev some useful points for defending the outcome of 2+4 at home. These elements, as I summarised them at the end of 1990, were 'NATO would stretch out the hand of friendship to the Soviet Union, no non-German NATO forces would be stationed in east Germany, the size of the German armed forces at 370,000 would be well below the existing level, Germany would permanently renounce nuclear, chemical and biological weapons and the German-Polish frontier would be recognized definitively'. To these points should be added another which was not part of the 2+4 agenda: Germany gave the Soviet Union DM 15 billion ($9.62 billion), intended mainly for the transfer home and rehousing of the Soviet forces in East Germany.

The Charter of Paris for a New Europe of November 1990 was another action which was designed partly to help Gorbachev. It was the result of many governments believing that the Helsinki Final Act should be strengthened by new content to reflect the end of the Cold War. I had myself made suggestions of this kind on 5 December 1989, as mentioned in the previous chapter.

The Paris Charter issued by the 34 states of CSCE built on the Helsinki Final Act, with much more detailed statements about the Rule of Law and the other principles and with many new elements. Some of the new content, for instance in the economic field, had been foreshadowed in Gorbachev's numerous statements about his idea of a Common European Home. But the Paris Charter was not a binding treaty and did not replace NATO. It came after German unification within NATO had been achieved and did not give the Soviet Union (or later the Russian Federation) a new platform for participation in the affairs of Europe as a whole.

A Broken (Verbal) Promise

James Baker, the impressive US Secretary of State, told Gorbachev in early February 1990 that the borders of NATO would not move further eastwards than united Germany. He offered a guarantee on this in the context of the 2+4 talks, on the assumption that Gorbachev would agree that NATO would continue to exist and US forces would be stationed in Europe under NATO. Prime Minister John Major made a similar remark to Gorbachev's Minister of Defence. The Russians never asked for these points in writing. They regarded the subsequent extension of NATO to bring in Poland and other Warsaw Pact states, and the three Baltic States when they left the Soviet Union, as a serious breach of faith.

The remarks of Baker and Major were not binding, but the Russian resentment at NATO's enlargement is understandable. I confess that I'm glad it happened because membership of NATO, with the guarantee that an attack on any ally will be treated as an attack on all allies, makes life much more comfortable for the new NATO members in the face of Putin's machinations now.

Looking Back on the Historic Year

The great transformation of Europe, with the unification of Germany as an essential part, was achieved in about a year.

As the change began in autumn 1989, the two superpowers still glared at each other in hostile rivalry across Europe. The continent was divided into two military blocs. The Cold War was still cold. The Berlin Wall still stood. The Soviet domination of Eastern Europe and the Iron Curtain were still in place. A year later the Cold War was over. The Berlin Wall had been torn down. Germany was unified. In Eastern and Central Europe, communism and Soviet domination had been swept away.

My feeling at the end of that momentous year was that the West had managed the great changes well. Quickly and peacefully, Europe had been transformed for the better. I regretted that the UK, in a plainly wrong-headed public stance, had been negative about

German unification. But it was great for Britain that the Soviet threat to Western Europe and the Soviet hold on Eastern Europe had ended: and that the German Question had been answered in a way fully consistent with western principles and interests.

This was the most important period of my career and I relished the experience. I had played an active role at my level. I thought that, despite my difference with the Prime Minister, I had reported events and prospects and intentions in Germany fully and frankly, and that I had made timely and useful proposals about British policy. The PUS wrote afterwards that this work was invaluable.

My colleagues in the Bonn Embassy had worked with flair and determination all through this extremely busy and important year. I am deeply grateful to them all. Pauline Neville-Jones and Colin Budd made especially distinguished contributions.

Inevitably, other problems have arisen in Europe in the quarter century since those events, but the multiple breakthroughs of the momentous year from autumn 1989 to autumn 1990 transformed Europe for the better.

Secret Police Trivia

I wanted to find out, before writing this book, whether the Stasi, the secret police of communist East Germany and the equivalent of the Soviet KGB, had kept a file on me. I applied to the authority in united Germany which holds the archives of the Stasi for information about whatever file there was. I received a full and helpful reply, sending me my Stasi file. It showed that little information was held about me and it was nearly all trivial and on several points inaccurate.

This was a small disappointment, for I had hoped that there might be accounts of my many visits to East Berlin and East Germany in the two years before unification, which I could recount to comic effect in this book. My file has 18 pages. Six are cards from a card index. They contain a few simple details about me – date of birth and so on – and a couple of lists of dates when I held meetings with Nigel Broomfield, the British Ambassador in East Berlin. Some of the other pages contain public information of similar triviality.

There is a report dated 20 February 1989 of my appearance in a talk show on West German television on 25 November 1988. This report is not only tardy but also inaccurate. It begins with another regurgitation of trivial information already published. This time it's a few facts about my working life, which I mentioned in the television programme. Then comes the first mistake: the Stasi say that I still own a house in West Berlin, though I've never owned one there at any time. Then comes another mistake: the Stasi say that my daughter Emily not only was born in West Berlin, which is true, but also that she still lives and works there, which is tripe.

Next there is a report of a telephone conversation between Nigel Broomfield in East Berlin and me in Bonn, clearly based on eavesdropping. It is headed Top Secret, so I was hopeful of some real content. Nothing of the sort. The report says that I began by asking how Nigel was and he replied that he was well. Then I asked whether Nigel could come for a drink with Pascale and me in West Berlin on the following Sunday, before a lunch which he has already accepted. The report says Nigel Broomfield accepted this invitation to a drink with pleasure, explaining that he would be riding in East Berlin that morning and would then come to the drink at noon. Unless we were talking in code, it's hardly a threat to national security.

Another Top Secret report dated 20 October 1988 says that Pascale and I met Nigel and Valerie Broomfield in Eisenach in East Germany on 18 October and gives the programme of our two-day trip in that area. Then it says that there is a point of operational significance – we are meeting the Protestant Bishop of Thuringen, Werner Leich. This is presumably considered operational because the Stasi are watching the Bishop.

The report goes on to list the guests at a lunch Nigel and Valerie are giving on 20 October for Pascale and me. There is an account of the conversation at lunch, presumably obtained from one or more of the East German guests. It says that I led the conversation. I evidently wanted above all to talk to Deputy Foreign Minister Moldt and the writer Stephan Hermlin. I asked pointed questions concerning the German nation and the overcoming of fascism in East Germany. I asked Moldt directly whether he was really convinced that the political, social and economic conditions in

East Germany were as stable as the propaganda stated. It was conspicuous that the lawyer Wolfgang Vogel was hardly involved in the conversation, which gave the impression that Vogel's relationship with the two Ambassadors was a distant one.

Vogel was well-known as the lawyer who had defended dissidents in several trials. I wonder whether the mention of his distant relationship with Nigel and me was an indication that he was the Stasi's source for this report.

The Stasi were a major power in communist East Germany. They did terrible harm to the citizens. The interest of their banal reports about me is that the Stasi also wasted time and money on unnecessary work without even being accurate in reporting facts. The only part of my file which might be slightly useful to the Stasi is the account of the conversation at Nigel Broomfield's lunch, which is one page out of eighteen.

16

GERMANY UNITED 1990–92

The unification of the two German states raised many important questions about the nature of the united country. Would united Germany be West Germany writ large? Or would some characteristics of communist East Germany remain? Would the country be embedded in the western world like West Germany? How long would it take to bring the East German economy to a level of prosperity comparable with West Germany?

On 2 October 1990, the day before unification, Patrick Eyers, our Ambassador in East Germany, and I sent the FCO a joint analysis of the likely answers to some of the new questions.

We wrote that there was a widespread belief that joining the east German to the west German economy would produce an economic miracle in east Germany. Views differed about whether it would take 5, 10 or 15 years. The advantages in this undertaking were west German entrepreneurial and technological skills, investment resources and know-how, and the reasonably well trained east German workforce. The difficulties in the east included tangled uncertainty about property ownership and severe environmental degradation. Half the population drew its water from sources polluted by industry and agriculture; and nearly all the power stations must in due course be replaced because they polluted appallingly or were based on risky Soviet nuclear technology. There would be major unemployment, not only as inefficient enterprises were rationalised or closed but also among the bloated civil service – 250,000 in East Berlin alone.

In west and east German society as a whole, the lessons of the Nazi era had been absorbed; and in the west there was complete commitment to the Federal Republic's successful system of democracy, decentralised federalism, market economics, social solidarity and the rule of law. The unification of Germany in 1870 had been the extension westwards of autocratic, nationalistic, militarist Prussia. The unification in 1990 was the extension eastwards of the democratic, western, outward-looking Federal Republic. This time united Germany was one third smaller than pre-war Germany; and virtually for the first time in German history, the country had definitive frontiers with which both a vast majority of Germans and the international community were content.

Patrick Eyers and I saw other important differences from earlier moments of major change in German history. Bismarck unified Germany in 1870 by 'blood and iron' or, more accurately, by trickery and war; and the empire was declared, on Prussia's defeat of France, in Versailles of all places. Kohl had done it by democracy and the Deutschmark and with international approval. The Weimar Republic was born in Germany's feeling of humiliation after the First World War and the peace treaty of Versailles. Germany's resentment provided humus for Hitler's rise to power. The Federal Republic in West Germany, unlike the Weimar Republic, was a genuinely new start. And the new united Germany was an enlargement of the Federal Republic, a respected member of the West, with 40 years of political and economic achievement behind it.

Whatever the cosmetic efforts to suggest a merger between equals, East Germany had been joined to West Germany. But united Germany would not acquire at a stroke *all* the characteristics of West Germany. East Germans feared that they might remain second-class citizens. Some knotty problems would have to work themselves through before east Germans could develop the open, self-confident civic and political culture of west Germany. Yet the west Germans outnumbered the 17 million east Germans by four to one and the east Germans had sought rapid unity because they wanted western democracy and prosperity. So Patrick Eyers and I concluded that united Germany should be very like West Germany had been.

We expected assertiveness in German foreign policy. With the national question solved and full sovereignty restored, Germany would expect to pursue its own interests without the rather deliberate restraint that was normal until a few years before unification. German interests would be pursued by peaceful and legitimate methods, but strongly, in the consciousness of German economic and political importance.

The European Community had been influenced from the start by Germany. Along with the close relationship with France bequeathed by Adenauer and de Gaulle, the Community was seen in west Germany as a permanent feature of foreign policy. Public support for European union – undefined – was strong. All the major political parties advocated it. And even without that factor, the hard-headed arguments of economic self-interest would continue to ensure a full German commitment to the European Community. There was no reason to expect east Germans to question any of this.

Germany had been Russia's leading trading partner long before the Soviet revolution. By the early 1970s West Germany had established itself as the most important western trading partner of the communist countries in Europe. United Germany was particularly well-placed to extend greatly its lead in trade with the east, through its location, its technical expertise, the experience of west German companies and the many eastern links inherited from East Germany. Eyers and I expected much greater investment and involvement (but not territorial expansion) in eastern Europe and probably in Russia to be the major new feature of German foreign policy. Germany's western orientation would be supplemented by strong eastern links.

This analysis, here greatly abridged, ended: 'There is no reason to expect reversion to the German behaviour which caused two world wars. Our German ally and partner will be much more difficult than before but not dangerous to deal with. Across the board united Germany will be a factor of the first importance in our foreign relations.'

In a report on 4 October I described the celebrations of unity in Berlin on the previous day as happy but sober. During the reception following the ceremony, I was approached by the Federal President, the leaders of the liberal and social democratic parties, the Defence

Minister and a dozen other Cabinet ministers keen to express thanks for the British role as a protecting power in Berlin and in the Two plus Four negotiations. The general mood of the politicians was one of great satisfaction. There was also much discussion of tasks ahead in eastern Germany and a preoccupation that united Germany must show that it would conduct a responsible foreign policy and that it did not wish to be a great power but a part of the European Community and an undivided Europe.

In the German media coverage of the celebrations there were many detailed analyses of the role of the Western Allies in Berlin, picking up comments such as one by Willy Brandt – that the Allies long ago had come to be regarded as friends rather than occupying forces. The French were described as having led the Federal Republic into the European Community, and the British as having brought it into NATO. All three Allies were described as having taught the Germans democracy again. The reports of the farewell ceremonies for the Allied Commandants in Berlin were full of warmth and nostalgia.

British Policy after German Unification

In my new role as Ambassador to united Germany, I made recommendations about British policy towards this important partner in Europe and ally in NATO. My comprehensive report on 30 November 1990 began with a reminder of the UK's assets in its relationship with Germany. Our foreign policy was recognised as serious and global. We were known to have influence in Washington and to have played an active role recently in East-West relations. The Royal Family was a focus of deep admiration and interest. English was Germany's first foreign language. Most of all, the strength and length of our democratic tradition and our political stability were respected, indeed envied. The Germans admired what they saw as the essentially 'civilised' quality of British public life, contrasting this with their own tragic failure in the past to achieve political morality alongside their notable cultural and intellectual achievements. There were many anglophiles in key positions in German public life.

So the UK was known and liked in Germany. Yet if we wanted to exert serious influence, we also needed to be considered important.

That was where we had work to do. Our European policy had for some time been the focus of much scepticism in Germany. The Germans knew that the British approach was different; and that we looked at proposals for new steps in the Community on their merits and not with sentiment about the European cause. The widespread view in Germany, however, was that there was a consensus among most members of the EC on the desirability of further major strides in integration, and that Britain would not be able to make its objections stick and in the end would accept major changes.

I argued that the single step which would most enhance our standing in Germany would be to make our policies in the Community more positive, in presentation and where possible in content. If we could make our overall style sound more constructive, if we could more frequently advance positive ideas of our own, the Germans would take our views much more seriously.

As for NATO, the reforms of the Alliance that were in hand should be a major help in maintaining German loyalty. One key element was the proposal I had supported for multi-national forces in the Alliance. If we could discard the concept of stationed or foreign forces in Germany, and talk only of multinational forces consisting of German and other allied units, public support for the presence of the foreign elements should have much more chance of lasting. If German generals had a fair and visible share of the command positions, that would help further.

I recommended that the British Government should consider an intensification of bilateral intelligence cooperation. For with the disappearance of communist East Germany, which had managed to collect considerable intelligence about government and policies in West Germany, the security threat in Germany had greatly diminished.

I saw many commercial opportunities in eastern Germany. In due course there would be an economic upsurge there. But even in the near term the export opportunities created by major infrastructure projects, new consumer demand and the foundation of service industries would be considerable. West German industry, already working at over 90% capacity, could not meet all the demand. My staff were working on a programme of trade missions, seminars and other events to promote British goods and services. Many more subjects were covered in this report and there was an annex with detailed suggestions.

My thinking at this time was that British-German relations had in recent years become less important to the Federal Republic than its relations with the United States and France. The United States was the leader of the free world and had borne the main responsibility for the security and freedom of West Germany. France was Germany's partner in the creation of the European Common Market and in making progress since then in European integration. The United Kingdom was seen as less important to Germany, and less important in general, than the US and France. The UK's standing had improved somewhat because of the recent success of the British economy but had been weakened by the perception that we were reluctant Europeans and latterly by the impression that Mrs Thatcher, and accordingly the United Kingdom, had been against the unification of Germany.

Now, with unification, several of Britain's important roles concerning Germany had succeeded and therefore come to a natural end. Our role as one of the Four Powers with reserved rights regarding the German Question had been completed on unification and those rights had ended. Our highly successful period of 45 years as a Protecting Power in Berlin was soon to come to an end. The presence of 75,000 British troops in the Federal Republic, contributing to the deterrence of Soviet aggression or threats of aggression in Europe, would now become less important because deterrence had been successful, and the size of our forces would soon diminish.

The United Kingdom had no important specific requirement to ask of Germany in the context of unification. We certainly did not want the prize which President Mitterrand obtained in return for agreeing to unification: a definite German commitment to the creation of the single European currency, the Euro. That was a proposition which we considered financially and economically destabilising and not in British interests.

What I did was useful rather than important: I tried to make an impact for Britain in the former East Germany, as I shall describe in a moment.

Prime Minister John Major

A pleasure of my last few years as a diplomat was to work sometimes with John Major. I found him likeable, pragmatic, moderate and full of common sense. He was also good company.

As he wrote in his memoirs, John Major accepted my view that he should make a speech on Europe at the Konrad Adenauer Foundation in Bonn.* I had argued in a report on 30 November 1990, quoted above, that the step by Britain which would most enhance our standing in Germany would be to make our policies in the European Community more positive, in presentation and where possible in content. I wrote that report just after John Major became Prime Minister. I participated in drafting the speech and I sat next to the new Prime Minister as he delivered it in March 1991.

That speech included a fateful statement: 'My aim for Britain in the Community can be simply stated. I want us to be where we belong, at the very heart of Europe. Working with our partners in building the future.' John Major thought that if Britain was to stay in Europe, we had to be at the heart of it to protect our own interests. If we let others dominate the debates we would be forever on the back foot. I shared this conviction.

John Major's expression 'the heart of Europe' proved to be a red rag to the eurosceptics among Conservative MPs. They took it, whether through ignorance or prejudice or political calculation, as showing that Major was an enthusiast for Europe, when in fact he was a patriot advocating the best way of advancing British interests. The people who objected to this remark ignored Major's statement in the same speech that he would 'bring forward our own proposals to the intergovernmental conference at Maastricht, since I didn't like what was on offer'.

To call John Major grey or weak is superficial and mistaken. In fact, his difficulty was that he had a narrow majority in the House of Commons and this majority included eurosceptic MPs, who opposed him on European and other matters. This made it extremely difficult for him to assemble a majority for important votes in the House. His ability to be effective in matters of policy

---

* *John Major: The Autobiography*, Harper Collins 1993. Pages 268–9.

of his own choice was greatly reduced by the need to fight within his own party for the decisions that were needed every week. His management of foreign policy was shown to be effective: he obtained the ideal result in the most important foreign policy subject and the most controversial, which was the European single currency. In the Maastricht Treaty of February 1992 he won agreement for Britain to opt out of the Euro, but also to opt in later if it ever wished. Major's double option gave the UK total flexibility.

Work in United Germany

With two years ahead of me as Ambassador to united Germany, I concentrated on building Britain's cooperation with the former East Germany. There had been a British Embassy in East Berlin during the communist period but because of the political system its activities had been limited. I had the first opportunity since 1933, when Hitler came to power, to make a real impact for Britain in eastern Germany. My thought was that this effort would be noticed in all Germany and would enhance our reputation and strengthen Britain's bilateral relationship. I knew that the creation of many more links with eastern Germany would not transform Britain's standing in Germany, but I was confident that it would improve things.

I made many visits to the New Länder, as the regions of the former East Germany were now called. I gave public lectures and seminars in universities, appeared in the newspapers and on television and visited many firms. I discussed my plans with the new political authorities from regional prime ministers to mayors. This activity attracted attention and approval in west as well as east Germany. Horst Ehmke, one of the senior politicians of the SPD and a noted intellectual, asked in Parliament why German Ministers were visiting the New Länder less than the British Ambassador.

One of my main purposes in these visits was to look for opportunities for direct investment by British companies. It had long been difficult for British companies to establish themselves in the Federal Republic, by acquisition of German companies or by starting new ones. I thought that acquisitions in eastern Germany could provide British companies with a base from which to expand sales in western as well as eastern Germany. When I left Germany at the end of 1992, there were about 80 British acquisitions of east German firms ranging from architects to hotels to concrete production.

One of my other purposes in the visits to the New Länder was to prepare the ground for various other British activities. I recommended to London that ministerial and parliamentary visits to Germany should henceforth include the New Länder. I was glad that the British Council, which already had cultural programmes in East Germany, intended to increase its activity considerably. A major priority was teaching English, responding to the thirst for the English language which was rapidly replacing Russian as the first foreign language in education in the New Länder. Youth exchanges were another field where much more could now be done. I urged that the BBC, already popular for its broadcasts during the communist period, should seize the opportunity to enhance its success, particularly in teaching English. I suggested that more British towns should make twinning arrangements with east German ones: there were 450 twinning arrangements between British and west German towns but we had only four with east German towns.

My pet aim of arranging the establishment in Germany of a postgraduate centre for the study of Britain was achieved after unification. In east German universities the faculties which had taught Marxist-Leninist views were closed down; that meant history, philosophy, politics and economics among other faculties. As a result, the budgets of the universities in the New Länder had money for new projects. We approached the Humboldt University in Berlin with our proposal. After thorough planning the Centre for British Studies was established in that prestigious university in the historic centre of Berlin. Many aspects of British life were covered in the courses and seminars and in research. In 2014 sixty students were doing Master's degrees and sixteen doing doctorates. I chaired the Centre's Advisory Council with much enjoyment for nine years after I retired from diplomacy.

The Queen's State Visit

I was over the moon when it was agreed that the Queen would make a State Visit to Germany in October 1992. Germans admire the Monarchy, and earlier visits by Her Majesty had been major public successes. I recommended that much of the visit should be devoted to Berlin and the New Länder. This was agreed.

We considered carefully whether to suggest that Her Majesty's programme in the New Länder should include Dresden. US and British bombing had destroyed the city in February 1945 and many bombed buildings were still to be seen. It would be a gesture of reconciliation for the Queen to visit the city on this, her first opportunity. There would be no question of a British apology for the bombing but the visit would be carefully designed to emphasise reconciliation. There were doubts on the British side about this idea. I favoured it because I believed that this eloquent gesture would strengthen British standing in Germany.

On the German side President von Weizsäcker was among those with doubts. He told me that the people of Dresden had been subjected for forty years to communist East German propaganda castigating the bombing as a vindictive crime against German civilians. Many probably believed this. There might be demonstrations against the Queen. If a single egg hit the Queen, this incident would make headlines across the world and would smother in the news, and in people's memories, all the positive parts of the Queen's visit to Germany.

I reported the President's thoughtful remarks to the FCO, reiterating my preference for Dresden to be included in the Queen's visit. I said that a visit there when the Queen was next in Germany, perhaps in eight years, would have far less impact than a visit now. This question was further considered in London. The Queen decided to go to Dresden.

In planning the State Visit, the British aim was to demonstrate Britain's interest in, and wish for, good relations with united Germany, so as to build up our standing and potentially our influence. In placing the emphasis on Berlin and the New Länder, we wanted to underline our commitment to unification and to highlight our effort to build cooperation with eastern Germany. In Dresden, our theme was reconciliation – a gesture designed to win hearts throughout Germany; in Leipzig, it was to show our admiration for the peaceful revolution of 1989 and the many demonstrations in the city which helped to end the division of Europe as well as Germany.

We wanted in particular to draw attention to our practical support for the development of the New Länder through numerous acquisitions of state enterprises by British companies, and through our efforts to promote English language teaching and cultural exchanges.

The Queen's remark in her speech on the first evening in Bonn that 'the Iron Curtain melted in the heat of the people's will for freedom' was widely quoted in the media and seen as a generous tribute to those who took part in the 1989 revolution in East Germany. In her speech in Berlin, the Queen described the day the Wall was opened as 'that great day in the history of freedom', a remark also received with widespread enthusiasm in the media. Another point which was popular was the Queen's emphasis on Britain's determination to maintain its special relationship with Berlin, built up over recent decades, through new arrangements, in particular the construction of our new embassy on our old site near the Brandenburg Gate, the British Council's new English language teaching Institute in East Berlin, and the establishment in the Humboldt University of the postgraduate Centre for British Studies.

The Queen's walk eastwards through the Brandenburg Gate into ex-communist Europe took place in splendid weather. It was registered by the German media as historic, with several editorials describing it as the final end of the Cold War. The Queen's attendance at the last in a long series of military tattoos mounted by our garrison through the years, and very popular with the Berliners, was also widely reported. Because of the special status of Berlin before unification, the West German Armed Forces had never before participated in our tattoos; this time there was not only a German army band, but one made up almost entirely of members of the former East German army.

To avoid the risk of criticism of the State Visit in the UK, it was made clear that the purpose of the visit to Dresden was reconciliation, not apology. We emphasised the twinning link between Dresden and Coventry, which was heavily bombed by Germany four years before the bombing of Dresden. The Bishop of Coventry conducted the ecumenical Service of Reconciliation jointly with the Bishop of Saxony, the cathedral choir of Coventry sang and the Lord Mayor attended.

There was a worrying moment when the Queen arrived at the church for the Service of Reconciliation. Two eggs were thrown which were hopelessly misaimed and never came near the Royal party. Walking towards the church just behind the Queen, I was unaware that anything had happened. There was no demonstration. The overall mood of the crowd was polite and curious rather than hostile, but the booing was at first louder than the clapping, even though the number of those booing was quite small.

The Service passed without incident. It was shown live on television and news broadcasts were unanimous in choosing as its high point the Duke of Edinburgh reading the first half of the Beatitudes in perfect German and the Prime Minister of Saxony completing them in English. The service was relayed by loudspeaker to the crowd outside the church. When the Queen came out of the church the mood of the crowd had changed. There was much more applause than before.

The Queen went next to Leipzig and then to Potsdam. Her drive through the centre of Leipzig became a triumphal procession, with people cheering from windows and balconies. The high point was a meeting in the Church of St Nicholas, the focal point of the demonstrations for democracy in 1989. Two pastors, who played key roles then, described the peaceful revolution to the Queen and the Duke of Edinburgh. In Potsdam Her Majesty walked slowly down the broad terraces in front of Frederick the Great's Palace of Sans Souci, greeting on the way many hundreds of local people including children. The Queen then went in an open carriage – a telegenic touch – through the Potsdam Park to have lunch in the Neues Palais. It was the first time that a royal visitor had been received in this royal setting for eighty years.

I was sure that we had been right to take the risk we did in Dresden. In a State Visit of 4½ days there was half a minute of worry before the church service. Otherwise the varied programme, featuring many events not previously included in any State Visit to Germany, was carried out successfully. There was blanket television and newspaper coverage and the overwhelming majority of comment was thoughtful as well as enthusiastic. The *Frankfurter Allgemeine Zeitung*, Germany's most thoughtful newspaper, wrote

> The Queen was received with friendship and joy wherever she had opportunities for direct contact with the public ... In Dresden she was received with great interest and restrained sympathy; in Leipzig with effusive joy ... The service in Dresden was one of the most moving moments of the visit. The visit had a clearly encouraging effect on Germans in the New Länder. Two factors contributed to this. One was the attention which the Queen directed to the participation of British firms in the renewal of east German industry. The second was the admiration which the Queen showed for the activists for freedom in East Germany. The monarch of the oldest democracy placed a seal of approval on one of the newest ones.

* * * * *

The rapid establishment of the West German system across East Germany and introduction of German monetary union on a basis which hugely overvalued the East German currency may have prevented the total collapse of the economy of East Germany and emigration to the west of even higher numbers of East Germans. But the rate of exchange, though politically necessary, had serious negative effects. East Germany was deprived of the chance, essential for early economic success, of being able to compete through lower wages and other costs than those in the West German economy. Its businesses were closed in large numbers. Unemployment rose fast.

There was also distrust between eastern and western Germans. The easterners thought the westerners, who arrived and told them how to do things, were domineering know-alls. The westerners, in a lapse into complacency, said the easterners were idle and feckless and should work hard to improve their economy, as West Germans had done after the war and ever since. The economy of the New Länder improved, but less quickly than many, including me, had expected. Nevertheless, life after unification was better from the start than life had been in the German Democratic Republic.

Germany at the end of 1992

When I left Germany at the end of 1992 my thoughts were focussed on the difficulties thrown up by unification but I was still confident about Germany's ability to overcome the problems. I concluded my final report with a word of caution:

> The great successes of 1989–1990 are heavily overlaid by the problems that followed. If the democratic political parties grip those problems there will be a period of self-absorption and strain. So long as Germany is preoccupied with dealing with the new problems, it will be an uncertain partner. We shall at times need strong nerves; but we should go on displaying our confidence that the generality of Germans are now real democrats and that democracy sooner or later will cope with the problems. The upward curve of prosperity will resume. Unification will succeed. Then Germany's confidence will grow further; but its consciousness of the Nazi past and fear of being compared with that time will diminish only slowly. Germany will be complex but not dangerous.

Dental Diplomacy

Our excellent family dentist in Bonn, who became a friend, was an active member of the FDP, the German liberal party. The Foreign Minister, Hans-Dietrich Genscher, was that party's outstanding personality, and our dentist knew him well. The dentist, savouring the possibility of involvement in foreign policy, would ask Genscher's office before my dental appointments to brief him on the points that needed to be made to the British Ambassador. When he had me gagged by whirring and hissing technology in my mouth, the dentist would declare loudly what was wrong with British foreign policy. I was relieved to be unable to reply, for I preferred to deliver my views to Genscher or his staff myself!

17

PARIS 1993–96

My appointment as Ambassador in Paris was a first in one particular way. Until a few decades ago, British Ambassadors with foreign spouses were not appointed to the country of the spouse. It was thought that the Ambassador's independence of judgement about the country might be skewed by the spouse's sympathies. I am glad to say that the British Diplomatic Service grew out of this prejudice in the late twentieth century. Ambassadors with foreign spouses would henceforth be trusted to do the job without personal bias. I was the first Ambassador in Paris to have a French spouse. A Conservative Member of Parliament, a backbencher whom we knew, was shocked at this and thought the Foreign Secretary must be unaware that my wife was French. He called on a Minister of State in the FCO, my friend Tristan Garel-Jones, to complain about the awful mistake that was being made. He made no headway!

As in Germany, my main role in France was political – to know the key politicians and understand their thinking and where possible to influence it, and thus to be able to advise London on dealing with France. In contrast to the great changes in Europe and Germany in my time in Bonn, the political work in France was less dramatic and thank goodness I had no differences with my government in London. What I did was to try to improve British-French understanding and cooperation in the post-Soviet world.

Sometimes this work was hindered by an intangible underlying difficulty. Despite all the links through trade and tourism and the thousands of citizens of each country living in the other, the British and the French can be mutually envious and suspicious. The French can be edgy because of past humiliations, especially the rapid defeat by Germany in 1940. They were liable to feel that the British were always thinking of that.

Some of the comment on these lines in the British and French media is good-natured teasing. But some is a nuisance in the bilateral relationship. The British and French can be hasty in criticising each other. One reason is that history weighs too heavily on present attitudes. Yes, the British and the French have fought, but the last time was in 1815 at Waterloo. In the 20th century we were on the same side in two world wars and the Cold War. Sometimes, when this subject is discussed on either side of the Channel, you might get the impression that Waterloo must have happened *after* the Normandy landings.

This was a harmful anomaly; I wanted to do what I could to reduce the influence of the past on the modern relationship between Paris and London. I thought I had a few advantages for this task. Pascale herself, for a start. A British Ambassador with a French wife made an intriguing novelty in Paris. My French was good enough to debate live on TV with French politicians and journalists. I had been steeped in French culture since school and university.

* * * * *

I asked the business people in charge of the Channel Tunnel project if I might travel through the tunnel when arriving in France to become Ambassador. This would be the first time a British Ambassador had travelled to France or any overseas country by land. It seemed mad to miss the opportunity. The media were full of stories about the financial problems surrounding the tunnel and were not saying much about the historic significance of linking the United Kingdom by land to continental Europe and the benefits for trade and tourism.

The interior of the newly excavated tunnel was an obstacle course of rocks and puddles. I got through much of it on a little buggy, like a go-cart, used by the construction teams. I walked and scrambled the first and the last mile or so. My hard hat and overalls were comfortable and the journey was enlivened by conversation with my friend André Benard, the head of the Channel Tunnel project on the French side.

This gambit caught the attention of the French media and gave me a good start as the new British Ambassador. In television interviews on arrival at Calais I emphasised the historic importance of the tunnel. Rather to my surprise the British media also took an interest, some romantic spirits presenting my trip as the first ever land journey by an Ambassador from London to any other country since England had sent occasional envoys to Scotland before the Union (a view which ignored the possiblility that an Ambassador in Dublin might have travelled there from Northern Ireland).

* * * * *

Pascale and I had three-and-a-half years in France, a happy time full of interest. Pascale was delighted to live in her home city again, after a gap of thirty years. She helped me greatly, especially in making contacts on the right of politics in France. Her father, Francois Thierry-Mieg, worked for General de Gaulle in London during the war. He had many friends among Gaullist politicians of his generation. Pierre Messmer, former Prime Minister and Minister of Defence, was one whom we met soon after our arrival. Another was Alain Peyrefitte, a former minister and still an active writer, who helped me with advice and introductions to my generation of political figures on the centre right.

France of course is a fascinating country and an important one. The landscape is beautiful and wonderfully varied. The country is less crowded than the UK: the populations of the two countries are similar but France is twice as large in area. The cathedrals, the chateaux and the museums are superb. The roads are excellent. French urban conversation is full of wit. The food and the wines are sublime. These attractions were already familiar, and I grew to enjoy them even more during our stay in Paris.

One difference from Britain is that intellectuals are revered in France. Some become popular celebrities. It is not too much to say that Bernard-Henri Lévy, the handsome and dashing philosopher and writer, enjoys the admiration and the fame in France of the handsome and dashing footballer David Beckham in Britain. The expression 'too clever by half' has been used disparagingly of exceptionally intelligent British politicians. There is no expression for this in the French language, for the simple reason that the very idea that it is possible to be too clever does not exist among the French. Another example of this difference comes from Major Thompson, the caricature of an English gentleman imagined by Pierre Daninos in his famous comic story of 1954, *Les Carnets du Major Thompson*. The Major says, in his drawling accent in French, that in Britain intelligence is respected more as a State Service than a human quality.*

Politics

Just after we arrived in Paris I went to the opening of a major exhibition of paintings by Matisse. When looking at a painting of a nude, I found President Mitterrand beside me. We talked for a time and I took the opportunity to tell the President about some new suggestions of the British government concerning the war in Bosnia. My staff also spoke to his office and to the French Foreign Ministry, confirming the same message. In reporting this to London, I took care to warn that the FCO should not expect me to be able always to beard the President on current business!

Early in our stay in Paris the centre-right won a parliamentary election. The new Prime Minister was an experienced Gaullist Minister, Edouard Balladur, with whom I was to work frequently. He was a moderate reformer. He often described France as a blocked society, meaning that every proposal for reform was blocked by interest groups and the public's dislike of change. Balladur himself experienced this in an episode which looked to me like a weak U-turn but in fact enhanced his popularity. He participated in drawing up a restructuring plan for the national airline, Air France, in late 1993, with the aim of reducing costs and increasing efficiency. He announced the plan, saw the risk of strikes and withdrew the plan, which had been presented by the government as the Prime Minister's personal project. I thought this instant retreat was feeble. But public opinion polls showed more

---

* Pierre Daninos, *Les Carnets du Major Thompson*, Hachette 1954.

than 70% approval. This demonstrated the difficulty of changing the way state enterprises were run in France. The contrast with Margaret Thatcher's success with privatisation and in handling the coal miners' strike is stark.

At this time Francois Mitterrand, a socialist, was President. The French know this situation, with the President from one side of politics and the Prime Minister and the government from the other, as Cohabitation. The duo of Mitterrand and Balladur showed care and forbearance towards each other. The President allowed the Prime Minister to take most decisions in domestic affairs. With these personalities, the system worked reasonably well.

I described Balladur to the FCO as 'the supreme administrator – careful, methodical and suave'. He was persistent and thoughtful as well as skilful, and he quickly became a much respected Prime Minister. 'Cohabitation' affected our working methods at the British Embassy. We needed to work with the President's advisers and those of the Prime Minister and with the ministries, especially the Ministries of Foreign Affairs and Defence. We explained British views to all and would assemble their various reactions in reports to London on the views of France. The quality of the officials we worked with was outstanding. It would be hard to find a better top level official than Jean-David Levitte, who was Chirac's diplomatic adviser.

Mitterrand showed great courage in facing terminal cancer. By mid-1994 he was playing only an occasional role in policy. He had been a fascinating figure: immensely clever and cultivated, a master of tactics, opportunities and cunning. But he was not a man of principle and sometimes put political advantage above honesty. At the same time he was a successful strategist on some things, notably Europe. His three main achievements were important ones. In a triumph of political technique he destroyed the public following and the power of the Communist Party, ending its many years as a strong force in France. Mitterrand's second achievement was that he was effective in advancing the integration of Europe, above all as a great protagonist of the single currency. Whatever one thinks of that fateful project, Mitterrand saw it as a major interest of France and played the key role in persuading Germany to agree to it. The third achievement was abolition of the death penalty. In his time as President there were also seriously negative themes. He left the French economy in dire need of structural reform. Extensive corruption in public life and parts of business became clearly visible.

By late 1994 Balladur had become the most important figure in the state and in politics. At that point he was the clear favourite to win the Presidency in May 1995. But his strong lead in the polls evaporated by mid-March 1995 and the Gaullist UMP chose not Balladur but Jacques Chirac as their candidate for President. Chirac, though a former Prime Minister and a longstanding public figure, managed to convince the voters that he represented change. He did this by his fresh and energetic style rather than by policies. One memorable thing about working with Chirac was his voracious appetite. I have seen him eat two large dinners in one evening while campaigning. His tearaway energy must have burned up the massive intake of calories.

I found Chirac impressive and charismatic as a person, and successful as a campaigner. To meet, he was good company in a rather overbearing way. He took one excellent decision in foreign policy: to refuse French participation in the Iraq war. When he was about to be elected I had breakfast with Dominique de Villepin, his close adviser who later was Foreign Minister and then Prime Minister. I asked Villepin how Chirac intended to change France in the coming years, when he would be President. Villepin did not answer. This I think revealed a truth about Chirac: he was better at politics than policy, an effective politician in some ways and rather good at managing his governments, but with no clear purposes or vision for France. He was not original or profound but strongly ambitious, and his foremost aim was to become President and then to win a second term.

The Presidential election brought the end of Cohabitation. The President and the new Prime Minister, Alain Juppé, were both Gaullists; indeed they were longstanding colleagues and friends. There were ministers from their party, the UMP, and some from the UDF, the centre party of Valéry Giscard d'Estaing. Giscard rang me with a tip before the list of ministers was announced. I was grateful that he took the trouble to call me on an extremely busy day. He said that Alain Lamassoure of the UDF, the new Minister for Europe, was the one whom I should get to know and treat as my regular contact in the new government. I did indeed do business with Lamassoure, and we became friends. But the minister whom we saw most was our friend Simone Veil, who was Minister for Social Security and Health.

The new government saw reform of the economy as the top priority. In November 1995 Prime Minister Juppé published his plan including changes to pensions in the public sector. This produced a crisis of public sector strikes. Air France, railways and public transport were paralysed for several weeks.

Balladur, when Prime Minister, said to me more than once that he believed that a major crisis which could endanger the regime itself, such as the storm of violent protests and demonstrations in 1968, could occur again. This view implied that the political system of France was fragile and might not endure. I doubted this. But what was certain and important was that Balladur and other French leaders believed that the risk of a really serious crisis was still present. So they were cautious in proposing reform and rapid to amend or withdraw their proposals if large demonstrations threatened.

Prime Minister Juppé stood up to the strikes and demonstrations for a month. One of the differences between the crises of 1968 and 1995 was that in the latter case there was no ideological fervour among the demonstrators; they were against some important policies, not against the political system. In the face of public dissatisfaction at the disruption of daily life and also widespread sympathy with the strikers, Juppé withdrew most of his plan, maintaining some changes to social security payments and benefits and carrying out some significant privatisations.

France during the Cohabitation period and then under President Chirac was very active in foreign policy, especially in the United Nations Security Council. France wanted to show that it remained worthy of its Permanent Membership of the Security Council and took seriously its responsibility in that role. As always in French foreign policy, prestige abroad and also at home was a major motive. French voters love international activism on the part of their leaders. One aim was to continue to be much more active and conspicuous in this field than Germany, so as to preserve after German unification the greater role of France on the international stage. Another purpose was to begin to develop the European Union under strong French influence into some kind of counterweight to the United States, the sole superpower in the post-Soviet world. France was the most active participant in the military deployments by western countries in crisis areas in many regions. Some 13,000 French troops were deployed in 20 countries in 1993. This was a bid for stardom on the new international scene after the end of the Cold War.

The French concern with Germany was understandable. Not only is Germany a powerful neighbour of France but also it had attacked and defeated France easily in 1870 and in the humiliating defeat in forty days in 1940. After that failure and then the war, France wanted to find a new way of coping with its neighbour. The European Common Market and a close partnership with Germany were embraced by de Gaulle as this new way. While Germany was weak and humiliated after the war, it was grateful and proud to become a close partner of one of its recent enemies. De Gaulle brilliantly saw and seized the opportunity to develop great influence over Germany, and French-German leadership in the Common Market and its successor organisations became a crucial, and for years a very popular, factor in the foreign policy of both countries.

In my time in France idealistic fervour for the European cause was diminishing. The French did not want a European Federation. But the great majority on the left and right in politics was still united in supporting further progress towards European unity. There was however another side to the French attitude. Douglas Hurd called this 'splendid ambiguity'. On the one hand, France wanted to develop Europe further; on the other hand France wanted, like Britain, to preserve the nation state. Balladur tried to reconcile the two horns of this dilemma. He proposed a Europe of concentric circles, with different groups of members of the EU making progress in different fields.

British-French Cooperation

I wrote to the FCO: 'while wanting to embrace Germany even more, because of the latter's greater power and assertiveness,

France I think realises that it will sometimes need British help in blocking German demands.' President Pompidou, who had opened the way for Britain to join the European Community, and also on occasion Mitterrand, had seen advantage for France in having two possible ways of dealing with controversial subjects in the European Community – a tactical alliance with either Germany or Britain, subject by subject. I thought also that there would be differences between France and Germany in the face of German predominance in the EU and at the same time a growing convergence of British and French positions, notably on defence matters. I suggested that these factors gave the UK the opportunity to make common cause increasingly with France.

There were important subjects where British and French interests and aims were not compatible, notably the European single currency. But my team in the embassy and I thought that Britain and France could do much more together in areas where cooperation would be in the interests of both. These two were the most active and capable members of the European Union in foreign policy and defence. The preservation of national sovereignty was an important common cause, and we both wanted intergovernmental cooperation among the members of the EU and were not keen on passing further powers to Brussels. This was true although France would sometimes make compromises between sovereignty and further European integration which the UK would not accept. These thoughts were the seed of much of what I tried to do in my time in Paris.

The Franco-German relationship is good in a fundamental sense for Europe, because Europe has suffered – and Britain has suffered – when France and Germany have fought in the past. On the other hand, it was a serious disadvantage for Britain that the diplomacy of the EU should be led by those two countries much more than by ourselves. There was therefore a key question for the UK: could Britain join France and Germany in leading Europe? I thought it impossible for the UK to do this so long as it was in a eurosceptic mood. But I thought that we would increase our influence in Europe if we could increase our cooperation on European matters bilaterally with Germany and with France. This view was readily accepted in London.

Prime Minister John Major did much to develop British-French cooperation, as he was also doing for British-German cooperation. The UK put ideas about greater cooperation to the French government in 1993. At first I found the going sticky. I remember a long meeting with Balladur's adviser on foreign affairs, when he took careful notes of my remarks but gave no comment. I kept on advocating the British view, in public speaking as well as private discussions with ministers and officials. After about a year, in early 1994, France responded to our message: French ministers and officials agreed that the convergent interests of Britain and France should lead to shared policies and projects.

The inauguration of the Channel Tunnel in May 1994 was seen as a symbol of the new emphasis. In media interviews and speeches I gave a British view of its significance, and we held in the Embassy major publicity events to encourage French people to take the Tunnel and visit Britain. We highlighted destinations in many parts of the United Kingdom.

The fiftieth anniversary of D-day on 6 June 1994 was another symbolic moment. The Queen and the Duke of Edinburgh and many senior people from the UK attended the British commemoration and my friend Simone Veil represented France. The weather in Normandy, where the Allied forces had landed in 1944 and begun their advance to victory eleven months later, was grey and drizzly, as it had been on D-Day. Seven thousand British veterans and widows, many of them in wheelchairs, paraded along the beach at Arromanches, where the British forces had landed fifty years before and many of their husbands or comrades had fallen. For me the most moving moment of that proud day was when the marching veterans sang in an audible whisper the songs of the soldiers then. Seven thousand people whispering in unison, to the soft accompaniment of the waves along the beach, left an indelible and deeply touching memory.

The main field of the new cooperation between Britain and France was defence. John Major personally worked hard on this. The British and French contingents in UNPROFOR, the UN peacekeeping force in Bosnia, were the largest. This force was set up to reduce the fighting and alleviate the suffering during an appalling regional war, when interracial fighting and atrocities including mass murder continued for months. The UK and France were the countries that did the most to get food and other vital supplies to the refugees and to limit the casualties. UNPROFOR undoubtedly did save lives and help to prepare the way for negotiations to end the war.

From the early stages of the fighting until NATO bombed the Serb forces, the UK and France made joint policy. I was involved in the coordination between the British and French Governments, speaking to French ministers, officials and generals. Pauline Neville-Jones, the senior FCO official in this affair, has described to me how British and French officials met alternately in the two countries, usually at military airports until towards the end, when the first confidential audio-visual conferencing link was set up in the two Ministries of Defence. The recommendations of these meetings were put to British and French ministers simultaneously. They would then consult together and take decisions. This degree of joint policy making was a first between the UK and France. The British and French governments presented the cooperation between our contingents in Bosnia to the media not only as an important effort to promote peace and reduce suffering in the Balkans but also as an example of the new cooperation between our two countries.

John Major decided to support President Chirac's decision to hold a series of nuclear weapons tests. There was no direct British interest in doing this and almost all the other international reactions were negative. But Major wanted to show solidarity with the other west European nuclear power and to give France a tangible demonstration of the UK's wish for closer cooperation. Chirac was glad of this and Major's gesture was welcomed in the French media.

The combination of tangible and symbolic cooperation between Britain and France was noticed by the French media. France's highest circulation newspaper commented on an interview of mine at the end of 1994 that Paris and London had not courted each other so actively since the Entente Cordiale Agreement in 1904.

In a joint statement at their summit meeting in London in October 1995 the President and the Prime Minister declared that they did not 'see situations arising in which the vital interests of either Britain or France could be threatened without the vital interests of the other also being threatened'. They spoke of a sea-change in British-French relations, stressing cooperation in defence, especially in Bosnia.

Our Life in France

The British Ambassador's residence in Paris is strikingly beautiful. It is an 18th-century mansion close to the Place de la Concorde and a few steps from the President's residence, the Elysée Palace. It was acquired by the first Duke of Wellington when he was ambassador in France in 1814, to be the British Embassy for the future. The decision of the Foreign Office to buy a mansion was a shrewd move at that time. Many of the grand houses of the aristocratic families had been put on sale during the revolution, when their owners were guillotined or impoverished. Some of the new aristocracy, created by Napoleon as Emperor, were also selling their grand houses in Paris after Napoleon was exiled. So it was a buyer's market. The house had been given by Napoleon to his sister Pauline Borghese, who filled it with handsome furniture and gilt bronze urns, candelabra and other pieces in the imposing Empire style. The house today still has much of that furniture and bronze.

This famous house, with its beauty and history, is an important element of Britain's prestige in France and a powerful asset for the Ambassador and his staff in their work. The social side of the job – the parties and events – was more important in this job than in any other post I've known and, I think, than any other post anywhere. The embassy and the parties there are a valuable tool in the substantive work. French people love being invited and even the most busy politicians, business leaders or indeed actors and writers will accept invitations if they possibly can. A person who has attended a party in that house will be well disposed to the embassy and glad to do business with it.

We often had members of the Royal Family to stay and British ministers galore. We had the staff for this: they kept the house in good condition and looked after our guests with skill and charm. One of the most agreeable parts of Pascale's life and mine was taking care of the house; several rooms were redecorated in the

Empire style while we were there and we selected, with expert advice, the colours and materials. The large garden was also a lovely setting for entertaining guests. I enjoyed my hobby of pottering there; and we improved the planting of the herbaceous borders. We also arranged for the trees to be tended properly and for one large Catalpa tree to be replaced by a young one which had time to reach adequate size before the old one became dangerously unstable.

The staff of the house were led by Ben Newick as butler, who started several years before we arrived and is still there more than two decades after we left. Ben and Mandy, who works in the Ambassador's office, are invaluable mainstays of the embassy's work. Our chef, James Viaene, was famous in Paris. He produced meals which were both delicious and magnificent in appearance. He had been lured 25 years earlier, by Christopher Soames as Ambassador, from the job of Deputy Chef in President de Gaulle's kitchen at the Elysée Palace.

Pascale enjoyed working with Chef. But even between two native French speakers there was room for misunderstanding. Once Pascale thought Chef was proposing langouste as the main course at a lunch we were giving for a British trade exhibition. But then Chef suggested that this dish be served with Yorkshire pudding. Langouste with Yorkshire? A heroic attempt to combine a British favourite with a French delicacy, but surely a contrivance too far? Then it became clear that Chef had said Angus; and Angus beef and Yorkshire pudding is an entirely British combination and exactly suitable for an event promoting British exports.

* * * * *

Before we left London for Paris, Pascale and I invited Lady Soames for lunch in London. She was the daughter of Winston Churchill and the widow of Christopher Soames, who had been a successful Ambassador in Paris. We wanted Mary Soames to feel free to visit the Paris Embassy, once her home and now to be ours for several years. We also wanted to celebrate Mary Soames by giving a dinner at the embassy in her honour. I knew that the guests Mary selected would include interesting personalities in public life in

France. On 11 September 1993 the dining room of the embassy was arranged in its most glamorous style, with the Empire urns and candelabra on the table and flowers everywhere. In my speech in Mary's honour, I recalled that her paternal grandparents, Lord Randolph Churchill and the beautiful Jennie Jerome, had held their wedding banquet in the embassy. And Mary herself had first met her husband in the house. As Ambassadress she had been loved by innumerable Parisians and by her staff. I said I was sure that the Household Gods of the house, who had seen countless powerful and beautiful people there, would be thrilled that evening to have their favourite Ambassadress among them once again.

Mary made a charming and generous speech in reply. Then came a surprise. Admiral Philippe de Gaulle, the son of the General, rose to speak. He said that the plight of the children of great men was not necessarily easy. They were not always as great as their fathers. This was just as well from the point of view of everyone else. Then the Admiral said that Winston Churchill had 'discovered' General de Gaulle; he meant that Churchill had recognised the talents and the potential of General de Gaulle in 1940 before the General was known and when many people were dismissive about him. The Admiral's remark was surprising because the usual French view about De Gaulle was that his rise was entirely his own achievement. Moreover, the French expression the Admiral used was that Churchill had 'inventé' General de Gaulle. Many people might mistranslate this as 'invented', which would greatly overstate the Admiral's meaning. Only one journalist was present on this private occasion, Kenneth Rose of the *Sunday Telegraph*. I pointed out the subtlety to him after dinner and he reported the Admiral's speech with perfect accuracy.

* * * * *

We rapidly came to know many fascinating people in politics, business, the media and the arts in Paris. Our closest friend was Maurice Druon, a distinguished and prolific writer and head of the Académie Française, which among other things is the guardian of the purity of the French language. Maurice was conservative in his tastes and his politics, and had been Minister of Culture under

President Pompidou. He had been in London with de Gaulle in the war and was a lifelong anglophile, and rather a dandy in the style of Savile Row and Jermyn Street.

Pascale and I have stayed many times with Maurice and Madeleine at their beautiful Abbey near Saint Emilion in the Bordeaux vineyards. He drove us (with panache and occasional disregard for the rules) around the Bordeaux countryside, showing us pretty villages and lovely chateaux and churches. Maurice died in 2009. We went on staying at Faize with Madeleine every summer until she died in 2016.

Maurice was highly cultivated, erudite and entertaining. His novels are well known in France, notably *Les Rois Maudits* (the Accursed Kings) which consists of seven stirring historical novels about the French kings in the 13th and 14th centuries. It has provided excitement and historical pageantry to many generations of French readers and has twice been adapted for television. Another successful novel, *Les Grandes Familles*, is a drama in three volumes set in the Paris bourgeoisie after the First World War, a tale of ruthless capitalism and family quarrels. It was adapted as a successful film starring Jean Gabin.

Another close friend of Pascale's and mine was Claude Pompidou, the widow of President Pompidou. She was tall and quietly humorous, a philanthropist and a collector and patron of contemporary art. Claude introduced us to many distinguished people, from politicians to painters. We shared her interest in modern painting and her insatiable appetite for sightseeing. Together we did a great deal of the latter among the churches and chateaux along the River Lot, where Claude had a modest, remote house high on a crag near Cajarc. We stayed there many times until Claude died aged 94 in 2007.

Simone and Antoine Veil were also special friends. Simone was a senior Minister in the government of Eduard Balladur, and in an earlier government in 1974 had led the legalisation of abortion, then a sharply controversial matter for Catholics in France. She was also famous for another reason; she had survived awful suffering during the war, as a Jewish child in the Nazi concentration camps at Auschwitz and then Bergen-Belsen, where her adored mother died. She had a soft spot for Britain because

British forces liberated Bergen-Belsen in April 1945. Simone was a powerful and extremely moving speaker on the Holocaust and a lifelong champion of women's rights. She was President of the European Parliament from 1979 to 1982.

A valued friend in our generation was Pascale's first cousin, Antoine Rufenacht, to whom she has always been close. He had been a very young Gaullist minister. He then devoted his work to his home city, Le Havre. The city had had communist mayors since the war. Antoine tried several times to win this position for the Gaullists. He won it in 1995 and was elected again in 2001 and 2008. Le Havre was transformed for the better by the policies and projects he introduced. He became a highly respected figure on the centre-right of French politics. We love Antoine and Liselotte's farm near Caudebec in Normandy and spent several summer holidays there when our children were small. This was a particular pleasure because Pascale had spent much time at the farm as a child and was delighted that our children should love one of her favourite places.

Our social life in Paris included many private dinner parties, as well as frequent public events. The French are well aware that many British people are keen on famous French products – Champagne, Bordeaux and Burgundy wines, Cognac and foie gras among others. So these delights were often on offer in the finest quality at the dinners we attended. When guest of honour, I could hardly turn down all such treats. My favourite among them is the claret from Bordeaux, and I had some memorable moments. My waistline duly expanded. I had some of my trousers enlarged at the waist. When we returned to London my waistline returned to normal. I had the altered trousers re-altered.

* * * * *

One of the pleasures of my work in Paris was to hold frequent conversations about French politics and international developments with the US Ambassador, Pamela Harriman.

Pamela's very first engagement on arrival in Paris was to come next door for a chat with me in the garden of our embassy. I knew she was a social celebrity, was 73 and had a reputation for being intelligent and attractive. I knew also that she was supposed to have had affairs, when living in Paris years earlier, with various men who now were friends of Pascale's and mine. After a few minutes of chitchat, I mentioned to Pamela that we were friendly with one of those men. Far from talking of him she plunged her hand Thatcher style into her large handbag and drew out the draft text of a resolution about Bosnia which was being discussed in the United Nations. She pointed to a few words in the resolution and suggested to me that slightly different words might be preferable. This was Pamela's way of making clear that she intended as ambassador to deal with the substance of the work and not to seek social stardom. Pamela could easily have been the top hostess in Paris, just as she had been in Washington, but she wanted to be a real diplomat and she threw her heart and her energy into the substantive work.

President Chirac himself and many other top people in France thought the world of Pamela and worked seriously with her. This was partly because she was fun and attractive but more importantly it was because she was known to be close to President Clinton and thus able to influence the White House. The top French ministers treated her as their direct channel to the President.

Pamela and I had weekly tête-á-tête chats and she often asked for my comments on reports which she was planning to send to Washington. Once I returned home after a particularly enjoyable conversation and said to Pascale that Pamela was 'so sweet'. Pascale laughed and said that Pamela had many qualities – elegance, energy and so on, but to call her sweet was really not on target. This was true. Indeed, Pamela was ruthless in getting her way on some occasions. At a major dinner at Versailles she managed to get into a small room where the guest of honour, the Princess of Wales, and a handful of others including Pascale and me were talking before dinner. Pamela did more: she placed herself right beside the Princess just as the photographers entered the room. Having ensured that she would feature next to the Princess in the media, Pamela slipped away from Versailles, leaving empty the very prominent place that had been reserved for her at the dinner, which began as she was leaving.

* * * * *

Ambassadors can have useful clout and I wanted to found a project which would help to improve the relationship between Britain and France and would last after Pascale and I left Paris. I had done this in Germany, when I helped to found the postgraduate Centre of British Studies in the Humboldt University in Berlin. I thought that the problem of mutual prejudice between Britain and France might be reduced if there were more people in influential positions on each side of the Channel who knew the other country well. That gave me the idea of a postgraduate scholarship scheme, with very able and ambitious young people from France and Britain studying for a year in the other country.

If people who studied across the Channel, doing a master's degree or a doctorate, advanced later to positions of influence, they would take account in making decisions on matters involving the other country of the knowledge they had gained as postgraduates. French views of British actions and policies would be based on greater knowledge, and that would reduce prejudice. This should also happen in the UK, and the reduction in prejudice on both sides of the Channel should bring lasting benefits.

The Entente Cordiale scholarship scheme was announced by Prime Minister Major and President Chirac at their summit meeting in London in October 1995. It was funded by businesses and foundations, and the two governments provided the administration. Many of our friends in Paris, above all Maurice Druon, helped me with advice on the scheme and in raising money. The first chairman on each side was a friend of ours: Simone Veil in France and Roy Jenkins in the United Kingdom. I succeeded Roy and Robin Janvrin succeeded me in 2008.

British scholars are still studying in France every year. The other side of the scheme – the French scholars coming to Britain – flourished for twenty years. In that time we had over 400 scholars, British and French combined. There is an active network of former scholars. Some, as I hoped, have worked in organisations where their knowledge of the other country might well influence significant decisions. For example, the French Ministries of Finance and Defence, the British Diplomatic Service and Department of Transport, the International Monetary

Fund, the UN Food and Agriculture Organisation, the Council of Europe, Friends of the Earth and Médecins Sans Frontières.

I was always on the look-out for gaps in cooperation or in mutual knowledge between Britain and France. I found one in a field of personal interest to me. The art world of France was ignorant of British art in the 20th century. People knew the sculpture of Henry Moore and not much else. I decided to try to correct this by arranging for three major exhibitions to take place: an exhibition of a wide range of modern British sculpture; a retrospective exhibition of Francis Bacon's paintings; and a major exhibition of David Hockney's work. Thanks to the efforts of the British Council in Paris, the sculpture exhibition was held in the Jeu de Paume gallery on the Place de la Concorde in Paris and the Francis Bacon exhibition was held at the Pompidou Centre, the foremost gallery of contemporary art in France. President Chirac himself opened it on my last day in Paris. David Hockney has become well known in France through numerous shows.

In France greater knowledge of the best of modern British culture can enhance the standing of Britain, as well as bringing tangible benefits, for instance for French tourism in the UK.

* * * * *

President Chirac's State Visit to Britain in May 1996 was a resounding success and a celebration of improved relations. There were warm-hearted speeches and friendly consultations. The private occasions also went well. I accompanied the President on a tour of Westminster Abbey, where historical links between England and France caught his attention, from the architecture of the Abbey, which was inspired by the Gothic cathedrals of Amiens and Reims, to the tombs of William I and of Mary Queen of Scots. Perhaps the reminder of the Conqueror made it easier for our French guests to make light of arriving through the two-year-old Channel Tunnel at a station called Waterloo and of the presence above the President's chair at a lunch in the City of London of an enormous monument to the Duke of Wellington.

The French love the British Royal family. But Chirac did not want pictures in the French media of himself on formal occasions, when he might look old fashioned or pretentious. Therefore he wore a suit for the public events when the male hosts were in tail coats. The Queen behaved as though she had not noticed. She also ignored the oddity of a member of Chirac's staff taking a call on his mobile telephone during the private lunch at Buckingham Palace. These departures from royal protocol did not spoil the enthusiastic atmosphere of the visit.

Chirac's visit to Glasgow was quite different from the formal events in London. He visited the infamous Easterhouse Estate, to see the urban renewal projects being carried out partly by the residents themselves. The Prince of Wales, whose Trust was involved in the work, accompanied the President. Chirac was visibly interested and impressed. He said the renewal work was 'wonderful, wonderful' and that he had picked up ideas which could help in the renewal of the rundown suburbs of French cities.

* * * * *

In my last weeks in France I had to deal with a complex and awkward subject. The outbreak in Britain of Bovine Spongiform Encephalopathy, known as BSE or mad cow disease, was a difficult subject for our relations with France. The outbreak raised the idea in France of banning imports of British beef. The French food industries, which Chirac as a former Minister of Agriculture knew and admired, had an interest in British beef being banned, for British farmers had won a considerable market share in France.

I put the case against an import ban to the French Minister of Agriculture and the Health Minister, Simone Veil. We won some delay, but France did ban British beef, following its own interest in protecting public health against possible risks to humans from contaminated beef and in excluding competition. In fact, I think the UK's position on BSE was never strong; it was not possible to prove that the beef was safe for humans. It was my job to defend our case in live interviews on radio and television- essential but not enjoyable.

Thoughts on Leaving France

On leaving Paris in July 1996, I wrote that the French greatly admired Britain's contribution to the victory over Nazism which, as they would admit, stood in sharp contrast to the defeat of France in 1940. Partly because of this contrast the French had a tendency to say disparagingly that the British had achieved nothing big since 1945. I wrote 'All through the post-war period, the immemorial sense of rivalry, the prejudices and the rapidity to criticise with which the British and the French have faced each other across the Channel, have persisted. You see it in the media of both countries, especially in ours.'

French people would point out that France had drawn 30% ahead of Britain in GDP. But France was well aware of the decisive reforms of the British economy in the 1980s and the consequent increase in our rate of growth. The French view of Britain had latterly become more positive. Our current efforts to increase cooperation with France were going well. The French fascination with the British Monarchy remained strong. So, as I left, I thought that British-French relations had improved and should improve further. The great gap in importance between British-French and German-French cooperation should diminish.

I still saw economic reform as the great necessity facing France. The state's dominance of the economy in many sectors and the uniform technocratic approach of the public service needed to change. Employers were spending on social security a sum equal to 41% of the salaries they were paying. The mismatch between social provision and the ability of the state to pay for it was growing. But there was another side to this. The French economy had been opened to Europe by the European Single Market and partially opened by the GATT agreements to the world. It had succeeded against the new competition. France had a positive balance of trade. The private sector was efficient, modern and successful.

Despite this success, the French mentality of defensiveness towards outside competition persisted, bringing calls for protectionism. The French still saw the state as the nanny to the people which should be responsible for dealing with their problems. Farming now provided only 5% of employment but the political debate seemed to assume that the percentage was still much higher. People had not noticed, and would jump out of their skins if they did, that one third of French shares were now in foreign hands.

French ministers were convinced that the risk of violent resistance to new policies remained real. I believed that the competitive pressures on France would intensify. How would French governments react to future protests against their attempts at reform? If they retreated, the problems of France would not be solved. But if they persisted in reform in the face of demonstrations and strikes they would need iron resolve to face the crisis and very likely would antagonise swathes of public opinion. The arguments for compromise would come loud and strong. Retreat might well seem yet again to be the better part of valour. Most likely there would be some economic reform but much less than required. Therefore France was likely to remain a country of high public expenditure and high taxation. I concluded that despite this major failing, France of course would always be a thrilling country.

* * * * *

Before I left Paris President Chirac invited me to call to say goodbye. He had not received any other departing Ambassador. In our conversation he said my work had been outstandingly successful. Franco-British relations were now excellent, thanks not only to their deliberate relaunch by the politicians but because of an admirable Ambassador who had always worked with skill and elegance. In the recent difficulty over BSE, my mediating role had been essential. It was quite wrong to say that diplomats no longer had a substantive role to play in the modern world. They could make all the difference. I had shown this in my decisive role in our now excellent relations.

I was tickled pink by this farewell bouquet! I received letters which were equally gratifying from Prime Minister John Major, Foreign Secretary Malcolm Rifkind and the PUS in the FCO, John Coles. Coles even wrote that I was 'one of the most remarkable and outstanding Ambassadors of the post-war period'.

At the end of my final despatch from Paris to the Foreign Secretary, the last words I wrote as a diplomat were 'What could be more fun?' That was my feeling about my 37 years in the British Diplomatic Service.

18

SUMMING UP THE COLD WAR

After the Second World War and the major Soviet part in the defeat of Nazism, Stalin was able to extend Soviet control in Europe as far westwards as the frontier between East and West Germany. His ambition was to advance Soviet influence even further westwards. He wanted particularly to end the western military presence in West Berlin, which from the Soviet point of view was a humiliating eyesore on the map of Europe. He tried first by blockading West Berlin, and Khrushchev then tried, by ultimatums, to threaten the western allies into withdrawing their forces from Berlin. These dangerous moves caused major crises between the Soviet Union and the West. Moscow failed because the West stood firm.

Khrushchev and the East German regime then built the Berlin Wall, a desperate measure to stop the haemorrhage of population from East Germany to West Berlin. In doing this they implicitly admitted two important things: that threats had failed to dislodge the Allied forces from West Berlin, and that East Germany could not keep its population without walling them in. For thirty years more West Berlin remained a democratic, prosperous city, a beacon of success surrounded by sad, dim communist East Germany.

Meanwhile, much had happened in Asia. China became communist in 1949. There were communist attempts to gain control of other Asian countries: the Korean War from 1950 to 1953 and the communist takeover in North Vietnam and then in 1975 in South Vietnam.

In 1960, as many colonies of the Western countries became independent, Khrushchev declared a new strategy: to outflank the West by gaining influence in important developing countries. The Marxist revolution in Cuba was seen in Moscow as the forerunner of further spread of Soviet-type regimes. In 1962, Khrushchev tried to install offensive nuclear missiles in Cuba, a few miles from Florida. President Kennedy's skilful diplomacy forced Khrushchev to withdraw the missiles, as described in Chapter 2.

The crises about Berlin and Cuba were the most dangerous moments of the Cold War. The Soviet Union started them and was forced to climb down. The West's level-headed determination prevented a third world war.

In the remaining 30 years of the Cold War the West continued to stand firm, maintaining nuclear forces sufficient to be able to retaliate if the Soviet Union committed aggression by conventional or nuclear attack. This made aggression or the threat of aggression too dangerous for the Soviet Union to risk. We were not too concerned that the Soviet Union built up sufficient nuclear forces to retaliate after a US nuclear attack, because the West had no intention of starting an East-West war. What would have worried the West would have been if the Soviet Union had drawn ahead of the US in nuclear weapons – in quantity or effectiveness – so that it might develop the ability to deliver a first nuclear strike which would leave the US and the West unable to retaliate. For many reasons that was highly unlikely and did not happen.

So western deterrence of the Soviet Union prevented the Cold War, despite acute tension at times, from becoming a hot war. The idea of creating forces which could destroy the world, in order to prevent nuclear aggression which would have caused immense destruction, was frightening. Some would say it was immoral. The important fact for me is that deterrence worked for forty years and nuclear destruction did not happen. The USSR collapsed because of its own failures.

In general, this policy of standing firm and maintaining deterrence was supported by public opinion in the United States and Western Europe. In the US, Senator McCarthy's panic campaign against alleged communist infiltration died away in the mid-1950s after much controversy. The second, lesser aberration was the scare in the US about a Missile Gap. This was a mistaken view in 1960 that the USSR had overtaken the United States in nuclear weapons. The revelations of a Soviet officer spying for the west showed that this theory was completely false. These two aberrations were pointing towards even tougher policies towards the Soviet Union, not questioning the concept of deterrence.

The widespread opposition in Western Europe in the 1980s to the stationing there of United States intermediate range nuclear forces was overcome by Kohl in Germany and Thatcher in Britain winning elections with policy platforms that included this deployment.

In these controversies in the West, democracy allowed full debate and in the 1980s major demonstrations; and governments won by argument the support of large majorities for sanity and security. In autocracies the system would have suppressed the alternative views without public discussion. Democracy has built-in shock absorbers, autocracy has only oppression.

Tension between the USSR and the West diminished gradually after the Cuba crisis. With deterrence working, the West launched the policy of détente. For over twenty years we worked to ensure that information about life in the west reached the peoples of the communist countries in Europe through broadcasting and cultural, commercial and other exchanges. The peoples realised increasingly that life in the West, with freedom and prosperity, was greatly preferable to their own condition. Large sections of the Soviet population ceased to believe in the doctrine of Marxism-Leninism and even the Soviet leaders' belief weakened – probably in the mid-1970s.

The USSR engaged in détente for its own reasons. It wanted, like the West, to reduce tension and the risk of war. Moscow also wanted better relations with the West because it had a major row with China on its hands from 1969. Its other important motive was to acquire western products and technology.

The Soviet Union did not give up other major components of its strategy of waging what it called the 'struggle against the West by all means short of war' or 'peaceful coexistence'. As shown in Chapter 9, it violated the Helsinki agreement by maintaining strict autocracy at home and domination in central and eastern Europe.

It continued to try to build influence in developing countries. Its invasion of Afghanistan in 1979 and the imposition of martial law in Poland two years later confirmed dramatically that détente was only a part of Soviet strategy and not the most important priority. The arrival in power of President Reagan, with tougher policies towards the USSR, caused concern in Moscow. These developments combined to cause a worsening of East-West relations.

The Soviet Union decided not to invade Poland in 1981 to crush the free trade union, Solidarity. Moscow preferred to run the clear risk of losing its hold on Poland to the disadvantages of invading. That enabled Solidarity to come to power in Poland by democratic means a few years later. Gorbachev's important move to reform major aspects of the Soviet system, combined with the change in Poland, began the rapid process of the collapse of European communism. The dominoes fell quickly and together.

The main lessons of this dramatic transformation of Europe are that:

- an economy run by an autocratic state lacks the flexibility and the incentives which bring growth through private enterprise in free economies;
- it is possible to make it unthinkable for one nuclear power to launch a war against another;
- modern communications enable information about other countries to reach the populations of autocratic states, and this is likely to create dissatisfaction with the dictatorial regimes;
- the biggest lesson of all is that successful free societies, if they maintain the strength to prevent aggression, can prevail by example over systems which are dictatorial and unsuccessful.

Leaders in the Transformation of Europe

The main reason for the collapse of Marxism-Leninism in Europe was its failure to give the citizens a life anywhere near as good as people enjoyed in the west.

The most important people in the overthrow of Marxism-Leninism included those in the region who first opposed it openly.

That means Solidarity and the Catholic Church in Poland; they started the unravelling which spread across central and eastern Europe, so Lech Walesa and the Polish Pope stand high among the heroes.

President Reagan's move, two years after the fateful Soviet decision not to invade Poland in 1981, to strengthen US military power by new technology on a grand scale was a major reason for Gorbachev's realisation that the Soviet system could not keep up and must reform.

Gorbachev is a crucially important hero. His reforms were a brave departure from the totalitarian Soviet system. The liberal intelligentsia in the Soviet Union contributed substantially to his policies for change.

In an historic act of statesmanship, Gorbachev decided not to use force to crush the changes in central and eastern Europe. His greatness is that he enabled the collapse of the Soviet empire in Europe to take place almost without bloodshed. He is a hero in the world and in history. He is unpopular in Russia because his reforms triggered unstoppable change, and that led to the end of European communism. But the reason why the system imploded is that it had failed and was no longer capable of controlled reform. Responsibility for that belongs to the preceding generation of Soviet leaders, who did not try to reform the autocratic and unsuccessful system before it was too late. They lacked the flexibility and the realism to consider major change. They preferred the inert option of stagnation, and that proved fatal.

In East Germany the heroes were the tens of thousands who demonstrated peacefully and responsibly, especially in Leipzig. President Bush senior and his Secretary of State, James Baker, saw the importance of German unification for ending the Cold War. Baker was the leader in accelerating progress on the international aspects of German unity. Kohl managed the huge project of unifying the two German states with astonishing speed and great success. The scandal after he left office about illegal party funding has affected his reputation. But the Chancellor who achieved unification in freedom and peace stands with Bismarck and Adenauer as one of the three greatest leaders in the past 200 years of German history.

Germany's transformation was a poor episode in British foreign policy, because the Prime Minister was against unification and her statements determined the public view in Germany of British policy. Mrs Thatcher wrote in her autobiography

> If there is one instance in which a foreign policy I pursued met with unambiguous failure, it was my policy on German reunification ... the desire for unity among Germans on both sides of the Elbe proved irresistible. So the policy failed.*

What Now?

Since the end of Soviet power in eastern and central Europe the liberated states there have made great progress. There are still problems but standards of living have reached or are approaching those in the West. They have become mostly stable democracies. They are part of the free world. Many are embedded in the West through membership of the European Union and NATO.

In the parts of the USSR which became independent in 1991 the record is mixed. The Baltic States have become democracies again and flourished economically. But in Ukraine there is conflict and Russian intervention, in Byelorussia economic crisis and in the Caucasus and Central Asia there is political instability in various countries and conflict in various places.

The post-Soviet history of Russia itself has been terribly disappointing to those inside and outside the country who hoped that the end of communism would lead to the development of a democratic system. Putin has taken control of nearly all the media and has suppressed many of the freedoms of the Yeltsin period. The courts obey the regime and the bribe-givers, and the rule of law is not even an aspiration. So Russia today has many of the characteristics of autocracy. Yet it appears for now (2017) that the system is paradoxically the least autocratic in the history of Russia, with the exceptions of the chaotic revolutionary transition between March and October 1917 and the Yeltsin interregnum

---

* Margaret Thatcher, *The Downing Street Years*, Harper Collins 1993. Page 813 of the 2011 paperback.

from 1991 to 1999. The Putin clique is increasingly autocratic but so far it is less so than the Tsars and the Commissars.

In contrast to the Soviet Union, private property is permitted in the Russian Federation; foreign travel too. Information from abroad is widely available. There has been real economic progress, which is felt by society as a whole. The range of goods available in the cities is far greater than at any time in the past. On the other hand, there is great economic inequality, as a minority of people have become extremely rich and many of these have gone to live abroad. There is also a massive problem of corruption at all levels of administration.

Another East-West Drama?

Putin's foreign policy is largely truculent. A central purpose is to restore the self-respect and the morale of the Russians after the humiliation of the collapse of the Soviet Union. In addition Putin, and indeed the Russian people, now see themselves as surrounded by a predatory west. They see the expansion of NATO up to the borders of Russia as a big example of the west's attitude; and they believe that the west wants to add Ukraine to NATO and they see this as another important proof of western designs against Russia.

Putin has won high approval in Russia. An early success in this process was the improvement of living standards, mainly through export of oil and gas. This may not succeed to the same extent in the future. The annexation of Crimea was illegal but a success in the policy of restoring self-confidence to Russia.

The outcome of Putin's current interventions in eastern Ukraine and Syria will provide more evidence to answer the crucial question whether he is a dangerous risk-taker. So far he has stopped short of taking the most dangerous risks.

One important point, in comparing Putin's foreign policies with Soviet ones, is that the Russian Federation is weaker in military terms than the Soviet Union was, though it is a nuclear power and an important player in the world. It has the forces for limited interventions in regional conflicts. It will cause sharp arguments with the West and some nasty moments.

Yet Putin is not reckless. He calculates carefully before taking risks. He is conscious of Russia's relative weakness, economically and militarily. Russia's conventional forces could no longer overrun western Europe, and its extensive military equipment programmes are not designed to restore the Soviet Union's preponderance in this important field. That means that Russia in an East-West crisis now would have few military options except the most dangerous ones, and I think he would not run the risk of provoking nuclear war.

In Syria the Russian Federation has intervened outside the frontiers of the former Soviet Union. It may do more of that, just as it may try to control more territories that were in the Soviet Union. The Moslem population of Russia and fear of further terrorism will be considerations in policy towards the Islamic world.

In the Cold War the Soviet Union would not have risked an adventure in non-communist Europe because of the possibility of American nuclear retaliation. But today would Moscow reckon that America would not use nuclear weapons for the sake of a smallish NATO territory, such as one of the Baltic States, where much of the population is ethnically Russian?

If Russia did attack and the US did not retaliate with strong actions as well as words, the membership of the victim state in NATO would be shown to be ineffectual, and NATO itself would be terribly discredited. Russia knows this and therefore would calculate that the US would feel obliged to take action. I think Putin could not exclude the possibility of a military crisis that might escalate if he did not withdraw from the territory he had just attacked. The presence of NATO forces in the region would make this calculation more likely.

Because of the risk of a nuclear crisis I do not believe that Russia would attack one of the Baltic States or any other country in NATO. Instead Moscow may resort to more cyber-attacks and other destabilising ploys.

EPILOGUE

In October 2015, I asked Deborah Bronnert, then Chief Operating Officer of the FCO, how far the role of an Ambassador has changed since my time.

Deborah's replies showed that the role of an Ambassador today is very similar. Advocating British policies, promoting British exports, getting inside the mind of the country where you are working, getting to know the key people – these are still the main tasks. The types of work are at least as varied.

But there are real changes. Brutal cuts in the budget of the FCO and its overseas posts have weakened our diplomacy and its ability to serve British interests. One of the many examples is that the number of career diplomats in the Embassies in Germany and France has been heavily cut back and locally engaged staff, whose remuneration is lower, make up the large majority.

Deborah Bronnert told me that the effort to bring more women into the Diplomatic Service and its senior positions has been intensified and the results are at last respectable. Women comprise 30% of senior management. That figure will rise further, with promotions from the other levels where the proportion of women is higher. The number of Ambassadors who are from ethnic minorities has reached a dozen and will go on rising.

Public diplomacy – the speeches and TV interviews in the local language, which I did more of than many of my contemporaries – has become usual for Ambassadors. The social media have added greatly to this activity, with Ambassadors tweeting their views in all directions.

The working hours are still demanding, probably more so today because email is the main means of communication and British diplomats may have to respond to messages at any hour. The pay is still below that of comparable jobs in the private sector.

One impressive innovation is the Crisis Management Department of the FCO. Response to a new crisis is far faster and more efficient than in my days as crisis manager, among other roles, in the FCO's Policy Planning Staff in the 1980s. The staff are specially trained and they include military, police and disaster relief experts. This may be among the best crisis-handling operations of all diplomatic services across the world.

INDEX